ETRURIA AND ROME

ETRURIA AND ROME

By R. A. L. FELL, M.A.

FORMERLY SCHOLAR OF TRINITY COLLEGE

THIRLWALL PRIZE ESSAY 1923

CAMBRIDGE

AT THE UNIVERSITY PRESS

MCMXXIV

CAMBRIDGE UNIVERSITY PRESS
Cambridge, New York, Melbourne, Madrid, Cape Town,
Singapore, São Paulo, Delhi, Mexico City

Cambridge University Press
The Edinburgh Building, Cambridge CB2 8RU, UK

Published in the United States of America by Cambridge University Press, New York

www.cambridge.org
Information on this title: www.cambridge.org/9781107687011

© Cambridge University Press 1924

First published 1924
First paperback edition 2013

A catalogue record for this publication is available from the British Library

ISBN 978-1-107-68701-1 Paperback

PREFACE

ANY study of the Etruscans and their place in Roman history must inevitably cover some ground on which much work has already been done. Thus on the "Etruscan question" I have no novel theory to offer, but have endeavoured to state the chief opposing views and to give my reasons for inclining to one of them. I have tried to investigate some of the underlying causes of the growth and the decline of the Etruscan supremacy in Italy, to make a fresh estimate of the manner and extent of the Etruscan contribution to Roman civilization, and to throw some light on the state of Etruria after the Roman conquest. I have made it my aim to visit all the sites and monuments in Italy to which I have occasion to refer, and I acknowledge with gratitude the assistance in this respect which I have had from Dr Ashby and Mrs Strong, of the British School at Rome, and from the inspectors of antiquities and directors of museums wherever I went.

My thanks are also due to the Electors to the Craven and Gilchrist Studentships, by which I was enabled to spend two years in Italy; to the Adjudicators of the Thirlwall Prize for accepting this

essay for publication; and to Prof. J. S. Reid, Mr
E. Harrison, Mr T. R. Glover, Mr A. B. Cook and
Dr P. Giles, Master of Emmanuel College, for
many valuable suggestions and references.

I am aware that I have not been wholly consistent
in the use of ancient and modern proper names.
But it has seemed natural as a rule to use the
ancient name when alluding to events in ancient
history, and the modern when alluding to modern
archaeological discoveries. I cannot bring myself
to speak either of "Lars Porsena king of Chiusi"
or of "the Civic Museum at Clusium."

R. A. L. FELL.

1924.

CONTENTS

PART ONE

THE ORIGIN AND GROWTH
OF THE ETRUSCAN POWER

§ 1

THE COMING OF THE ETRUSCANS TO ITALY

THE ETRUSCANS, like some other peoples in history, have suffered both from undue disparagement and from an exaggeration of their importance. In the early part of last century there was a wave of "etruscomania" when enthusiasts represented the Etruscans as the parents of European civilization: even Greek art was derived from Etruscan. An exaggerated reaction set in, and the Etruscans were relegated to a place of unimportance, largely through the great authority of Mommsen, who ranked their art lowest in the early art of the Italian peoples[1], and dogmatized on the question of the origin of the Etruscans as one hardly worthy of serious enquiry. That Etruscan art is little but debased imitation is maintained by Martha in his great work on the subject: all that is good in it is Greek; thus a particularly fine mirror bearing an Etruscan inscription "ne peut être que d'une main grecque[2]." Even Dennis, whose *Cities and Cemeteries* is still a classic, and who does not usually err on the side of underrating the Etruscans, adopts the familiar phrases of

---

[1] *Roman History* (E.T.), I. pp. 242, 248–9; cf. Fowler, *Religious Experience of the Roman People*, p. 309.
[2] *L'Art Étrusque*, p. 547.

"the dark and gloomy character of the Etruscan super-stition" and "the juggleries of priestcraft[1]." Now the tide appears to be turning once more; modern historians such as De Sanctis, Pais and Meyer give a prominent place to the Etruscan power in the early history of Italy; while archaeological discoveries such as that of the Apollo-group at Veii have renewed interest in the Etruscan contribution to later Roman art.

The loss of all histories of the Etruscans (even those by Romans, such as the Emperor Claudius and others) cannot be too much regretted: this unique and remarkable people only appears fitfully in histories of Rome, always in a hostile light, and in scattered allusions in other Greek and Latin authors, which have been dealt with exhaustively in Müller's *Die Etrusker* (revised by W. Deecke, 1877). Apart from this fragmentary literary evidence our know-ledge of the Etruscans has to be gleaned from their surviving monuments.

The Etruscans have formed the subject of abundant research and controversy in modern times. The most dis-puted question in this connexion is that of the origin of the Etruscans, and of their possible affinities with other peoples. On this, "the Etruscan question" *par excellence*, it is necessary to say a few words, as the view taken of this cannot but influence deeply our whole view of early Italian history.

As is well known, practically all ancient authors follow Herodotus in asserting that the Etruscans came from Asia or more particularly from Lydia. The story in Herodotus (I. 94) of the great famine which the Lydians tried to meet by taking food only on alternate days and occupying them-selves on the other days with games of dice, knuckle-bones, and ball, till after eighteen years the King Atys had recourse to the expedient of sending half the population under his

[1] *Op. cit.* I. pp. lvi–lvii; cf. Momm. *R.H.* I. pp. 189–90.

son Tyrsenus to find a fresh home overseas, is of course
not to be pressed too far; but it does at least point to a
tradition current in Lydia in the fifth century B.C. of a
great migration thence by sea in an earlier age, even if the
connexion of the historic Tyrseni with Lydia is due to
a verbal mistake, and the mention of the 'Ομβρικοί in whose
land the Lydians settled to a false inference on the part of
the historian. The unanimity of later Greek and Latin
writers (with a single exception) concerning the Lydian
origin of the Etruscans seems to rest solely on the authority
of Herodotus; but it may be taken as evidence that they
knew of no other tradition which they considered prefer-
able.

Dionysius of Halicarnassus (1. 30)[1] alone rejects the
Herodotean account, on grounds of the difference between
the Etruscans and the Lydians of his own time in language,
religion and customs; and records[2] (without, however,
accepting it as true) a different account given by Hellanicus,
namely, that the Pelasgians landed in the Ionian Gulf,
settled at Croton in the interior of Italy, and thence conquered Tyrrhenia and changed their name to Tyrrhenes.
The story of the Pelasgians, driven out of Thessaly,
founding Spina on the Adriatic (Dionys. 1. 18) is probably
also derived from Hellanicus, and by him from Herodotus
who also mentions Pelasgians living now at Creston
(identified with Croton, later called Corthonia, i.e. Cortona
in Etruria, by Dionys. 1. 29) and formerly in Thessaly,
but does not identify them with the Etruscans[3]. The

[1] Dionysius speaks of the Etruscans as "not having the same language or manners as any other nation (οὐδενὶ ἄλλῳ ἔθνει οὔτε
ὁμόγλωσσον οὔτε ὁμοδίαιτον)"; and so far none of the partial resemblances which have been found between the Etruscans and other
peoples amounts to a proof of identity.
[2] Dionys. 1. 28. 3.
[3] Hdt. 1. 57: Πελασγῶν τῶν ὑπὲρ Τυρσηνῶν Κρηστῶνα πόλιν οἰκεόντων.
If Herodotus were here following Hellanicus, he would surely not
have passed over the latter's identification of Pelasgi and Tyrseni,

1-2

landing of these Pelasgi on the Adriatic coast of Italy
seems to be simply a deduction of Hellanicus from their
presence at Cortona and their previous abode in Thessaly,
and therefore of no value as evidence as to the entrance
of the Etruscans into Italy; and he suggests no reason why
these Pelasgi changed their name to Tyrrheni. The statement of Hellanicus, that the people who owned the land
in Italy which was known in historic times as Tyrrhenia
or Etruria came thither from Thessaly across the Adriatic,
has found no followers in ancient or modern times, and
appears to be due to the vague untrustworthy use of the
name Pelasgi. It is not too much to say that no historical
conclusions can be based on any of these legends of
Pelasgic migrations and settlements.

These mysterious Pelasgians appear again connected
with the Tyrrhenes as early inhabitants of Lemnos and
Athens. Thucydides says of the barbarians of the Chalcidic
peninsula τὸ δὲ πλεῖστον Πελασγικὸν τῶν καὶ Λῆμνόν
ποτε καὶ 'Αθήνας Τυρσηνῶν οἰκησάντων, and Herodotus
speaks of the Pelasgians being driven out of Attica and
settling, amongst other places, in Lemnos where they
remained till its capture by Miltiades[1]. Now as to what
fact, if any, may lie behind the solitary allusion quoted
above to a Tyrrhene settlement in Athens, it is useless
to speculate[2]; as to Lemnos we are on somewhat firmer
ground, through the discovery of an inscription[3] there in

which is contrary to the Lydian story of Hdt. I. 67. (Grenier, *Bologne
Villanovienne et Étrusque*, p. 466.)

[1] Thuc. IV. 109. 4; Hdt. VI. 137-8.
[2] Cf. Callimachus *ap.* Schol. Ar. *Aves*, 832: Τυρσηνῶν τείχισμα
Πελασγικόν.
[3] Pauli, *Eine vorgriechische Inschrift von Lemnos* (= *Altitalische
Forschungen*, Bd. II); Karo (*Bull. Paletn. Ital.* XXV (1904), p. 25, n. 4)
describes it as similar to the Etruscan inscriptions but distinct from
them; cf. Brizio in *Atti e Mem. R. Deputazione di Storia Patria per la
Romagna*, 1886, pp. 240-1. See further *Inscr. Graec.* XII. 8. 1, and the
literature there quoted.

a language not far removed from that of the Etruscans of Italy. It is natural, too, to identify with these Tyrrhenes of Lemnos the "Tursha," a maritime folk who appear in Egyptian inscriptions of the fourteenth and fifteenth centuries B.C.[1], but it does not of course follow that the Tyrrhenes of the eastern Mediterranean are identical with the Tyrrhenes of Italy, unless it can be shewn that there are other grounds for this identification. Of the native legends little or nothing survives to shew what tradition the Etruscans themselves held concerning their early history. It is not certain that they believed their ancestors to have entered Italy by sea from Asia Minor, nor yet by land from Central Europe; the myth of the lawgiver Tages, who sprang from the soil a child yet gray-headed with wisdom[2], does not imply that the nation as a whole claimed to be autochthonous as the Athenians did, but the localization of the myth at Tarquinii, which also figures in the other confused legends of Tyrrhenus and Tarchon as the metropolis of Etruria, points to the diffusion of the Etruscans from the south-west northwards rather than to a migration across the Apennines.

The theory of the Lydian origin of the Etruscans was first seriously challenged in modern times by Niebuhr[3], who advanced the contrary opinion that the Etruscans entered Italy across the Alps—an opinion supported as was claimed by the existence of inscriptions in an Etruscan[4] dialect in the Trentino, by some parallels in place-names

[1] Meyer, I. 2, § 515; Pauli, *op. cit.* pp. 227 ff.
[2] Cic. *de Divin.* II. 23–50, who pours scorn on the legend: "estne quisquam ita insipiens qui credat exaratum esse, deum dicam an hominem?"
[3] *Röm. Gesch.* (ed. 1853), pp. 62 ff.
[4] But it is doubtful whether the Raetic dialect really is Etruscan: see J. Whatmough in *Class. Quart.* XVIII (1923), pp. 61–72, who argues that the Raeti were Indo-Europeans of mixed Celtic and Illyrian stock, the Etruscan elements in their language being due to the Etruscan domination in N. Italy.

of Raetia and Etruria, and by the passage of Livy which asserts the Etruscan origin of the Raeti[1]. This Raetian theory was accepted by Mommsen[2] as "not wholly improbable" on the grounds of the survival of the Etruscan dialect in the Alps, and of the similarity of the names "Raeti" and "Rasenna" (the name by which the Etruscans called themselves[3]); and though Mommsen dismissed the question of Etruscan origins as on a par with that of Hecuba's mother—"neither capable of being known nor worth the knowing"—his authority gave the Raetian theory a considerable vogue. It was further supported on better grounds by the school of Helbig[4] and Pigorini, who claimed that the Etruscans were "Italic," not different in race from (e.g.) the Umbrians, and that these Italici were the people who lived in the "terremare" of North Italy, that in the early iron age they produced the civilization which takes its name from Villanova, and that later the same people produced under Aegean and Ionic influences the civilization known as Etruscan. It was especially maintained by this school that in certain places in Tuscany, such as Tarquinii, there was no break of continuity between the tombs of the Villanova and Etruscan types[5], but on the contrary a clear development from the primitive well-tombs to trench-tombs and from these to corridor and chamber-tombs. The same con-

---

[1] Livy, v. 33. 11: "Alpinis quoque ea (*sc.* Etrusca) gentibus haud dubie origo est, maxime Raetis; quos loca ipsa efferarunt ne quid ex antiquo praeter sonum linguae nec eum incorruptum retinerent."

[2] *History of Rome*, I. pp. 154 ff.   [3] Dionys. I. 30.

[4] Helbig, "Der Italiker in dem Poebene," and "Sopra la provenienza degli Etruschi," in *Annali dell' Instituto di Corrispondenza Archeologica*, 1884, pp. 108 ff.

[5] But cf. Falchi, *Vetulonia*, pp. 214–5, on the clear distinction there between the "Italic" well-tombs with hut urns or Villanova urns and local products only and the circle-tombs which contained scarabs, coloured glass and other foreign ornaments; he speaks there of a complete antagonism of civilization and customs between the two peoples.

tinuity appears in some cemeteries of the Faliscan territory[1]:
the same furniture was found in the earliest trench-tombs
as in the well-tombs (vases of rough black *impasto* sometimes with incised geometrical decoration, bronze fibulae
and crescent-shaped razors), while the latest trench-tombs
contained material of the "orientalizing" type found in
early chamber-tombs (imitations in pottery of bronze
supports for cauldrons, and decorative motives of lions,
winged horses, sphinxes, lotuses, etc.).

Of late years there has been a clear reaction towards
the Lydian theory[2]. The arguments from the similarities
of Asiatic and Etruscan culture have often been pointed
out[3], and need not be pressed here: it will be enough to
mention the Etruscan love of music, jewelry[4], bright
colours, games, dancing and feasting, and in general their
luxury as oriental rather than Italic in character. Their
architecture and skill in metallurgy, their physiognomy
and their dress find their closest parallels in Asia Minor.
The Etruscan use of matronymics was foreign to the Italic
peoples, but was customary among the Lycians[5]; their
science of divination by the entrails of animals was almost

[1] The finds from the Ager Faliscus which are now to be seen in the
Villa Giulia Museum shew this clearly.
[2] Brizio, "La provenienza degli Etruschi," in *Atti e Mem. della R.
Deput. di Storia Patria per le provincie di Romagna*, 1885, pp. 120–237;
Modestov in *Atti Congr. Stor.* 1903, II. pp. 23 ff. Cf. Kannengiesser
in *Klio*, VIII (1908), pp. 252–62, who gives a survey of the position of
the Etruscan question.
[3] See especially Dennis, I. pp. xxxv ff.; Müller, I. pp. 81 ff.
[4] The earliest Etruscan jewelry shews striking similarities to that
of Lydia and of Ephesus and Rhodes, e.g. the oriental motive of the
"Persian Artemis"—a goddess flanked by two lions—appears on the
gold bracelets of Vetulonia; cf. Marshall, *Catalogue of Jewelry, Greek,
Etruscan and Roman in the British Museum*, pp. xxiv–xxvi; Karo in
Revue des études anciennes, VII (1905), p. 196. Pausanias (VII. 6. 6)
mentions a Lydian shrine of the Persian Artemis.
[5] Hdt. I. 173; cf. Schrader's *Reallexikon der indogermanischen
Altertumskunde* (2nd ed.), s.v. "Mutterrecht," "Namen."

certainly derived from Chaldaea[1]; the extravagant gestures of grief common in Etruscan tombs (e.g. the Tomba del Morto at Tarquinii) suggest the emotional Asiatic, and are quite alien to the "gravitas" of the Latins. These facts have a strong cumulative effect; and it is hard to believe that the distinctive features of Etruscan civilization were entirely due to contact through trade with Phoenicians and Greeks, and to the acquisition in Tuscany of a rich soil and a subject population; that the Villanova and Etruscan civilizations are only different phases in the life of a single race which migrated from the Po valley across the Apennines[2]. We must notice further several other points of resemblance between the Etruscans and the peoples of Asia Minor.

The "beehive" tombs of Etruria (such as the tomb from Casal Marittimo which has been reconstructed in the garden of the Florence Museum[3], the Tomba Pietrera at Vetulonia, and others at Populonia and elsewhere) are of the same type as the "Treasury of Atreus" and other Mycenaean θόλοι; while the anthropoid cinerary urns of Chiusi recall the Egyptian Canopus-urns and the Mycenaean death-masks[4]. These similarities are striking, but neither is quite conclusive. A "beehive" tomb has been found at New Grange in Ireland[5], and the type might therefore

---

[1] Cf. Ezekiel xxi. 21: "The king of Babylon...shook' the arrows to and fro, he consulted the teraphim, he looked in the liver"; Deecke in *Etruskische Forschungen und Studien*, iv. p. 79; G. Blecher, *De extispicio capita tria*, with Karl Bezold's supplement (pp. 246–52) on Babylonian *extispicium*.

[2] So De Sanctis maintains (*Storia dei Romani*, i. pp. 124 ff. and esp. 143 ff.).

[3] Milani, *Il R. Museo Archeologico di Firenze*, p. 286, tav. cxxiv. Montelius, *Civilisation Primitive*, ii. pl. 166, illustrates a similar tomb.

[4] Milani, *Italici ed Etruschi*, p. 9. In the Civic Museum at Chiusi there are some bronze masks originally attached to cinerary urns, a closer parallel still to the Mycenaean death-masks. See Montelius, *op. cit.* ii. pls. 220–3.

[5] S. Müller, *Urgeschichte Europas*, pp. 74–5.

be regarded as characteristic of the Bronze Age rather than
of Mycenaean culture in particular; and anthropoid urns
appear from eastern Germany as well as from Etruria and
the East[1].

It has further been maintained by Patroni[2] that the
characteristic Pompeian house, with its atrium and rectangular rooms, was introduced by the Etruscans from the
eastern Mediterranean. The Pompeian house, he thinks,
was not derived directly from the Greeks of historical
times, but resembles rather the Homeric house with its
μέγαρον (tablinum) and αὐλή (atrium) and (on a smaller
scale) the Minoan and Mycenaean palaces. But I do not
agree with Patroni that the atrium could not have developed
out of the round thatched hut which is characteristic of
the Italic peoples of north and central Italy. The atrium
is reproduced in the form of some Etruscan tombs (e.g.
Tomba dei Pilastri at Cerveteri) and in a funeral urn from
Poggio Gaiella near Chiusi, now in the Florence Museum[3].
These shew the "displuviate" type (Vitruv. VI. 3), which
may easily have developed from the hut with a smoke-hole
in the roof. The next step would be to make the roof slope
inwards instead of outwards (so that the rainwater should
not run off on to the outer walls), and so we get the
"Tuscan" atrium, which may really be an Etruscan
invention, as it is not known outside Italy. The tetrastyle
and Corinthian forms would represent later stages of
development due to an increase in the size of the atrium.

Thus Patroni's theory cannot be regarded as proved,
though it is not impossible; he accounts for the difference
between the open αὐλή and the nearly closed atrium by

[1] J. Schlemm, *Wörterbuch zur Vorgeschichte*, pp. 173–5, s.v.
"Gesichtsurnen," describes and illustrates anthropoid urns from
Pomerania, Posen and Silesia.

[2] "L'Origine della Domus" in *Rend. Linc.* 1902, pp. 467 ff.

[3] Martha, *L'Art Étrusque*, p. 290; Durm, *Baukunst der Etrusker*,
pp. 22–3.

the difference between the mean temperatures of (e.g.) Tiryns and Pompeii, and supposes that the atrium developed in the reverse direction, from the Corinthian to the Tuscan type[1].

Milani in his *Italici ed Etruschi* and elsewhere appears to have gone much further than the facts warrant in seeking to prove a connexion between the Etruscans and the "Minoans" of Crete. There is no evidence that either the round stone "shields" which covered some of the Vetulonian well-tombs, or the small figures with crested helmet, round shield and drumstick which were found at Vetulonia[2] are derived from Crete—the characteristic shape of the Minoan shield appears to have been a figure of eight[3]—while the ivory arms from Praeneste, now in the Villa Giulia Museum, which Milani regards as symbolical and akin to the long tridental rods which appear on a vase of Hagia Triada, are probably simply handles for fans. Nor, with the exception of the double axe, is there anything Cretan in the archaic Vetulonian stele of Aules Pheluskes[4]; the warrior's round shield and crested helmet recall far more closely the figures on Corinthian vases.

The double axe itself which appears so often in Minoan art is found also in Hittite sculpture[5], and there are many other similarities in the monuments of the Etruscans and of the Hittites. In particular we may note as common to both the high caps, and shoes with upturned toes; the curved rods and folding chairs; the hunting scenes and

[1] *Rend. Linc.* 1902, p. 503; 1903, p. 384.

[2] *Italici ed Etruschi*, pp. 12–13.

[3] Burrows, *The Discoveries in Crete*, p. 182; Ridgeway, *Early Age of Greece*, p. 312, says that "on no monument of the true Mycenaean Age is a circular shield to be seen."

[4] *Not. scav.* 1895, p. 26; Montelius, *Civilisation primitive en Italie*, II. pl. 189. 11. Cf. Karo in *Ath. Mitt.* XXXIII. 1908.

[5] Garstang, *Land of the Hittites*, p. 288 and pl. LXXVII. 2; Meyer, *Geschichte des Altertums*, I. 2, § 479.

processions[1]. Of the stele of Larthi Atharnies from Volterra[2], representing a warrior with a low helmet, long
tunic, curved shoes and scimitar, Hall says that it is purely
Hittite; the stele of Larthi Aninies from Fiesole[3] exactly
illustrates what Garstang describes as a Hittite characteristic—"the arrangement of the hair, which falls away
in a single cluster or curl behind the neck[4]."

These resemblances do not justify us in identifying
Hittites and Etruscans; but they do give some support
to the tradition that the Etruscans were an Asiatic people.
Modern researches into the earliest history of Asia Minor
tend to shew that it was inhabited in the south and west
by a stock which was neither Indo-European nor Semitic
but was in some degree influenced by or akin to the Hittites
in the centre and east, and which was represented in
historical times by the Lydians, Carians, Lycians, Pisidians,
Isaurians, Lycaonians and Cilicians; and that peoples of
the same stock also inhabited Crete (perhaps their original
home), the islands of the Aegean, and parts of the Greek
mainland[5]. It is among these peoples that we must look
for the origin of the Etruscans[6]; and besides the archaeo-

[1] Garstang, *op. cit.* pp. 114 ff.; Conder, *The Hittites and their
Language*, pp. 101, 120; Hall, *Ancient History of the Near East*, pp.
331–6; Herbig in *Deutsche Literaturzeitung*, 1916, p. 424.
[2] In the Florence Museum, Room VI; Milani, *R. Museo Archeol.
di Firenze*, p. 224, tav. LXXV.
[3] Florence Museum; Milani, *op. cit.* p. 278, tav. CXVI.
[4] *Op. cit.* pp. 119–20, cf. p. 231: "the short tunic characteristic of
the Hittite soldiery."
[5] Meyer, *Gesch. des Alt.* I. 2, § 476, quoting Kretschmer's *Einleitung
in die Geschichte der griechischen Sprache*, ch. x. Cf. too Sundwall,
"Die einheimische Namen der Lykier," in *Klio*, 1913, Beiheft II, and
a review of it by Danielson in *Göttingische gelehrte Anzeigen*, 1916,
pp. 490–532. Indo-European elements in the native languages of Asia
Minor may be due to the Phrygians, an Indo-European people akin to
the Thracians and Armenians (cf. Hdt. VII. 73; Meyer, § 473).
[6] It would appear, however, that the evidence of ethnology is against
a complete identification of the Etruscans with the "Kleinasiaten"
(i.e. Lydians, Carians, etc.): the former being dolichocephalic or

logical evidence there are certain resemblances in proper
names which appear to connect Etruria with the lands
which border on the Aegean. Already in 1886 in his
Vorgriechische Inschrift von Lemnos Pauli noted that names
in -*nd*- (-*d*-, -*nth*-) and -*ss*- (-*s*-) were common in Lycia,
Caria, and Lydia, and were also found on the Greek
islands and mainland; such names he called "Pelasgian"
and regarded the Etruscans as a branch of the widespread
Pelasgian race, whose home was in Asia Minor[1]. Pauli
admits that the name-forms which he regards as characteristic of the Pelasgians are not common in Etruria; he
says, however, that they occur in the Etruscan language[2].
More recently the proper names which appear to be
common to Etruria and Crete or Asia Minor have been
studied by Kannengiesser and by Herbig[3]. The former
shews that many non-Greek names found in Crete
(especially in coast-towns) and the Aegean lands have
parallels in Etruria; e.g. Σύρνας (one of the Cyclades),
Σύρνα (in Caria), Σύρινθος (Crete) = *sure, surna* (*C.I.E.*
918, 3508, etc.), Sora (Volscian town), Surrentum, Surri-
nenses (*C.I.L.* XI. 30:2); Gortyn = Cortona (cf. *curthutes*,
C.I.E. 2470); Praisos = *presu, presnte* (*C.I.E.* 2605, 667, etc.)
(? Praeneste). From the number and closeness of these
parallels Kannengiesser infers that there must have been
a strong influx into Italy from Crete or from lands whose

dolichomesocephalic (Sergi, *Arii e Italici*, p. 108; Mosso, "Crani
etruschi," p. 270, in *Atti R. Accad. Sci. Torino*, 1906), while the latter
were markedly brachycephalic (Schrader, *Reallexikon* (2nd ed.), I. 608,
s.v. "Kleinasiaten"). But the Caucasians are said to have been dolichocephalic in antiquity (*ibid.* 570, s.v. "Kaukasusvölke").
[1] Pauli, *op. cit.* I. pp. 41 ff., 72 ff. On the names formed with -*nd*-
and -*ss*- see also Meyer, *loc. cit.*
[2] *Op. cit.* I. pp. 52-3.
[3] Kannengiesser, "Aegäische, besonders kretische Namen bei den
Etruskern," in *Klio*, XI (1911), pp. 26-47; Herbig, "Kleinasiatisch-
etruskische Namengleichungen," in *Sitzungsberichte der k. bayer.
Akad.* (Hist.-Philol. Klasse), 1914.

inhabitants were akin to those of Crete. Herbig notes that many suffixes are common to Etruscan names and to those of Asia Minor, e.g. -a, -na, -enna (= -ηνος): Asiatic -i = Etr. -i, -ie = Gk. -ιος, -ις, -εις = Lat. -ius: As. and Etr. -u = Gk. -ω, -ων, -ου, -υ = Lat. -o, -onius. Also stems are often formed in the same way in both lands, e.g. in -l- (Κώγλ-ως Κόκκαλ-ος cucl-nies Cocl-es), in -r- (Τούβερ-ις Τυβέρ-ισσος thupr-e Tuber-o; ? thepr-i Tiber-is), in -s- and in -t-. Again he gives instances of parallel variations on the same root: e.g. from the root Trqu- come Tarku (name of a god in Asia Minor[1]) = tarchu Ταρκύνιος Tarquinius; As. Τάρκνα = Etr. tarchna; As. Τέρκανδρος = Etr. tarchntes. In Asia Minor as in Etruria there are personal names formed (a) from words denoting relationship, e.g. the Asiatic words and names papa, mama, cf. Etr. names papa[2]; claniu, clante (clan = "son"); (b) from racial names, e.g. kara luda luka kata (= Hittite) in Asia Minor; creice latini sapini umria velsca maruce venete in Etruria; (c) from names of gods and heroes, e.g. Τύλος (Lydia), Ῥῶμος (Lycia) = Etr. tule, *ruma. These resemblances are remarkable, particularly if we remember that our evidence for Etruscan names practically does not go back beyond 600 B.C., for native Asiatic names not so far; so that on both sides there were several centuries of independent development. Some resemblances have also been found between the Lydian and Etruscan languages[3]: e.g. Lyd. -k = Etr. -c = Lat. -que; the Lydian ethnicon sfardak ("Sardian") corresponds to the Etruscan rumach ("Roman"); both languages have an oblique case in -l, -s, -ls; the sign for -f- is similar in both languages. Thus

---

[1] Meyer, I. 2, § 476; Kretschmer, Einleitung, pp. 362 ff.
[2] Schulze, Zur Geschichte lateinischer Eigennamen, p. 332.
[3] Schrader's Reallexikon der indogermanischen Altertumskunde (2nd ed. 1923), II. 1, s.v. "Lyder," where it is argued that the Lydian language is probably not Indo-European.

both in art and in language we find considerable points
of contact between Etruria and Asia Minor.

If, as was maintained by Helbig and his followers, the
Villanova and Etruscan cultures appear to blend with one
another in Tuscany, north of the Apennines they are
clearly distinct. The ancient town at Marzabotto[1] was
purely Etruscan with (as far as has been discovered) no
Italic substratum; the cemeteries there, though the dead
were mainly cremated, have not yielded a single Villanova
urn or ornament. The Villanova and Etruscan cemeteries
of Bologna are clearly separated topographically, and the
figured stelae, Attic and local pottery, and rich bronze-
work which are characteristic of the latter find no parallel
in the former[2]. Nor can any intermediate phases be traced;
the evidence points not to the gradual evolution of an
elaborate civilization from a simpler, but to the introduction from outside of something different and already
well-developed. No Greek vases of any period are found
in the undoubtedly Villanova tombs, whereas in tombs
which inscriptions on the stelae[3] prove to be Etruscan
they are plentiful, beginning with black-figure Athenian
ware of the end of the sixth century B.C. It is a reasonable
assumption that the first traces of contact with Greece,
much later in the Bologna area than in Etruria proper,
coincide with the settlement in the former of Etruscan
invaders from across the Apennines; even if we dismiss
as a mere deduction from the Herodotean tradition the
plain testimony of Livy (v. 33. 7)[4]: "Tusci...in utrumque

---

[1] On this see Brizio in *Monumenti Antichi*, I (1891), pp. 249 ff.

[2] Grenier, *Bologne Villanovienne et Étrusque*, pp. 312–3. The contrast between the two sets of tombs is evident in the Bologna Museum.
Cf. too Brizio, "La Provenienza degli Etruschi," pp. 184 ff.

[3] On these stelae see Ducati in *Monumenti Antichi*, XX (1910),
pp. 360 ff.; also Brizio, *op. cit.* pp. 198 ff.

[4] Similarly Diod. XIV. 113. The detail of the twelve cities of trans-
Apennine Etruria is unimportant.

mare uergentes incoluere urbibus duodenis terras prius cis
Apenninum ad inferum mare, postea trans Apenninum
totidem, quot capita originis erant, coloniis missis...."
We have still to face the possibility of a migration from
the Po valley into Tuscany in the Villanova period followed
after some considerable time by a return across the
Apennines of members of the same race bringing with
them the superior "Etruscan" civilization which they had
evolved in the meanwhile on the west coast of Italy. The
primary objection to such a theory is that it involves an
almost complete cessation of intercourse between the two
branches of the same race during the necessarily long
interval between the two migrations. This follows from
the absence in the Po valley of signs of transition between
the Villanova and Etruscan epochs: the latter begins at
the end of the sixth century, and the former continues
into the fifth[1]. But the alleged continuity of the two epochs
in Etruria proper is itself doubtful. It is true that in many
places (e.g. Tarquinii, Volci, the *ager Faliscus*) the same
furniture is found in well-tombs and trench-tombs, and
also the same in trench-tombs and chamber-tombs; but
this does not necessarily imply identity of population. No
one claims that the invading Etruscans displaced the
existing population any more than the Normans displaced
the English: the two races would naturally live side by
side, their mutual influence varying in different parts of
the country, according to the proportions in which they
were mixed. Each race would react on the other, and such
reaction would appear in their tombs. Hence it is credible
that in general the well- and trench-tombs are those of
the Italic subjects, and the different types of chamber-
tombs (e.g. the tumuli of Cerveteri, Veii and Volci, the
tholoi of Vetulonia, the "corridor-tombs" of Orvieto,
besides the ordinary form found at Tarquinii, Cerveteri,

[1] Grenier, *op. cit.* p. 176.

Chiusi, Orvieto, etc.) belong to the Etruscan conquerors. These latter might well not disdain to bury with their dead some of the vases and utensils used by the natives, just as the natives might put in their tombs articles which were first introduced by the Etruscans[1]. And it is significant that in general the chamber-tombs contain richer material than even the trench-tombs which appear to be contemporary or later.

No certain conclusion can be drawn from differences of funeral rite. Cremation is characteristic of cemeteries of the Villanova type, but the Etruscans undoubtedly used both cremation and inhumation at an early time. It is difficult to see why if the Etruscans were merely the same Italic stock as the Villanova people in a later stage of culture, they should have adopted a different rite in south Etruria[2] almost universally, and to some extent north of the Apennines; whereas the prevalence of inhumation in the south agrees with the hypothesis that a foreign race which practised inhumation had its chief settlement there. Further north (especially round Chiusi, Perugia and Volterra) cremation was far commoner; but the large rectangular "ash-chests" found in these places may be a survival of the earlier practice of inhumation[3]. Beyond the Apennines, at Marzabotto cremation is prevalent though not universal, and the large stone-lined tombs in which the ashes were put (mainly about 4 feet long by 3 wide) again look like a development from inhumation-tombs: the Etruscan necropolis of Bologna, according to Grenier[4], shews both cremation and inhumation in the proportion of 2 : 3. It is particularly remarkable that while in the "circle-tombs" of Vetulonia the remains were nearly always cremated, in

---

[1] E.g. trench-tombs containing Corinthian pottery at Tarquinii, Volci and elsewhere (Gsell, *Fouilles de Vulci*, pp. 315, 430).

[2] E.g. Tarquinii, Cerveteri, Volci, etc.

[3] Karo in *Bull. Paletn. Ital.* xxx (1904), pp. 19–20.

[4] *Bologne Vill. et Étr.* p. 161.

the large necropolis of Marsiliana which has yielded precisely similar furniture inhumation predominates, and there is no distinction in locality or contents between the cremation and inhumation tombs[1].

The problem of the Etruscan language lies outside my scope. Suffice it to say that the attempts which have been made to connect that language with the Graeco-Italian family have now been almost entirely abandoned[2]. Even Mommsen, though inclining to the conclusion that "the Etruscans may be on the whole included among the Indo-Germans," at the same time held that "the Tuscan language differed as widely from all the Graeco-Italian dialects as did the languages of the Celts or of the Slavonians." And De Sanctis, the latest opponent of the oriental origin of the Etruscans, admits a clear distinction between them and the "Italici" (i.e. the Umbrian and Sabine stocks) on philological grounds[3]. Nor do I propose to discuss the affinities of the Etruscan religion, which shews, as far as our fragmentary knowledge of it goes, a synthesis of various elements. Thus the science of *haruspicina* appears to be of Babylonian origin: and the Italic deities Minerva and Neptune were adopted by the Etruscans. We also find in Etruria the Greek Olympian deities, either with purely Etruscan names[4] (Tinia, Turan, Turms, etc., corresponding

[1] Falchi, *Vetulonia*, p. 218; Minto, *Marsiliana*, pp. 29, 297.
[2] Conway, *Italic Dialects*, I. p. xi: Skutsch in Pauly-Wissowa, VI. 773 ff., s.v. "Etruskische Sprache."
[3] Mommsen, *R.H.* I. p. 152; De Sanctis, *Stor. Rom.* I. p. 124, n. 2.
[4] *Tinia* is connected with *tins*, "day," which occurs in the Agram text and elsewhere (Torp, *Etr. Beiträge*, I. 99; II. 20), rather than with the Cretan Τῆνα = Ζῆνα. *Tinthun* and its Greek equivalent Τιθωνός may come from the same root; a town Tintunia appears in Cappadocia, cf. Apollonia from Apollo (Bugge, *Verhältnis der Etrusker zu den Indogermanen...*, p. 229). For *Turan* Herbig (*Sitzungsb. k. bayer. Akad.* 1914, p. 28) compares the name Τούραννος in Asia Minor, and suggests that Archilochus introduced the word τύραννος from that region: thus *Turan* = "Queen." *Fufluns* (Dionysus) may be derived from Βίβλινος (Βύβλινος) οἶνος and this from the river Biblos in

to Zeus, Aphrodite, Hermes) or with adaptations of their Greek names, as Aplu (Apollo), Eita and Phersipnai (Hades and Persephone), just as we find frequent representations on late Etruscan urns of scenes from Greek mythology, without any obvious religious significance. On the other hand the monstrous demons of the Etruscan underworld shew no derivation from anything in Greek or Italic religion, both of which were less concerned with the nature of the after-life. The dim and dreary Hades to which the Homeric heroes come is very different from the existence which the Etruscans vividly imagined as one of joyous feasting and games[1], or of inexorable torment.

I will conclude this outline of certain aspects of the Etruscan question with the brief statement of a working hypothesis. The germ of the Etruscan nation was a body of invaders from Asia Minor who landed about 850 B.C. on the west coast of Italy, north of the Tiber, where their oldest monuments are found[2] and their civilization was most fully developed. The chief Etruscan cities of this region—Caere, Tarquinii, Vetulonia, Volci, if not directly on the sea, were not far inland, and the two former are still within sight of it[3]. Caere had a port at Pyrgi (Strabo, v. p. 226; Diod. xv. 14) and Tarquinii perhaps at Graviscae. The invaders may have been racially connected with the Hittites, and had certainly come under the influence of

Naxos; cf. Olck in Pauly-Wissowa, *R.E.* III. 405–6; Thulin, *ibid.* VII. 211.

[1] But this Etruscan belief has some parallels in Greek religion, e.g. the μέθη αἰώνιος (Plat. *Rep.* 363 *d*) of the Orphists, and the picture in Pindar, *frag.* 95.

[2] De Sanctis (I. p. 130) overlooks this fact when he states that the chief Etruscan cities were inland.

[3] The sea at that time covered the flat marshy land below the hill of Vetulonia, cf. Falchi, *Vetulonia*, p. 7, n. 2. In this region was the river Umbro (Ombrone) and the "tractus Umbriae" of Plin. *N.H.* III. 51. Cf. Hdt. I. 94, on the arrival of the Tyrrhenes ἐς Ὀμβρικούς. The ancient settlement at Marsiliana in the Albegna valley was also within sight of the sea. (Minto, *Marsiliana*, p. 4.)

the pre-Hellenic Aegean culture; hence their artistic development was greater than that of the other Italians, and also they were far more susceptible than these to the influence of Greek art, which itself was largely sprung from the same Aegean source. The partial affinities of Greek and Etruscan religion may also be due to an original common element in the two civilizations rather than to a direct borrowing by the one from the other.

The date of the Etruscan migration cannot be determined with any exactitude; Roman legend as shewn in the *Aeneid* and Livy (I. 2) represents the Etruscans as already established at Caere in the time of Aeneas, and the absence of any Greek or Roman tradition as to the date of their arrival suggests that it was assigned to a remote period. In agreement with this, Montelius[1] maintained that the Etruscans came in the eleventh century B.C., and dated the Regolini-Galassi tomb in the ninth; while Milani assigns the Vetulonian stele of Aules Pheluskes to the ninth or tenth century and the Volterran stele of Larthi Atharnies to the eighth or ninth[2]. In view of the fact that these stelae bear inscriptions in the Etruscan alphabet, which is generally held[3] (though Milani denies it) to be derived from the Chalcidians of Cumae, such dates may

[1] *Journ. Anthrop. Inst.* 1897, pp. 261 ff.
[2] *Italici ed Etruschi*, pp. 19, 22; *R. Mus. Arch. di Firenze*, p. 219.
[3] Of course this view falls to the ground if the Lemnos inscription is Etruscan and previous to the arrival of the Etruscans in Italy, as is maintained by Karo in *Bull. Paletn. Ital.* 1904, pp. 25-6, who there recants his own previous opinion that the Etruscan alphabet was derived from Cumae. Cf. M. Hammarström, *Beiträge zur Geschichte des Etruskischen, Lateinischen, und Griechischen Alphabets*; he concludes (I quote from Prof. R. S. Conway's review in *Class. Rev.* 1922, p. 126) that the Latin alphabet is derived from the Etruscan with additions from the Greek rather than from the Greek with Etruscan modifications; that the Etruscan alphabet is derived from that of Corinth and Phocis, which may have reached Italy before the foundation of Cumae (which he dates 720 B.C.); and that the Latin names of the letters are derived from Etruscan.

be too early. But the date of the Chalcidian settlement
at Cumae being itself uncertain affords little indication
with regard to the Etruscans. It is maintained by Gabrici[1],
who puts the colonization of Cumae about the end of the
ninth century, that if the Tyrrhenes had begun to occupy
the Tuscan coast from the middle of the ninth century,
Chalcidian trade could not have been as prevalent as it
was in maritime Etruria in the eighth owing to "the
antagonism which always existed between Cumans and
Etruscans." He adds that the art of the Etruscans is
essentially Ionic, which did not appear in Asia Minor till
the end of the eighth century; and concludes that the
Etruscans arrived in several waves of immigration during
that century. It may, however, be doubted whether the
prevalence in maritime Etruria of eighth-century Cuman
pottery is any evidence that the Etruscans were not already
established there. Further a pre-Hellenic stage of Etruscan
art can be discerned: witness the stelae alluded to above,
and the gold ornaments found in early tombs at Vetulonia,
which are shewn by Karo[2] to be indigenous products
(their technique being rare or unknown outside Etruria,
but paralleled in e.g. the pectoral from the Regolini-
Galassi tomb) of the late eighth and seventh centuries[3].
Thus the Etruscans may well have settled in southern
Etruria before the Chalcidians in Cumae; otherwise we
should expect some record of their passing to be preserved
by the Greeks[4]. But the extant Etruscan monuments
cannot be dated with any confidence earlier than about the

---

[1] "Cuma" in *Mon. Ant.* XXII. pp. 415–6.

[2] *Studi e materiali di arch. e numism.* I. p. 237.

[3] Modestov (*Introd. à l'hist. rom.* p. 453) asserts that no Greek
objects were found in the Regolini-Galassi tomb; but cf. Pinza, *La
Tomba Regolini-Galassi*, p. 137, and Lorimer in *J.H.S.* 1912, p. 336,
on proto-Corinthian pottery (from Cumae?) found in that tomb.

[4] Modestov in *Atti del Congresso Internaz. di scienze Storiche*
Rome, 1903), II. p. 46.

middle of the eighth century; so we may tentatively place
the Etruscan invasion round about 850 B.C. to allow time
for the development in Italy of their civilization.

We have seen that the original settlements of the
Etruscan invaders were on the coast from Caere northwards to Vetulonia, with Tarquinii as their leading town.
Later the chief place appears to belong to Volsinii, with
the Fanum Voltumnae as a religious centre—both places
situated (though their exact locality is disputed) in south
Etruria which remained the main home of the nation.
Gradually the Etruscan power spread to Clusium, Perusia,
Cortona, Arretium, and the outlying strongholds of Volaterrae and Faesulae; but the prevalence in the north (e.g.
especially at Clusium, Perusia and Volaterrae) of the rite
of cremation seems to shew that the Etruscan stock in this
region was blent with the Italic population to a greater
degree than in the south. In the latter half of the sixth
century part of the Etruscan nation crossed the Apennines
and settled in the Po valley, their chief town in this region
being Felsina (Bologna)[1]. That they had also some
dominion in Campania is asserted by ancient tradition
(e.g. Polyb. II. 17. 1, Vell. I. 7 (quoting Cato), Plin. *N.H.*
III. 70, Strabo, V. pp. 247 and 251, etc.), and the scarcity
of clearly Etruscan remains in this region need not shew
more than that the invaders were not numerous, and were
therefore strongly influenced by their neighbours[2]. The
chief piece of archaeological evidence for the presence of
the Etruscans in Campania is a tile bearing an Etruscan
inscription, found in a Capuan tomb and now in Berlin[3];

[1] The imported vases of the Felsinean necropolis begin with those
of the end of the sixth century.   [2] De Sanctis, I. p. 444.

[3] Duhn in *Riv. di Stor. Ant.* 1900, pp. 35 ff. pronounced this to
have been the work of an Etruscan in Campania, though he had
previously denied the presence of the Etruscans there. Beloch, *Campanien*, 2nd ed. pp. 443 ff., defends the tradition and remarks on the
rarity in Etruria itself of inscriptions previous to the fall of the Etruscan
rule in Campania.

while the rectangular street-planning of ancient Capua and Pompeii may be due to the Etruscans.

We have no clear evidence of the date of the Etruscan invasion; probably it was about 600 B.C. There were different Roman traditions concerning the antiquity of Capua, and they are not of great value[1]. The earliest extant building at Pompeii is the sixth-century Doric temple, but we cannot argue from this that the Etruscans were or were not established there when the temple was built; their presence at Pompeii at some time is attested by Strabo (V. p. 247). Patroni puts the Etruscan invasion of Campania as far back as the end of the ninth century, but as his argument is mainly based on the *bucchero* ware (which he holds to be of Etruscan manufacture) found in early Campanian tombs it seems somewhat precarious[2]. Since Capua and Nola, which appear in tradition as the two chief Etruscan cities in Campania, are situated at some distance from the coast, it seems likely that the Etruscans arrived in Campania by land, especially as we hear of no conflict between them and the Greek colonies on the coast till towards the end of the sixth century.

If this be so, it is in agreement with the indications which we have of an Etruscan supremacy continuous in some form or other between Etruria proper and Campania. The wide extent of the Etruscan dominion is twice asserted

[1] Beloch, *op. cit.* p. 8, attempts to shew that when Cato (*Orig.* frag. 59, *ap.* Vell. I. 7. 2) says that Capua stood 250 years before it was taken by the Romans he is referring to its capture in 338 B.C., i.e. Capua was founded about 600 B.C., perhaps on a site already partially inhabited; see, however, De Sanctis, I. p. 445, n. 1. Velleius tells us that according to others Capua was founded "830 years ago," i.e. 800 B.C.

[2] Patroni, "Buccheri campani," in *Stud. e Mat.* I. pp. 290 ff. and "La colonna etrusca di Pompei," in *Rend. Linc.* 1903, pp. 367–84. The column, which is unfluted and has a round base (see also Mau in *Röm. Mitt.* XVII (1902), pp. 305 ff., pl. VIII), may be Etruscan, but its age remains uncertain. Cf. De Sanctis, I. pp. 443–4, who denies the Etruscan origin of the Campanian *buccheri*.

by Servius[1], and various place-names south of the Tiber such as Tusculum, Velitrae (cf. Velathri = Volaterrae), Tarracina (cf. Tarquinii) seem to point to an Etruscan origin[2]; while Roman tradition itself admits that Rome was at one time ruled by an Etruscan dynasty, the Tarquins.

§ 2

THE BASES OF THE ETRUSCAN POWER

There is little indication of the manner in which the Etruscans reached the dominant position which they held in the latter part of the sixth century B.C., or how far it was due to force of arms, how far to the gradual penetration of a more highly-developed people. In war, the superior weapons of the Etruscan invaders must have given them an undoubted advantage: thus at Vetulonia arms are rare in the well-tombs, abundant in the circle-tombs, which certainly belong to a different people[3]. At Tarquinii belts and helmets occur in well-tombs, together with gold and silver ornaments, amber and scarabs which are extremely rare in such tombs at Vetulonia[4], but it appears probable that at Tarquinii the use of well-tombs continued to a

[1] On *Aen.* x. 145: "Tuscos omnem paene Italiam subiugasse manifestum est," and *Aen.* XI. 567: "in Tuscorum iure paene omnis Italia fuerat," where he also quotes Cato for the statement that the Volscians were ruled by the Etruscans (Cato, frag. 62, in Peter, *Hist. Rom. Reliquiae*, p. 73).

[2] Martha, *op. cit.* p. 7. But some resemblances in names may be due to a pre-Etruscan and pre-Italic substratum of population.

[3] Falchi, *Vetulonia*, pp. 41, 44, 162, 171, 193, 258, etc. Many of the circle-tombs contained horses' bits and other pieces of harness (*ibid.* pp. 100, 108, 114–5, etc.) which suggests that the Etruscans were already strong in cavalry; cf. too the remains of chariots in early tombs, e.g. at Caere (Pinza, *Röm. Mitt.* 1902, p. 85); Marsiliana (Minto, *Marsiliana*, pp. 167 ff.) and Populonia (*Not. scav.* 1914, pp. 453 ff.).

[4] Falchi, *op. cit.* p. 41.

later date and the Italic *plebs* had a larger share in the
material prosperity of the Etruscan aristocracy. At Bologna,
though bronze was largely worked in the Villanova period,
iron was scarce; swords and lances are rarely found in
the Villanova tombs, the commonest weapon being an axe[1].
Perhaps the axe which the Etruscan warrior Larthi Aninies,
in the stele of Fiesole[2], bears in his left hand (having a
lance in his right) represents a trophy taken from the
aborigines in war rather than an Etruscan weapon. The
early use by the Etruscans of defensive armour[3] is shewn
by the very archaic Vetulonian stele of a warrior with a
round shield, and the frequency of such shields in early
Etruscan tombs[4]. It appears, too, that helmets of a certain
type were characteristic of the Etruscans[5]—a type represented by the helmet from the battle of Cumae dedicated
to Zeus by Hiero (in the British Museum), several from
seventh- and sixth-century tombs of Vetulonia, over a
hundred (probably later in date) found in a deposit on the
arx of Vetulonia[6], and reliefs of similar helmets (with
the addition of side-pieces) in the Tomba dei Rilievi at
Cerveteri[7]. It is not unlikely that the use of the metal
helmet (*cassis*) was introduced into Italy by the Etruscans.

The supremacy of the Etruscan aristocracy was secured

---

[1] Grenier, *Bologne Villanovienne et Étrusque*, pp. 263, 270, 309.

[2] Milani, *Mus. Arch. di Firenze*, tav. CXXI. 1, p. 279; *Italici ed Etruschi*,
fig. 77.

[3] Milani, *Ital. ed Etr.* p. 19, fig. 76. Cf. the fine set of bronze armour
from a fourth-century tomb at Orvieto, in the Florence Museum,
Room IX. (Milani, *Mus. Arch.* pp. 238–9.)

[4] E.g. T. Duce (Falchi, *op. cit.* p. 118), and Regolini-Galassi
(Pinza, *Röm. Mitt.* XXII. 1907, p. 108).

[5] Cf. Isid. *Orig.* XVIII. 14: "cassidam autem, a Tuscis nominatam
(dicunt): illi enim galeam cassim nominant."

[6] Falchi, *op. cit.* pp. 122, 171, 197: tav. IX. 23, XV. 17, XVII. 8.
Pernier in *Ausonia*, IX (1909), p. 15.

[7] Other variations of the Etruscan helmet at Vetulonia (Falchi,
p. 163, tav. XIV. 2), and in the stone warrior's head from Orvieto (*Not.
scav.* 1887, tav. VII. 9).

by the foundation of large cities, some on hill-tops girt
with massive walls such as Vetulonia, Volaterrae, Faesulae,
Cortona, others isolated by precipitous ravines, as Veii,
Sutrium and many other towns in the south. The
Etruscans, it seems, were accustomed to live in cities,
each commanding a wide area, at a time when the earlier
inhabitants lived in villages formed of groups of huts,
unwalled and without political cohesion. There is a marked
contrast between the Villanovan settlement at Bologna,
with its circular hut foundations and no trace of a wall[1],
and the Etruscan town of Marzabotto which had a wall,
paved streets intersecting at right angles, elaborate houses,
five temples, and a system of drainage[2].

But the Etruscan ascendancy was not maintained solely,
perhaps not mainly, by superior force: arms and armour
and walled cities were only some of the outward indications
of the cultural superiority—greater mental development
and command over natural resources, greater power of
adapting means to ends—which made the Etruscans the
natural leaders of the Italic tribes among whom they settled.
The Etruscans brought with them much of the civilization
of the East; they were expert in navigation and in the arts
of building and metallurgy, working iron freely: the Italici,
as revealed by their most primitive tombs at Vetulonia,
were rough and uncultivated, without industry, trade or
art, fashioning in the simplest manner the bare necessities
of pottery and bronze utensils[3].

Thus the natives were reduced to serfdom; the Etruscan
chieftains formed a governing class, each having a considerable body of these retainers to fight at his command
in war[4], and to work in his fields or mines, to build his

[1] Grenier, *Bologne*, p. 42.
[2] Brizio in *Mon. Ant.* I. pp. 249 ff., esp. 285–324.
[3] Falchi, *op. cit.* p. 258.
[4] Cf. Dionys. IX. 5. 4: συνεληλύθεσαν ἐξ ἁπάσης Τυρρηνίας οἱ
δυνατώτατοι τοὺς ἑαυτῶν πενέστας ἐπαγόμενοι. We read of "Um-

fortresses or row in his galleys in peace. The power of the aristocracy was further supported by the religious pre-eminence which was hereditary in their families, perhaps, too, by the possession of what passed in primitive times for science or magic[1]. We hear nothing of discontent or revolts among the subject population of Etruria till the close of the fourth century, and no doubt the conquered and conquering races, except for the highest princely and sacerdotal families, were early blended by intermarriage: thus it was possible for deities of Italic origin[2] such as Neptune and Minerva to be adopted by the Etruscans. The numerous household slaves, dancers and musicians of the Etruscans whom we meet in their tomb-paintings may have been partly natives of the land, partly aliens acquired by trade and piracy; and even they were reported to have shared in their degree the luxury of their masters[3].

As the supremacy of the Etruscans in Etruria proper was originally won and then maintained through their higher culture and superior armament, so it was extended in Emilia to the north and Campania to the south in the same way, and also by means of the large bodies of subjects whom the Lucumones could now lead to battle. But we may fairly conjecture that this was not all, and that the way to political dominion was largely prepared by the penetration of Etruscan trade. A body of merchants might settle in some place which gave them a good opening for their business, form a colony, and gradually become the dominant power, particularly as the native inhabitants

brians, Daunians and other barbarians," who may have been either serfs or mercenaries, as taking part in the Etruscan attack of Cumae in 524 B.C. (Dionys. VII. 3. 1). Cf. too the retainers of the king of Veii, Livy, V. 15.

[1] Cf. Diod. v. 40: γράμματά τε καὶ φυσιολογίαν καὶ θεολογίαν ἐξεπόνησαν ἐπὶ πλεῖον.

[2] Wissowa, *Religion und Kultus der Römer*, pp. 225, 252.

[3] Diod. *loc. cit.* on the number of slaves which the Etruscans had, clothed ἐσθῆσι πολυτελεστέραις ἢ κατὰ δουλικὴν ἀξίαν.

whether in north or south Italy were at that time less
advanced in civilization. Thus at Bologna a stone head and
two stelae with primitive sculptures are thought to date
from the Villanova period but yet to be inspired by archaic
Etruscan art, and the same applies to some of the forms
of the late Villanova pottery and bronze-work[1]. The bronze
itself which is plentiful in the Villanova tombs of Emilia
doubtless came from the copper and tin mines of Tuscany[2];
and the very rare silver and gold fibulae of the same period
came from Etruria (being analogous to those which are
common at Vetulonia), perhaps, too, the few glass and
amber ornaments[3].

Similarly a remarkable tomb at Cumae[4] shews close
parallels with the "orientalizing" tombs of Vetulonia,
Caere, Veii, Volci and Praeneste, which appear to date
from early in the seventh century B.C., a period that is
previous to the Etruscan dominion in Campania, which in
any case never subdued the Greeks of Cumae. The gold
fibulae and clasps of the Cuman tomb find exact parallels
in Etruria and at Praeneste, and shew the same filigree
technique which is characteristic of the Vetulonian jewelry,
but was not used by the Greeks; so that we may regard
the gold jewelry of Cumae as imported from Etruria[5].
The same may be true of the silver vessels and the bronze
cauldrons and supports, and the bronze shield, of the
Cuman tomb; Karo, however, (p. 23) though admitting
that the metal-working industry was already flourishing

[1] Grenier, *Bologne*, pp. 421–31.
[2] Grenier (*op. cit.* pp. 265–6) says the bronze was brought from
Cyprus, asserting that tin is not found in Italy, but this, as we shall
see, is an error.
[3] Grenier, *op. cit.* pp. 299–305; he gives reasons for doubting
whether the Baltic amber came direct to the Adriatic before the end of
the sixth century.
[4] Pellegrini, *Mon. Ant.* XIII. pp. 225 ff.; Karo, *Bull. Pal.* XXX (1904),
pp. 1–29 (see p. 25, n. 3, on the date of this and similar tombs).
[5] Karo, *op. cit.* pp. 26–8.

in Etruria at the beginning of the seventh century, ascribes the bronzes to Greek importation. But in any case the identity of contents of this tomb with those of Etruria makes it highly probable that in Campania as in the Bolognese district Etruscan products and traders were penetrating, to be followed at a later date by the establishment of a definite Etruscan dominion.

It would be rash to attach too much importance to the wealth of the Etruscans as a cause of their conquests; it may have enabled them to employ mercenaries (as they certainly did in their last struggles against Rome[1]), but in general riches were far less important in ancient than in modern warfare. But the development of Etruscan art may be traced in a large measure to their wealth; for Etruscan art in spite of its national characteristics was throughout indebted to the Greeks—not merely to an original Hellenic influence, but to a constantly-renewed contact with Greece whether through the immigration of Greek artists or the importation of Greek products, both of which came to Etruria because it possessed an aristocracy which could pay a high price for them.

The prosperity of the Etruscans was due in the first place to the richness of their soil[2]. There was a large body of serfs to till it and considerable attention was paid to the draining of the soil and the regulation of streams[3]. Thus some of the most flourishing cities of ancient Etruria such as Tarquinii and Volci were in regions which are only now being reclaimed from the fever-stricken condition into which they were already sinking in Roman

---

[1] Livy, x. 10. 6 (299 B.C.), etc.

[2] Diod. v. 40: πάμφορον καὶ παντελῶς εὔγειον νεμόμενοι χώραν παντὸς καρποῦ πλῆθος ἀποθησαυρίζουσιν. Cf. Virg. G. II. 533 (in praise of country life), "sic fortis Etruria creuit."

[3] E.g. drainage and similar works to the north of Veii, and north of Prima Porta. Cf. the legend of the lawgiver Tages who was ploughed up from the soil of Tarquinii. (Cic. de Div. II. 23. 50–1.)

times[1]. There are frequent references to exports of corn from Etruria to relieve famines at Rome, and many of the Etruscan cities contributed corn for the army and crews of Scipio in 205 B.C.[2] The land was not too hilly for breeding horses, a fact which here as in Thessaly contributed to the support of an aristocratic system; horse-races appear commonly in Etruscan tomb-paintings and as we have seen remains of chariots and of horses' bits are found in many early tombs.

Of greater significance was the mineral wealth of Etruria and the extensive trade in metal goods to which it gave rise[3]. The fondness of the Etruscans for gold jewelry is evident from their tomb-paintings and sepulchral effigies —in the latter both men and women are not infrequently represented with a ring on every finger—and from the treasures of gold necklaces, armlets, bracelets, rings, brooches, clasps and other ornaments which are found in the great seventh-century tombs of southern Etruria, especially at Vetulonia and the Regolini-Galassi tomb at Caere. From the methods[4], rare or unknown outside Italy, but applied constantly to different forms of gold-work at Vetulonia, it is almost certain that they were local, and that the Etruscan goldsmiths' industry had already attained a high level of skill in the seventh century B.C.[5] Even in Athens, it appears, in the fifth century Etruscan

[1] Plin. *Ep.* v. 6. 2: "est sane grauis et pestilens ora Tuscorum quae per litus extenditur."
[2] Livy, II. 34; IV. 13, 25 and 52; XXVIII. 45.
[3] On this cf. Müller, II. pp. 254–60; on the sources of metals in the ancient world, Blumner, *Technologie*, etc. IV. pp. 10–1000; on Etruscan methods in mining, Reyer quoted by Nissen, *I.L.* II. pp. 297–8.
[4] Some of the forms of these ornaments also appear to be peculiar to Italy, e.g. the Caere "pectoral" (Pinza, "La Tomba Regolini-Galassi," in *Röm. Mitt.* XXII. 1907, pp. 50–1, 84; Montelius, *Civ. Prim.* II. pl. 341. 15) now in the Museo Gregoriano (Vatican) with the other contents of the Regolini-Galassi tomb.
[5] Karo, "Le orificerie di Vetulonia," in *Studi e Materiali*, I. pp.

gold-work was highly valued[1]. It is possible that the Etruscans procured their gold ore from some local source which has since become disused and unknown; otherwise it probably came from across the Apennines, or was imported from Ischia opposite Cumae, or from Spain[2]. Both gold and silver appear to have been coined by the Etruscans, especially at Populonia, the port and centre of the mining district, in the fifth century; about 200 years, that is, before the earliest silver coinage of the Romans[3].

Silver vessels also were widely used by the Etruscans, in marked contrast to the Romans of the early Republic[4]. Of the early silver treasures of Etruria, the most important comes from the Regolini-Galassi tomb at Caere, and some similar objects were found in tombs of Vetulonia and Praeneste. Some of these are doubtless of Phoenician importation: such are the bowls and paterae[5] with decoration in concentric bands shewing Egyptian or Assyrian scenes. One of these bowls (from Praeneste) bears a Phoenician inscription[6], and two cups belonging to the same series as those found in Italy were found in Cyprus[7].

233 ff., II. pp. 97 ff.: on the similar gold-work from Narce in the *ager Faliscus*, Karo in *Stud. e Mat.* III. pp. 143 ff.

[1] Critias *ap.* Athen. I. 28 *b*: Τυρσηνὴ δὲ κρατεῖ χρυσότυπος φιάλη | καὶ πᾶς χαλκὸς ὅτις κοσμεῖ δόμον ἔν τινι χρείᾳ.

[2] Gold in the bed of the Po: Strab. IV. 208, Plin. XXXIII. 66; near Vercellae: Strab. V. 218, Plin. XXXIII. 66; near Aquileia: Polyb. XXXIV. 10; in Pithecusae (Ischia): Strab. V. 247.

[3] Sambon, *Monnaies antiques de l'Italie*, I. pp. 37 ff.; Head, *Historia Nummorum*, pp. 10 ff.

[4] Diod. V. 40: ἐκπωμάτων ἀργυρῶν παντοδαπῶν πλῆθος, among the Etruscans: the same words in Poseidonius *ap.* Athen. IV. 153 *d*. Cf. Livy, *Epit.* XIV, on the expulsion of a consular from the Roman Senate: "quod is decem argenti pondo facti haberet."

[5] Montelius, II. pl. 338 (from Caere).

[6] Curtis in *Mem. Amer. Acad.* III. 1919, pp. 43–4, pl. 22 (= Montelius, II. pl. 369. 7): the bowl is in the Prehistoric Museum at Rome.

[7] Now in the Louvre (Salle de Suse). Cf. Perrot-Chipiez, *History of Art in Phoenicia and Cyprus*, II. pp. 341–59; Poulsen, *Die Orient u. frühgriech. Kunst*, pp. 20 ff.

However, several cups and a small amphora in silver from the Caere tomb have an Etruscan inscription "Larthia" or "Milarthia" (read from right to left) scratched upon them, and are noted by Pinza as common in the Tyrrhene area (being found also at Vetulonia and Praeneste) but not found elsewhere[1]. Also the form of skyphos which is found in gold at Praeneste, in silver at Vetulonia, Caere and Cumae is common in "proto-Corinthian" pottery (cf. e.g. Lorimer in *J.H.S.* 1912, p. 328, fig. 3 *a*), but is rarely if ever found in the precious metals outside Italy[2]; which suggests that they were made in Italy in imitation of imported Greek pottery, and probably in Etruria, a more likely centre for their production at an early date than Cumae or Praeneste. There are some indications that silver was mined in Etruria in early times, in the mineral region between Populonia and Volaterrae[3]; it may also have been procured from Sardinia or the rich mines of Spain[4].

More important, however, was the Etruscan bronze and iron industry for which abundant materials were present in the country. The copper and iron mines were in the island of Elba and in the mountain country between Volaterrae, Populonia and Vetulonia; they are still worked at several places in these regions (e.g. Montecatini near Volaterrae, and Campiglia Marittima near Populonia), and the name Montieri is clearly derived from Mons Aeris[5]. It appears from the resemblances in form and in marking of some copper ingots from Sardinia with similar ingots

[1] Pinza, *op. cit.* pp. 79–81; Montelius, II. pl. 339, nos. 1, 3, 7, 9; Falchi, *Vetulonia*, tav. XIV. 13 and XVI. 3; Curtis, *op. cit.* pls. 27. 3 and 29. 1.

[2] Pinza, *op. cit.* p. 84.

[3] Dennis, II. p. 209, n. 8; Müller, I. p. 225.

[4] Cf. Sidon. Apoll. v. 49: "Sardinia argentum, naues Hispania defert." Silver in Spain: Diod. v. 35, etc.

[5] On the copper mines of Tuscany, cf. Gabrici, "Cuma," in *Mon. Ant.* XXII. p. 168; Mosso, *Le origine della civiltà mediterranea*, pp. 301 ff.

found in Cyprus, Crete, and in the sea near Chalcis that copper and perhaps bronze already fused was exported from Cyprus to the west[1], and it has therefore been suggested that the plentiful bronze of the Villanova tombs in the region of Bologna was imported from Cyprus and not fused locally[2]. However, numerous bronze ingots found in various places in Italy differ from those of Cyprus and Sardinia both in shape and in markings[3], and may well have come from the mines of Tuscany; especially as there is good evidence that tin, necessary for making a bronze alloy, was worked by the Etruscans in several places near Populonia[4].

It is not improbable that copper and perhaps tin were mined in Tuscany before the period of Etruscan rule; but from the much greater abundance of iron in Etruscan tombs than in those of the Villanova type, it seems that the Etruscans were the first to work iron on a large scale in Italy. The iron mines of Elba were especially famous: it was believed that they were inexhaustible owing to the iron ore growing afresh where it had been excavated, and they were still worked in the early Empire[5]. Strabo, however, speaks of certain abandoned mines (of copper or iron)

[1] Pigorini in *Bull. Pal.* xxx (1904), pp. 91 ff. The Cyprian and Sardinian ingots contain about 98 per cent. copper and no tin.

[2] Grenier, *Bologne*, pp. 225–6.

[3] Pigorini, *Bull. Pal.* xxi (1895), pp. 5 ff., who then regarded the ingots as mined and distributed by the Etruscans.

[4] *Bull. Pal.* ii (1867), p. 79, and Blanchard in *Atti dei Lincei*, i. 1878, p. 186, on the discovery of large quantities of tin, with indications that it was worked in antiquity at Cento Camerelle near Campiglia. The place is named from the chambers connected by small galleries where iron ore was also extracted in antiquity. Mosso (*op. cit.* pp. 307–8) also mentions ancient tin mines at Montieri and Monte Valerio.

[5] Ps.-Arist. *de mir. ausc.* 93, p. 387 (mentions earlier copper mines there); Diod. v. 13; Strab. v. p. 223 *fin.*; Virg. *Aen.* x. 173: "insula inexhaustis Chalybum generosa metallis"; Rutil. Nam. i. 355: "ferri fecunda creatrix." Most of the other mines in Etruria probably ceased to be worked after the Roman conquest of Spain.

near Populonia, and the iron of Elba was at that time not
smelted on the island, perhaps through exhaustion of the
necessary wood-fuel, but on the mainland opposite, where
excavations in the Populonian necropolis have revealed
deep layers of iron refuse[1].

The possession by the Etruscans of practically all the
copper, tin, and iron which is found in Italy, together with
abundant timber for fuel[2] and with a remarkable ability
in working metals, must have contributed largely towards
their early predominance in Italy, and to their high place
among the trading and manufacturing peoples of antiquity.
Thus we find Etruscan utensils employed at Athens in the
fifth century[3], and the tombs of Etruria proper and those
of the Etruscan necropolis of Bologna have yielded bronze
articles of all kinds in large numbers—jars, cauldrons and
other vessels, tall candelabra, lamps, beds, tripods, cistae,
and incised mirrors—of which perhaps the finest extant
example is the bronze lamp of Cortona.

Besides these industrial products, many of which shew
great beauty and technical skill, the Etruscans produced
large quantities of bronze statues and statuettes—the
"Tyrrhena sigilla" which Horace mentions among articles
of luxury, and which had a very wide diffusion[4]. Many of

[1] *Not. scav.* 1908, p. 200, 1914, p. 446. Cf. the bronze coins of
Populonia bearing a head of Vulcan with a hammer and tongs (Sambon,
Monnaies antiques, I. p. 72).
[2] Strab. v. p. 222.
[3] Athen. xv. 700 c quotes from Pherecrates: *A. τίς τῶν λυχνείων ἢ
'ργασία; B. Τυρρηνική,* and adds *ποικίλαι γὰρ ἦσαν αἱ παρὰ τοῖς
Τυρρηνοῖς ἐργασίαι, φιλοτέχνων ὄντων τῶν Τυρρηνῶν.* Cf. Critias
ap. Athen. I. 28 b quoted above, and the supplies furnished to Scipio
in 205 B.C.—iron from Populonia, 3000 shields, 3000 helmets and
50,000 other weapons from Arretium (Livy, xxviii. 38).
[4] Hor. *Ep.* II. 2. 180; Plin. xxxiv. 34: "signa quoque Tuscanica per
terras dispersa quae quin in Etruria factitata sint non est dubium,"
and the 2000 statues said to have been taken at Volsinii. Tert.
Apol. 25: "ingenia Tuscorum fingendis simulacris urbem inun-
dauerunt."

the existing statuettes are of little artistic value, but such masterpieces as the Capitoline Wolf, the Chimaera of Arezzo, and the Orator of Lake Trasimene may with strong probability be laid to the credit of the Etruscan artificers[1].

Doubtless the gold and silver vessels and the bronze and iron work of the Etruscans formed the main basis of their sea-borne trade. The Etruscan mariners are almost always described by Greek and Roman writers as pirates; but we need not assume from this that they entirely neglected the more peaceful side of their profession. No doubt the earliest foreign goods found in Etruscan tombs were brought by Phoenician traders, who appear in Homer as the great sea-traders of the time[2], and the local trade indicated by the presence of vases with linear decoration, of the type common at Cumae, which we may therefore regard as the centre of distribution, was also carried on by sea, since these vases were found in Etruria most commonly in the coast towns such as Tarquinii, Volci, Caere, and in Latium they are commoner at Satricum close to the coast than at Rome[3]. In return the Etruscans exported to Cumae gold jewelry and perhaps bronzes, but there is nothing to indicate whether the trade was done by Cuman or Etruscan ships.

But the Etruscans, if it is once admitted that the nucleus of the nation came to Italy by sea from the east, must always have had a certain amount of shipping, though of the extent of it in the earliest times we know nothing. The

[1] Cf. Plin. xxxiv. 43: "uidemus Tuscanicum Apollinem in bibliotheca templi Augusti L pedum a pollice, dubium aere mirabiliorem an pulchritudine."

[2] Cf. *Il.* xxiii. 743, *Od.* xv. 403 ff. etc.: Kahrstedt in *Klio*, xii (1912), p. 451, on Phoenician trade on the west coast of Italy: De Sanctis, however (i. 329), thinks that the oriental goods found in early cremation-tombs were brought by the Greeks before the arrival of Phoenician traders.

[3] Gabrici, "Cuma" (*Mon. Ant.* xxii), pp. 382 ff.

country produced timber for shipbuilding in abundance, and in later times we hear of sails manufactured at Tarquinii[1], but it was deficient in good harbours. Hence Populonia was the only important city situated directly on the coast, though Tarquinii and Caere were not far distant from the open roadsteads which served as their ports. Populonia was regarded as later in origin than the twelve leading cities, whether it was a colony from Corsica or from Volaterrae or taken by the latter from the former[2]; yet it appears to have been a place of some importance already in the seventh century, and to have been inhabited before that[3]. Its importance lay in its proximity to the mines of Elba and of the mainland (Campiglia and Massa), and in the harbours facing in different directions which it possessed.

By the early part of the seventh century B.C. there was an active trade between Greece and Etruria, and the influx of Greek vases into Etruria was increasing. The tombs at Gela (founded in 689 B.C.) contained hardly any imported pottery earlier than Corinthian, and the same is true of Volci in Etruria, which yielded Corinthian ware in abundance[4]. Lorimer finds a cause for this wide diffusion of Corinthian pottery in the development of the carrying trade of Syracuse[5]; but there is no other sign of the maritime

---

[1] Livy, XXVIII. 45. The inland cities of Perusia, Clusium, and Rusellae on the same occasion provided Scipio with pine for building ships.

[2] These different traditions are preserved by Servius ad *Aen.* X. 172.

[3] Villanova tombs at Populonia: *Not. scav.* 1908, pp. 211 ff.; 1915, pp. 73 ff. A vaulted tomb with dromos, like those of Vetulonia and with remains of similar contents (gold, ivory, etc.): *ibid.* 1914, pp. 447 ff.

[4] Lorimer in *J.H.S.* XXXII (1912), pp. 340–4.

[5] Cf. on this Helbig in *Rend. Linc.* 1889, pp. 79 ff. who regards Syracuse as intermediary in the trade between Athens and Etruria in the sixth and fifth centuries.

activity of the Syracusans at so early a date[1], and from the scarcity in Sicily of the earliest Attic vases, which are common in Etruria, it seems probable that in the sixth century Athens traded with Etruria direct and not through Sicily[2], and that in the seventh century Etruscan ships carried the trade with Syracuse and the other Dorian colonies in Sicily. The fact that the Greeks in general seem to have known so little about central Italy and the Etruscans, whereas the Etruscans received a profound impression from Greek art, religion and mythology, strongly suggests that as a rule Etruscans came to Greek ports rather than Greeks to the coast of Etruria[3].

An exception must be made with regard to the Ionians of Asia Minor, particularly the Phocaeans[4], who according to Herodotus discovered the Adriatic, Tyrrhenia, Iberia and Tartessus. Their colony of Massalia dated from about 600 B.C. and they naturally touched at the Italian ports which lay on their route thither. Apparently the earliest true coins used by the Etruscans were those of the Ionian cities; for instance 65 silver coins of types which belong to Asia Minor (Phocaea, Lampsacus, etc.) were found at Volterra[5]. Ionian influences, too, are strongly marked in the Etruscan art of the early sixth century, such as the Tori, Auguri, Pulcinella, and Iscrizioni tombs at Tarquinii, and the terracotta sarcophagi and painted tiles of Caere[6]. There was no opposition between the Greeks

---

[1] We might except the Συρακόσιος λιμήν in Corsica (Diod. v. 13. 3): but there is no evidence for the antiquity of this name.

[2] Furtwängler, *Antike Gemmen*, III. p. 172.

[3] Furtwängler, *loc. cit.* holds that in the sixth and early fifth centuries Etruscan ships came to Athens, remarking that Herodotus' knowledge of Etruria is all derived from Phocaean sources.

[4] Hdt. I. 163.

[5] Deecke in Müller, I. p. 382; now in the Florence Museum.

[6] E.g. the winged creatures carrying human figures in their arms, which appear on some of the tiles from Caere (now in the Louvre), recall the famous "Harpy tomb" in the British Museum.

and the Etruscans as yet, and according to Herodotus
the Phocaeans had founded Alalia in Corsica 20 years
before their final departure from Asia Minor[1]. But the
Etruscans and Carthaginians were not prepared to leave
the Tyrrhenian islands to the Greeks, and the Phocaeans
attacked by their united fleets were driven out of Corsica
about 538 B.C.[2] The island passed to the Etruscans, who
founded there the city of Nicaea[3], while the Carthaginians
retained Sardinia.

Thus the command of the Tyrrhene Sea by the Etruscans, which had its origin at a much earlier period[4], was
firmly established. Diodorus (v. 40) speaks of the Etruscans
as πολλοὺς χρόνους θαλαττοκρατήσαντες, and the Etruscan
coins with representations of a sea-horse, polypus or
dolphin, or with an anchor or trident and dolphins on the
reverse[5], point to the sea as the source from which the
town which coined them derived its wealth. To the sixth
century belongs the agreement between Carthage and the
Etruscans which put a stop to any further development of
Greek colonization in the west, and only lost its force when
the sea-power of the allies in the Tyrrhene was broken by
the Syracusans under the leadership of Gelo and Hiero.

[1] Hdt. I. 165; Diod. v. 13, says the Phocaeans founded Calaris in
Corsica but later were driven out by the Etruscans.
[2] Hdt. I. 166, five years after the migration *en masse* of the Phocaeans, which followed the conquest of Ionia by Harpagus. Herodotus
describes the battle as a "Cadmean victory" for the Phocaeans since
their ships were either sunk or rendered useless for further warfare.
[3] Diod. *loc. cit.*
[4] According to Ephorus (*ap.* Strab. VI. p. 267) the Greek colonies
in Sicily were founded in the tenth generation after the Trojan War,
τοὺς γὰρ πρότερον δεδιέναι τῶν Τυρρηνῶν τὰ ληστήρια, which seems
to shew that the Etruscans were already a naval power in the period
of colonization.
[5] Sambon, *Monnaies antiques*, pp. 39, 46–7, 73 ff. etc.

PART TWO

THE ETRUSCANS IN LATIUM

§ 1

ETRURIA AND THE ORIGINS OF ROME

THE fact of the Etruscan dominion in Latium during the sixth century is now so generally[1] accepted that I will only attempt here to consider its nature and some of its effects. In the first place, its political significance must not be exaggerated. For instance, to speak of the Etruscan conquest as "the first attempt to unite the north and south of the peninsula to the centre," and of the "unifying work of the Etruscans" later resumed by Rome[2], is the fancy of a patriotic historian under the influence of the union of Italy in modern times. The Etruscans were not even in Etruria a united nation under a single ruling power as Republican Rome was; much less were they consciously or even unconsciously aiming at uniting all Italy. We are not to imagine the Lucumones in their council at the shrine of Voltumna resolving on an expedition into the Po valley or Campania or Latium; rather were such expeditions the work of individual cities or chieftains with their dependents[3]. It is clear, too, that Latium never became an Etruscan land as the region of Bologna did, probably it had fewer Etruscan immigrants

---

[1] See e.g. Körte in Pauly-Wissowa, VI. p. 752, s.v. "Etrusker"; De Sanctis, I. pp. 445 ff.; Pais, I². pp. 790 ff.; Meyer, II. § 435.

[2] Pais, I². p. 791.

[3] Meyer, *loc. cit.*, cf. e.g. Vibenna in the Roman legend.

—a small number of powerful families[1] who were driven out towards the end of the sixth century, and left the native population to reassert itself, stimulated by contact with a more advanced culture, but maintaining its Latin character[2]. Thus the archaic inscription (of disputed date) found under the *lapis niger* in the Forum is Latin and not Etruscan, nor do the early cemeteries of Rome on the Esquiline and in the Forum afford much evidence of an Etruscan occupation; a few chamber-tombs have been found resembling those of Etruria and containing fragments of the same imported pottery with linear decoration as is found in Etruria in early tombs, one such fragment bearing a Greek inscription[3]. The rare gold and silver ornaments and a large part of the bronze ware in the Roman tombs were probably imported from Etruria, but are not in themselves evidence of Etruscan rule[4].

[1] W. Schulze, "Zur Geschichte lateinischer Eigennamen" (in *Abhandlungen der k. Gesellschaft der Wissenschaften zu Göttingen*, Philol.-Hist. Kl. v. 2, 1904), shews that there was a large common element in the Etruscan and Latin name-systems; but as the borrowing of names was reciprocal (Schulze, pp. 64, 263, 434, etc.) the historical significance of the facts which he collects is uncertain; cf. Lattes in *Klio*, XII. pp. 377 ff.; Herbig in *Indog. Forsch.* 1909, pp. 357 ff.

[2] On some possibly Etruscan elements in the early constitution of Rome see A. Rosenberg, *Der Staat der alten Italiker*, and a review of this by E. Körnemann in *Klio*, XIV (1913), entitled "Zur altitalischen Verfassungsgeschichte." It seems probable that the "imperium" of a single magistrate was a characteristically Etruscan institution, and this appears at Rome in the dictatorship; there is no trace in Etruria of the Roman principle of collegiality. But many of Rosenberg's conclusions regarding the names and ranks of the federal and local magistracies in Etruria seem to me to rest on insufficient evidence.

[3] *Bull. Comm.* 1874, pp. 47–52; 1875, pp. 55–6, and tav. VI–VIII. *Not. scav.* 1877, p. 81; 1883, p. 47. The chamber-tombs were found underneath the small pit-tombs ("puticoli") common in the Esquiline necropolis. On the Greek inscription (originally considered to be Etruscan), cf. Pinza, *Mon. Ant.* XV. p. 195, n. 2. Chamber-tombs have also been found recently on Monte Mario, immediately across the Tiber from Rome.

[4] *Bull. Comm.* 1896, pp. 32, 35; Pinza in *Mon. Ant.* XV (1905), pp. 431 ff., 560 ff.

On the other hand we are not entitled to treat the period of foreign dominion as a transient phenomenon with no particular significance. It may, I think, be asserted that her Etruscan rulers first made Rome a city both materially and morally; that under them the Romans were given a wider outlook and introduced into a more developed civilization than they had previously known; and that in religion and social life, in art and architecture, and perhaps also in industry and trade the Romans owed more to the Etruscans than they were accustomed to admit in later times. On the material side we see in this period the building of the first wall of Rome, an event of the highest importance for implanting a sense of unity in the uncivilized peasants of the hill-villages which it enclosed, and as the religious symbol of this union, the Capitoline temple[1]. We see the primitive Latin religion modified by Greek and Etruscan elements; the assertion of the supremacy of Rome among the Latin cities; the beginnings of the Roman Forum; and there is ground for believing that the very names of Roma and the Tiber are of Etruscan origin[2], as was asserted by the Romans themselves of the names of their three primitive tribes[3].

The influence of Etruria on Rome certainly lasted long after the fall of the Etruscan hegemony, and may have begun in an earlier period. But our knowledge of Roman history before the Tarquins is so vague and fragmentary that it is risky to dogmatize on this point. An attempt has been made by Carlo Pascal[4] to claim for the Etruscans a share in the original settlement on the Palatine, round which

[1] Cf. Carter, "Evolution of the City of Rome," in *Proc. Amer. Philos. Soc.* XLVIII (1909), pp. 129–41.

[2] Schulze, *op. cit.* pp. 218, 247, 579 ff.

[3] Varro, *L.L.* v. 55: "sed omnia haec uocabula Tusca, ut Volnius qui tragoedias Tuscas scripsit dicebat." Schulze (p. 218) accepts this tradition as true.

[4] "Le divinità infere e i Lupercali," in *Rend. Linc.* 1895, pp. 138 ff.

ran the original pomerium[1] which was regarded as an
Etruscan institution. This was also the course of the Luper-
cales[2], and Pascal (*op. cit.* pp. 145–6) regards "Faunus-
Lupercus" as an Etruscan deity on the strength of the
identification of Pan or Faunus with Inuus[3], and the
existence of a "Castrum Inui" near Ardea (Virg. *Aen.*
VI. 775) in the land of the Rutuli, whom Appian[4] calls
Tyrrheni, and also near Caere, the latter being mentioned
by Rutilius Namatianus (I. 225–32). Pascal also (p. 154)
speaks of "walls of the Romulean pomerium" still extant
on the Palatine and built "in the Etruscan manner," i.e.
in the style known as "headers and stretchers." The same
writer elsewhere[5] speaks of the tribe occupying the Palatine
as a fusion of the primitive Ramnes with the Luceres, the
followers of "the Etruscan king of Ardea" Lucero, who
settled first on the Caelian hill, which (it is claimed) is
connected in all the myths and legendary traditions with
an Etruscan settlement.

But this somewhat elaborate argument has serious defects.
In the first place, the wall "in the Etruscan manner"
which Pascal ascribes to the Romulean pomerium belongs
to the fourth-century wall of Rome (or a separate fortification of the Palatine of the same period), and in all probability the earliest wall of Rome was built in the sixth
century and enclosed a much larger area than the Palatine.
Another dubious point is the Etruscan origin of the
Lupercalia, of which there is no other trace[6]. The Palatine

[1] Tac. *Ann.* XII. 24; Gellius, XIII. 14. 2. Cf. Varro, *L.L.* v. 143:
"oppida condebant in Latio Etrusco ritu multi, id est uinctis bobus
tauro et uacca interiore aratro circumagebant solum"; Livy, I. 44. 4.
[2] Varro, *L.L.* VI. 34.   [3] Livy, I. 5. 3; Serv. ad *Georg.* I. 16.
[4] Βασιλ. I. I.   [5] *Rend. Linc.* 1895, pp. 546–7; 1896, pp. 147–8.
[6] Wissowa, *Religion u. Kultus der Römer*, p. 211, n. 7, denies that
Inuus had anything to do with the Lupercalia and that Inuus was an
Etruscan deity, the mention by Rutilius of Castrum Inui being due to
a mistake for Castrum Novum (Bormann, *C.I.L.* XI. p. 531). Cf. too
Warde Fowler, *Roman Festivals*, pp. 312 ff.

might from its position be compared to the isolated towns of south Etruria (Falerii, Sutrium, Nepet), but equally well to the Italic "terremare" settlements of north Italy.

The tradition of an Etruscan settlement on the Caelian is somewhat stronger though by no means as universal as Pascal claims; in a famous passage of the speech of Claudius preserved at Lyons (*C.I.L.* XIII. 1688), Servius Tullius, the Etruscan Mastarna, is said to have brought thither the army of his friend Caelius Vibenna; other writers[1] refer to an Etruscan Caelius who came to help Romulus against the Sabines, and Tacitus was aware of the different versions of the legend[2]. But it appears that originally Caelius Vibenna was quite distinct from the Etruscan hero Lucumo or Lucerus or Lycomedius who was supposed to have joined Romulus in the Sabine war[3]. Here is a clear case of an etymological myth; the connexion of the Tities with the Sabine Tatius and the Ramnes with the Latin Romulus being once assumed, what was more natural than to regard the Luceres as an Etruscan element[4] and introduce into the legends of Romulus an Etruscan Lucumo from whom they could take their name? That there may have been some Etruscans in Rome from the earliest times is, in view of the important position of

[1] Dionys. II. 36. 2 (but cf. *ibid.* 50. 1: Ῥωμύλος τὸ Παλάτιον κατέχων καὶ τὸ Καίλιον ὄρος); Festus (*ap.* Paul. Diac.), p. 44; Varro, *L.L.* v. 46, who identifies this Caelius with Vibenna, and ascribes the name *Tuscus uicus* to a settlement of his followers.

[2] *Ann.* IV. 65. 1: "Caelium appellatum a Caele Vibenna qui dux gentis Etruscae cum auxilium portauisset, sedem eam acceperat a Tarquinio Prisco seu quis alius regum dedit; nam scriptores in eo dissentiunt. cetera non ambigua sunt, magnas eas copias per plana etiam ac foro propinqua habituisse, unde Tuscum uicum e uocabulo aduenarum dictum."

[3] Cic. *de Rep.* II. 8. 14; Varro, *L.L.* v. 55; Festus, p. 119 (who all derive the tribe of Luceres from these foreign allies); Dionys. II. 37. 2; Prop. IV. 2. 49 ff. who derives the "Tuscus uicus" from them.

[4] Cf. Dionys. III. p. 6; Flor. III. 18, for the idea of a fusion of Latins, Sabines, and Etruscans in Rome.

Rome at the crossing of the Tiber, not impossible; but the tribal division (as among the Dorians or Ionians) does not necessarily imply a distinction of race. Furthermore, Livy and Plutarch shew no knowledge of the Etruscan derivation of the Luceres[1], and according to some other legends the Caelian hill was assigned to the people of Alba Longa by Tullus Hostilius[2], or first added to the city by Ancus Marcius[3]. Thus on the question of an original Etruscan element in Rome we must maintain an agnostic attitude.

Of Caelius or Caele Vibenna, however, there is more to be said; for though his name is preserved by Roman tradition for purely etymological reasons, yet he appears in a small group of Etruscan monuments associated with his brother Aulus and (in one of them) his friend Mastarna. I refer to a mirror from Bolsena, now in the British Museum[4]; three Etruscan urns[5] shewing the same subject with some variations as the mirror but without the names of the characters; and the famous painting[6] from the François tomb at Volci (copied in the Vatican), which represents the release of Caile Vipinas by Macstrna and the slaying of four men (apparently barely roused from sleep) by four armed assailants, among the latter being Aule Vipinas, and among the victims being Cneve Tarchu Rumach, which can only stand for Cnaeus Tarquinius (or Tarquitius) Romanus. With the mirror and the urns

[1] Livy, I. 13. 8: "Lucerum nominis et originis causa incerta est"; Plut. *Rom.* 20: Λουκερήνσης διὰ τὸ ἄλσος ("lucus," i.e. the Romulean Asylum).

[2] Livy, I. 30. 1; 33. 2; Auct. *de vir. ill.* 4. Cf. Dionys. III. 1. 5.

[3] Cic. *de Rep.* II. 18; Strabo, V. p. 234.

[4] Walters, *Bronzes in B.M.* no. 633; Körte in Gerhard's *Etr. Spiegel*, V. pp. 166–72, tav. 127.

[5] Körte, *Rilievi delle urne etrusche*, II. pp. 254–8, tav. CXIX.

[6] Garrucci, "Pitture Vulcenti," in *Dissertazioni Archeologiche* (Rome, 1886), II. pp. 57 ff.; Pais, I². pp. 510–8; De Sanctis, "Mastarna," in *Klio*, II (1902), pp. 96–104; Körte in *Jahrb. k. d. Arch. Inst.* 1897, pp. 5 ff.; Petersen, *ibid.* 1899, pp. 43 ff.

(shewing the surprise of the minstrel or seer Cacus[1] by
the Vibenna brothers) we are not here concerned; but the
wall painting gives a different version of the Etruscan
tradition to which the speech of Claudius refers, when he
speaks of Servius Tullius:

si Tuscos (sequimur), Caeli quondam Vivennae sodalis fidelissi-
mus omnisque eius casus comes, postquam uaria fortuna exactus
cum omnibus reliquis Caeliani exercitus Etruria excessit, montem
Caelium occupauit et a duce suo Caelio ita appellitauit [appelli-
tatus *inscr.*] mutatoque nomine (nam Tusce Mastarna ei nomen
erat) ita appellatus est ut dixi, et regnum summa cum reip.
utilitate optinuit.

Alongside of this must be placed the fragmentary sentence
of Festus (p. 355) in explanation of the name "Tuscus
uicus"; after (as it seems) giving the derivation from the
remains of Porsena's army (as in Livy, II. 14. 9) he continues—I quote the text as supplemented by Garrucci—
"[Tusci, quod Volci] entes fratres Caeles et [A.] Vibenn[ae,
quos dicunt ad regem] Tarquinium se cum Max[tarna
contulisse, eum incolue]rint[2]."

The Volci fresco is dated from its style about the end
of the fourth century B.C., the period, that is, when the
Etruscans were engaged in their final struggle against Rome,
and represents a victory of the national heroes over the
Romans, who are surprised after a raid in which they had
captured Caele Vibenna, and their leader Tarquin is killed.
This appears as De Sanctis says[3] a more genuine version

[1] The tradition of Gellius in Solinus, I. 8, quoted by Körte (*Spiegel*
and *Rilievi, locc. citt.*) and Petersen, throws little light on this obscure
legend, and none on Roman or Etruscan history.
[2] Garrucci also discusses at length the passages which refer to the
head of Olus or Aulus of Volci which was found when the foundations
of the Capitol were laid, viz. Arnob. *adv. Nat.* VI. 7 and Serv. *Aen.*
VIII. 345 (both in Peter, *Hist. Rom. Reliqu.* pp. 23–4), identifying this
Aulus with Aulus Vibenna. But the story of the human head (also
in Livy, I. 55. 5, Dionys. IV. 59, Plin. XXVIII. 15, Zonar. VII. 11, etc.) is
merely etymological, explaining the name Capitolium.
[3] *Op. cit.* p. 100.

of the Etruscan legend than that given by Claudius, in which the army of Caele after his death settles in Rome, and its leader Mastarna later becomes king—there being no apparent motive for either event. Further, the identification of Mastarna with Servius Tullius causes difficulties, as the exploit of Mastarna depicted in the Volci tomb is quite at variance with the various Roman legends concerning the origin and work of Servius[1], and accordingly De Sanctis regards Mastarna as a duplicate of Porsena, who in the most trustworthy Roman tradition gains possession of Rome after the expulsion of Tarquin, but does not restore the latter. Undoubtedly the Mastarna of the fresco corresponds better with Porsena (if we put out of mind the official Roman account of the latter) than with Servius Tullius; but where all the figures are so wrapt in legend identifications are dangerous, and Claudius may have known of other Etruscan traditions which are lost to us.

Of the number or the names of the Etruscan rulers of Rome we know nothing. For Lucius Tarquinius Priscus is simply "the Lucumo from Tarquinii" according to Roman legend[2], surnamed "The Elder" to distinguish him from a later L. Tarquinius, who is in reality merely a duplicate of the same legendary figure, since the same deeds in peace and war are ascribed to both kings (e.g. the Latin wars, the Capitoline temple, the cloacae, etc.)[3]. "Tarquin" is well attested as an Etruscan family name; thus it occurs repeatedly in the "Grotta dei Tarquinii" at Caere[4] both in Etruscan (usually "Tarchnas") and in

[1] Legends of the birth of Servius: Livy, I. 49; Dionys. IV. I. 2; Plin. XXXVI. 204; Ov. *Fast.* VI. 631 ff. But as he was said to have married a daughter of Priscus he may in any case be counted as a member of the Tarquin dynasty.

[2] Livy, I. 34; Dionys. III. 46.

[3] Pais, I². pp. 519–21; De Sanctis, *Klio*, II. p. 102; *Stor. dei Rom.* I. p. 371.

[4] Dennis, I. pp. 242–4, quotes other examples, to which may

Latin ("Tarnca," "Tarquitius," *C.I.L.* XI. 3626–32). It
is therefore not improbable that a dynasty of this name
coming from Caere may have ruled in Rome (especially
as in one tradition the Tarquins take refuge at Caere after
their expulsion[1]), and there is no ground for dismissing
the Etruscan origin of the Tarquins as "an etymological
myth[2]." Alternatively we might regard the Tarquins as
the personification of the Etruscan metropolis Tarquinii,
and their conquests as the reflexion of a real hegemony
of Tarquinii over a large part of Etruria and Latium[3]; but
such a theory is at variance with the appearance of an
individual Tarquin at Rome in the Volci wall-painting, and
the political hegemony of Tarquinii is purely conjectural.

The date and the manner of the Etruscan conquest of
Rome are equally unknown to us. We may date it pro-
visionally about 600 B.C.; but whether it came about by force
of arms or by peaceful settlement, there is no indication.

But in one point we can claim for our legendary tradition
a high degree of accuracy—the Greek connexion of the
Tarquins. When legend[4] represents the elder Tarquin as
the son of a Greek father, who brought with him the artists
Euchir, Diopos and Eugrammos[5], and an Etruscan mother,
it well symbolizes one of the chief consequences of the
Etruscan rule in Rome. Somewhat as England was brought
by the Norman conquest into the orbit of French (and so
Latin) civilization, so the Etruscan rulers were the medium
by which Greek influences first entered Rome. On this
we have the testimony of Cicero who prefaces his account[6]

perhaps be added, "L. Tercenna" (*C.I.L.* XI. 3371 *b*) from the Tomba
del Tifone at Tarquinii. The name of Tanaquil the wife of Tarquinius
Priscus (Liv. I. 34) also occurs in Etruscan inscriptions (Deecke,
Etr. Forschungen, III. pp. 156–62).

[1] Liv. I. 60. 2; but in Dionys. IV. 85. 4 they go to Gabii.
[2] De Sanctis, I. pp. 371–2, who, however, believes in the Etruscan
dominion over Latium (p. 446).   [3] So Müller, I. p. 113.
[4] Polyb. VI. 11 *a*. 7; Cic. *de Rep.* II. 19; Dionys. III. 46; Liv. I. 34, etc.
[5] Plin. *N.H.* XXXV. 152.   [6] *de Repub.* II. 19. 34.

of the Tarquins with the words "influxit non tenuis quidam
e Graecia rivulus in hanc urbem, sed abundantissimus
amnis illarum disciplinarum et artium, fuisse enim quen-
dam ferunt Demaratum Corinthium... etc." and of the
sons of Demaratus he tells us "omnibus eos artibus ad
Graecorum disciplinam erudiit." Greek trade had long
flourished in the maritime cities of southern Etruria—we
can trace it by the pottery with linear decoration (apparently imported from Cumae)[1] which is found in large
quantities at Tarquinii, and also at Caere, Volci and other
sites—and it was followed by the settlement of Greek
artists who powerfully affected all but the very earliest
Etruscan art. The so-called "mare clausum" policy of
the Phoenicians and Etruscans by no means involved the
total exclusion of Greeks from Etruscan cities.

Of this Hellenic influence Caere, which we have suggested
as possibly the place of origin of the Tarquins, seems to
have been a particular centre. It early had relations with
Delphi[2]; according to Strabo "it was in good repute among
the Hellenes for its valour and righteousness; for it re-
frained from piracy though it had full power to practise it,
and it dedicated at Pytho the treasury called the treasury
of the Agyllaeans." It is surely not by accident that we
find the earliest Roman embassy to Delphi ascribed by
tradition to the reign of a Tarquin king, and also the
introduction of the Greek Sibylline oracles[3]. Pais (I[2]. p. 527)
regards the latter event (like nearly all the recorded events
of the Tarquinian period) as belonging in fact to the fourth

[1] Cf. Gabrici, *Cuma (Mon. Ant.* XXII), pp. 382 ff.; but the Cuman
origin of the geometrical pottery found in central Italy is not certain.

[2] Hdt. I. 167, on the games instituted at Agylla (Caere) in obedience
to a response from Delphi, to atone for the stoning of Phocaean
prisoners; Strab. v. 222; Plut. *Cam.* 21, refers to it as τις τῶν Ἑλληνίδων
πόλεων.

[3] Cic. *de Rep.* II. 24. 44; Dionys. IV. 69. 2 (quoting Varro on the
Sibylline books); Liv. I. 56. 5 ff.

century B.C. and wrongly thrown back to the sixth; and De Sanctis (I. p. 374) suggests that the oracles were only connected with the Tarquins because they were kept in the Capitoline temple. But there are traces in Rome of trade-relations with Cumae (whence the Sibylline oracles came) in the sixth century or earlier[1], and it is not incredible that a collection of Greek oracles may also have come to Rome at that time[2]. If so, we may see in the temple dedicated to the Greek triad Demeter, Dionysus and Kore (Ceres, Liber and Libera) in 493 B.C.[3], on which Greek artists were engaged, the first of many honours paid to Greek or other foreign divinities by command of the Sibylline books. We also find traces in tradition of Roman relations with the Greek city of Massalia in the time of the Tarquins[4], and it may have been at this time that Rome became known to Greek writers, who called it Τυρρηνὶς πόλις[5].

In the field of Roman religion we can see clearly the working of Graeco-Etruscan influence. It is well known that the gods of the primitive Romans were vague "powers" (numina) without images or temples[6]; the first and decisive step towards anthropomorphism was taken under the Tarquin kings, who built the Capitoline temple with its statue of Jupiter. The Etruscans had already identified

[1] Gabrici, Cuma, p. 381. A doubtful legend connects the Tarquins with Aristodemus the tyrant of Cumae: Liv. II. 21. 5; Dionys. VI. 21. 3.

[2] Perhaps, however, we should speak of a Sibylline influence entering Rome, rather than an actual collection of oracles, cf. W. Fowler, Religious Experience of the Roman People, p. 257.

[3] Plin. XXXV. 154; Dionys. VI. 17.

[4] Strab. IV. 180: τὸ ξόανον τῆς Ἀρτέμιδος τῆς ἐν τῷ Ἀβεντίνῳ [cf. Liv. I. 45] οἱ Ῥωμαῖοι τὴν αὐτὴν διάθεσιν ἔχον τῷ παρὰ τοῖς Μασσαλιώταις ἀνέθεσαν. Just. XLIII. 3. 4.

[5] Dionys. I. 29. 2; but as Greek writers did not discriminate clearly between the different peoples of Italy the fact is of little importance.

[6] Plut. Numa, 8; Aug. de Civ. Dei, IV. 31: "(Varro) dicit antiquos Romanos plus annos CLXX deos sine simulacro coluisse."

their thunder-god Tinia with the Greek Zeus, and they now gave a new turn to the conception of the Latin Jupiter. Juno was already known to Roman religion; Minerva was a stranger whose original home was probably the half-Latin town of Falerii, whence her cult had spread in South Etruria[1]. The "Capitoline triad" seems to have been evolved in Etruria, its only appearance in Greece being in Phocis where the several cities met at the shrine of Zeus, Hera and Athena[2]. More important in its results was the humanizing process first applied to the old Latin deities under Graeco-Etruscan influences; for it paved the way for the long series of Greek divinities which in later times entered Rome, it formed the starting-point for the artistic development of Rome as shewn in numerous temples with their statues and paintings, and led ultimately to the quite non-Roman idea of the deified man. And the building of the Capitoline temple marked the transition from the exclusive worship of the many minor powers connected with the home and with pastoral and agricultural pursuits to the national religion of Jupiter Optimus Maximus—a transition which was the religious side of the growth of the civic and patriotic sense in the Romans of the sixth century.

On the possible Etruscan affinities of other deities worshipped at Rome not much need be said. The Fors Fortuna, whose cult was said to have been introduced by Servius Tullius[3], is sometimes regarded as a Latin form of the

[1] Wissowa, *Religion u. Kultus der Römer*, pp. 252–3; W. Fowler, *Religious Experience*, etc. p. 233. Juno had a special cult in Falerii (Ov. *Am.* III. 13, etc.) and Veii (Liv. v. 22).

[2] Pausan. x. 5. 1. According to Servius (ad *Aen.* I. 422) the "Etrusca disciplina" prescribed temples of Jupiter, Juno and Minerva as essential to a properly founded city. On the stone of Terminus, perhaps of Etruscan origin (cf. the Etruscan round stones marking graves or boundaries, e.g. Montelius, *Civ. Prim.* II. pl. 168. 6), which was found *in situ* when the Capitoline temple was built and survived in representations of Jupiter, see A. B. Cook, *Zeus*, I. pp. 53 ff., pls. vi–vii.

[3] Varro, *L.L.* VI. 17; Dionys. IV. 27. 7; Ovid, *Fasti*, VI. 569, etc.

Etruscan goddess Nortia, worshipped at Volsinii[1], and Müller (I. p. 115) built on this identification a theory that the reign of Servius represented the temporary overthrow of the supremacy of Tarquinii in Rome by a less aristocratic band of invaders from Volsinii. But this derivation of Fors Fortuna is uncertain; she may have been originally a fertility-goddess as Warde Fowler suggests[2], or connected with the mysterious Fortuna Primigenia of Praeneste. Whether the practice of driving a nail annually into the wall of the Capitoline temple was directly derived from the similar practice in the temple of Nortia at Volsinii[3], we cannot say. It appears to have had no original connexion with the reckoning of time, but to be a survival from the dedication of some object representing the offerer[4]: thus the community in the person of its highest magistrate ("praetor maximus" in the ancient law to which Livy refers) annually dedicated itself. Vortumnus, another deity of Volsinii, was apparently introduced at Rome only after the capture of Volsinii in 264 B.C.[5]

It was inevitable that in religion Etruria, "genetrix et mater superstitionis[6]," should leave some imprint on Rome.

[1] Juv. x. 24: "si Nortia Tusco fauisset," and Schol.: "Fortunam vult intellegi." Tertull. *Apol.* 24.

[2] *Roman Festivals*, pp. 67 ff., 166 ff.; cf. Carter, *Religion of Numa*, p. 51; A. B. Cook, *Zeus*, I. pp. 271–2.

[3] Liv. VII. 3, who says the Roman practice was based on an ancient law, "priscis litteris uerbisque scripta" (i.e. perhaps akin to the archaic inscription found under the *lapis niger*).

[4] Cf. the nail and rag driven into the sacred tree, A. B. Cook in *Folklore*, XVII (1906), pp. 321 ff.; and Syracusan coins shewing Nike with hammer and nail fixing a trophy, *Catal. Coins in the Brit. Mus. (Sicily)*, pp. 195 ff. Warde Fowler (*Roman Festivals*, p. 172) suggests that the ritual nail-driving may have been connected with the Fortune of Antium and the "claui trabales" of Horace, *Odes*, I. 35. 18. But there is no real evidence for this idea; if it were true, we should expect the ceremony to have been performed in the Temple of Fortune.

[5] Wissowa, *op. cit.* p. 287.

[6] Arnob. *adv. Nat.* VII. 26, cf. Liv. V. 1. 6: "gens ante omnes alias eo magis dedita religionibus quod excelleret arte colendi eas."

A purely Etruscan element in Roman religion was the *haruspicina*, or science of divination by examining the entrails of sacrificial victims, which the Romans used till a late period though they seem never to have made it fully their own; hence we constantly hear of haruspices being summoned from Etruria to explain "prodigies" and give directions for their expiation[1]. The science was connected with another distinctively Etruscan doctrine, that of the celestial "templum" by which the sky was divided into sixteen parts, each the domain of a particular deity[2]. The famous liver of Piacenza is similarly divided into forty areas, each marked with Etruscan characters[3]. The idea of the templum made more complex the science of divination by the flight of birds (a method more widely spread among Greeks and Romans than the *haruspicina*), and it also involved various ritual rules with regard to the foundation of cities and division of land. Thus the Romans took over from the Etruscans the pomerium and the idea of the terrestrial templum or sacred area.

§ 2

ETRUSCAN INFLUENCES IN ROMAN ARCHITECTURE

Especially important was the Etruscan influence on Roman architecture—an influence by no means confined to the period of the Tarquins. To this period, however, tradition largely borne out by archaeological evidence

[1] Cf. Diod. v. 40: γράμματά τε καὶ φυσιολογίαν καὶ θεολογίαν ἐξεπόνησαν ἐπὶ πλεῖον καὶ τὰ περὶ τὴν κεραυνοσκοπίαν μάλιστα πάντων ἀνθρώπων ἐξειργάσαντο.

[2] Cic. *de Div.* II. 18. 42; Plin. *N.H.* II. 143.

[3] Deecke, *Etruskische Forschungen* (1880), IV. pp. 1 ff.; cf. a terracotta liver from Babylonia in the British Museum, and an urn of Volterra representing a haruspex holding a similar liver. See G. Blecher, *De extispicio capita tria*, with Bezold's supplement (pp. 246–52) on Babylonian *extispicium*.

assigns various important constructions, such as the earliest walls of Rome, the Capitoline temple, and the drainage of the Forum. It is generally agreed that the so-called "Servian Wall" is subsequent to the Gallic invasion[1]; but it does not follow that the tradition of a wall built in the regal period[2] is entirely false.

It is probable in itself that Rome, being the centre in the sixth century of a fertile and densely populated district, would already possess some form of fortification[3], especially as its position was not as strong naturally as that of most of its neighbours, such as Veii practically isolated by precipitous ravines, or Praeneste on its hill-top. Further, there exist fragments of an earlier wall than the better-known structure ascribed to Servius; it follows the same line as the latter (except that there is no trace of it on the Aventine) and in places seems to have been restored to form an inside facing to it. But the walls are different in style and material. The later wall (probably dating from the fourth century[4]) is of yellow-brown tufa in large blocks measuring about $4 \times 2 \times 2$ Roman feet and arranged so that in alternate courses the sides and ends of the blocks are visible—the style known as "headers and stretchers[5]"; the largest

---

[1] Cf. e.g. Pinza in *Mon. Ant.* xv. pp. 746 ff.; *Bull. Comm.* 1912, pp. 68 ff.; Richter, *Die Alliaschlacht und Serviusmauer*, pp. 15 ff.

[2] Dionys. III. 67. 4: Tarquinius Priscus first built λίθοις ἀμαξιαίοις εἰργασμένοις πρὸς κανόνα; Liv. I. 36. 1; 44. 3.

[3] T. Frank, "Notes on the Servian Wall," in *Amer. Journ. Arch.* XXII (1918), pp. 177 ff.

[4] Frank, *op. cit.* pp. 181–3, shews that the stone came from the territory of Veii and Fidenae and perhaps partly from the walls of those towns after their capture. On the dates of the two walls cf. Graffunder, "Das Alter der servianischen Mauer in Rom," in *Klio*, XI (1911), pp. 83 ff., who deals largely with the use of the Roman and the earlier Oscan foot.

[5] This style is common in S. Etruria, e.g. Sutrium, Nepet, Caere, the Roman Falerii; Pinza (*Bull. Comm.* 1897, p. 250) says it is found also in the walls of Dionysius at Syracuse (and elsewhere in Sicily), but I have not found any traces of it there.

portions of this wall extant are in a yard of the railway
terminus and on the south side of the Aventine, and there
are fragments on the Palatine and elsewhere. The earlier
wall is built of a gray flaky tufa known as "cappellaccio"
in thin slabs; there are fragments of it at the north-west
corner of the Palatine, under the late German Embassy
on the Capitol, a large portion in Via Giosuè Carducci and
another in Piazza dei Cinquecento (i.e. on the northern
edge of the Quirinal and the plateau of the Viminal respectively)[1]. There are remains of *cappellaccio* masonry in
the lowest stratum of the temples of Jupiter Capitolinus,
the Castores, and Apollo[2] (which date respectively from
the late sixth century, from 484 and from 431 B.C.) and of
the Lacus Curtius, the shrine of Venus Cloacina, the temple
of Saturn, the Tullianum, the Comitium, and it is noteworthy that in all of these the *cappellaccio* is the lowest and
therefore earliest element[3]. Furthermore this gray-green
tufa lay near the ground-surface in most parts of Rome,
and appears to be peculiar to Rome[4]; thus it would naturally
be used at an earlier date than stone which came from a
distance, and judging from the extant evidence it may be
maintained that all structures in which it occurs date from
the fifth century at latest. No indication of date can be
drawn from the style of the masonry, as owing to the
flakiness of the stone it could only be cut in relatively thin
horizontal strata, the depth of which varies considerably.

The area enclosed by this earliest wall was in the main

[1] *Not. scav.* 1909, p. 221; *Bull. Comm.* 1876, p. 37. Other smaller
fragments which I have not seen are enumerated by Delbrück, *Der
Apollotempel auf dem Marsfelde*, p. 15 n. Cf. also *Not. scav.* 1907,
pp. 438, 504.   [2] Delbrück, *op. cit.* pp. 12, 14.

[3] In places the brown tufa wall cuts across the *cappellaccio* wall:
Pinza, *Bull. Comm.* 1912, pp. 68–70.

[4] Frank, *op. cit.* pp. 185–6. Lanciani (*Bull. Comm.* 1872, p. 6;
1875, pp. 178–9) says the only known quarry of this stone is near
Porta S. Lorenzo. It was therefore in the possession of the Romans
from the earliest times.

the city of the "four regions" of Varro (*L.L.* V. 45–55), and
the Capitoline hill which apparently lay outside them, that
is to say, the "urbs et capitolium" of the Roman historians. It thus coincided with the line of the pomerium
which remained unchanged during the Republic till the
time of Sulla—the same line which was followed by the
procession of the Argei[1]—except that it may have included
a strip of ground outside the pomerium where the Quirinal
and Viminal hills join[2]. This strip was doubtless included
in the wall for strategic purposes, a wall across the table-
land giving a stronger line and being easier to build than
one which cut across the heads of the valleys. There is no
evidence for the existence of a wall round the four regions
which did not run as far east as the existing remains on
the Quirinal and Viminal plateaux[3]. The Aventine lay
outside the four regions and till the time of Claudius outside the pomerium[4], and so was outside the wall of Servius,
being first included in the city-wall in the fourth century
B.C. or later. A large portion of the brown tufa structure
is extant on the Aventine with no traces of the earlier
cappellaccio masonry; but a gateway and an adjoining wall
of the latter material were found (and destroyed) near
S. Maria in Cosmedin, i.e. close to the point where the
pomerium and the original Servian wall (running along
the south-west edge of the Palatine) met the river[5].

Two main objections are urged against the existence of
any stone wall at Rome previous to the fourth century B.C.

[1] Jordan, *Topographie*, I[1]. p. 288, II. pp. 237 ff.; Graffunder in
Pauly-Wissowa, s.v. "Rom," I A. I, p. 1022.

[2] See Kiepert and Hülsen, *Formae Urbis Romae Antiquae*, Map I;
but Graffunder (*loc. cit.*) says there is no ground for excluding the
north corner of the Quirinal from the four regions city.

[3] Carter, "Evolution of the City of Rome," in *Proc. Amer. Philos. Soc.*
XLVIII (1909), pp. 134 ff. supposes such a wall built by the Etruscans.

[4] Gell, *N.A.* XIII. 14. 7; cf. Merrill, "The City of Servius and the
Pomerium," in *Class. Philol.* IV (1909), pp. 420 ff.

[5] Lanciani in *Not. scav.* 1886, p. 274; Frank, *op. cit.* p. 175.

—the existence of tombs inside the wall, and the capture of Rome by the Gauls. But the intramural tombs which are assigned to the fourth century or later are few and their chronology is not always certain; further, it is possible, as Prof. Frank suggests, that they were outside the pomerium and the inhabited area. And the rule against burials inside the walls was not always rigidly enforced[1]. As to the Gallic catastrophe, it is possible that the Romans were too panic-stricken to offer a serious resistance; or we may accept the more attractive conjecture of Graffunder that the gray tufa wall built by the Tarquin kings was in places destroyed by Porsena, when the city was surrendered to him and the use of iron weapons forbidden to the Romans[2], a parallel to the demolition of walls of conquered cities which frequently occurs in Greek history. With the date of the wall of brown tufa we are not here concerned; but the phrase "saxum quadratum" applied to the wall begun according to Livy (VI. 32. 1) in 378 B.C.[3] is more applicable to the brown tufa blocks of the later wall than to the thin slabs of *cappellaccio*. And as there is no mention in any of our records of any walls being built under the Republic before 378 B.C., there is, if not a convincing proof, at least good ground for the belief that the wall of gray tufa was the work of the later kings.

We are not, however, justified in regarding on grounds of style all the ring-walls of polygonal masonry found in various parts of central Italy as the work of the Etruscans, as Martha does[4], asserting that they are only found in territory formerly occupied by them. This assertion appears

[1] Frank, *op. cit.* p. 177; cf. Graffunder, *op. cit.* pp. 116–23; *Not. scav.* 1907, pp. 189–90, on a tomb on the Palatine perhaps of the fourth century; De Sanctis, I. p. 183, n. 6. Cf. too Cic. *de Leg.* II. 23. 58: "Quid? qui post XII in urbe sepulti sunt clari uiri?"

[2] Graffunder, *op. cit.* p. 105.

[3] Repairs are recorded in 353 B.C. (Liv. VII. 20. 9) and 212 B.C. (XXV. 7).

[4] *L'Art Étrusque*, p. 141.

too definite in view of the existence of polygonal walls at
Alba Marsorum, and at Cesi and Spoleto in Umbria. Such
walls are found chiefly in the Latin, Volscian and Hernican
regions, and only at four places in Etruria—Cosa, Orbetello, Pyrgi and Saturnia. In other Etruscan city-walls the
blocks are laid horizontally—almost untrimmed in the
"Cyclopean" walls of Vetulonia, huge but roughly rectangular at Volterra, and progressively smaller and more
regular at Cortona, Fiesole and Perugia. It has been usual
to claim a high antiquity for the polygonal style: thus
Noack[1] says that "there is no doubt of the age" of the
walls and gates of Segni, Norba, Praeneste, and other
towns, and appears to regard those of Orbetello as previous
to the Etruscan occupation; and Deecke (on Müller,
I. p. 234, n. 8) claims the polygonal style as Pelasgian and
pre-Tuscan[2]. But the impossibility of ascribing such walls
to any one period or people is now being recognized[3]; thus
the Romans used polygonal masonry in embankments of
the Via Valeria near Tivoli and the Via Appia near Tarracina. Excavations at Norba shewed that the polygonal walls
and terraces there date only from the third century, as
was proved by the Etrusco-Campanian pottery, Latin inscriptions and coins which were found behind or inside
them; nothing certainly pre-Roman, and no Greek or
Etruscan pottery was found, and the walls were roughest
where the natural position was strong, and most solid and
finely worked where it was most open to attack—clearly
not a question of date[4]. It is probable that the polygonal

[1] *Röm. Mitt.* 1897, p. 188, on the walls and gates of Perugia.
[2] Durm, *Baukunst der Etrusker und Römer*, p. 22, regards the walls
of Cosa as Etruscan, those of Orbetello Pyrgi and Saturnia as pre-
Etruscan; cf. Dennis, II. p. 241.
[3] Cf. Choisy, *Histoire de l'Architecture*, I. p. 229: "l'influence
dominante est celle des matériaux eux-mêmes: un fait géologique bien
plus qu'une question d'époque."
[4] Savignoni and Mengarelli in *Not. scav.* 1901, pp. 548–52, and in
Atti Congr. Stor. (Roma, 1903), V. pp. 259 ff.

walls of Cosa and Signia (Segni) are also Roman work of the fifth and third centuries B.C.[1] I do not mean to deny that some of the polygonal ring-walls of central Italy may have been built by the Etruscans or under Etruscan rule, but only that they can be taken as evidence of the Etruscan dominion.

That it was from the Etruscans that the Romans learnt the principle of the arch is highly probable, even if it cannot be proved. The Cloaca Maxima in its present form dates from the late Republic or early Empire, and its fine arched mouth, still visible, cannot be regarded as an Etruscan work[2]. But it appears that the true arch was widely used in Etruria at an earlier date than elsewhere in Italy[3]. It appears in various Etruscan tombs, such as the Deposito del Granduca near Chiusi, which is a perfect barrel-vault, but apparently had a horizontal lintel (now restored) over the door[4], and the "Tempio di San Manno" near Perugia[5], a similar vault with a long Etruscan inscription on one side of it, and with two small arches in the side walls leading into smaller chambers. An approach to the principle of the arch appears in various early tombs, which have flat courses projecting one above the other with a flat top or a rudimentary keystone in the middle; such are the Cam-

[1] At Cosa I could see no trace anywhere of the distinction of style (polygonal below, rectangular above) referred to by Dennis (II. p. 249). Delbrück, *Das Capitolium von Signia*, p. 13, dates the Capitolium of Segni with its polygonal podium in about 500 B.C., but it is probably much later, see "Cronaca delle Belle Arti," p. 14, in *Bollettino d'Arte*, x (1916), *ad fin.*

[2] See below, pp. 72–3.

[3] Delbrück, *Hellenistische Bauten in Latium*, II. pp. 84–5, says the few pre-Hellenistic arches in Italy are all in Etruria. Cf. A. Garroni, "Cronologia della volta in Etruria," in his posthumous *Studi di Antichità* (Rome, 1918), pp. 91 ff.

[4] Dennis, II. p. 338; he also mentions (p. 339) a similar arched vault in the Deposito della Vigna Grande, which I have not seen. The urns in the former of these are of the fourth and third century type.

[5] Dennis, II. p. 450.

pana tomb of Veii[1], the Regolini-Galassi and other tombs at Cerveteri, and those in the early necropolis of Orvieto[2]. All these are previous to the fifth century B.C., as appears from their contents.

The chronology of the arched gateways found in Etruria is a matter of dispute, but one of the best examples, the Porta di Giove at Falerii noui (S. Maria di Falleri), can be dated with confidence about 240 B.C.[3] or later. The famous Porta all' Arco at Volterra is to be regarded as an Etruscan work probably of the fourth century, even if the existing travertine arch is due to a later restoration; the gateway is too wide (13 feet) to be spanned except by an arch, and it appears (with the three heads which are still in place) in the relief of a third century urn in the Volterra Museum representing the death of Capaneus[4]. Other extant Etruscan arches are to be seen (as I believe) in the Arco di Augusto and Porta Marzia at Perugia[5], in which the awkward position of the Latin inscriptions (in the one, carved on the actual voussoirs, in the other above and below the frieze representing Jupiter, the Dioscuri and their horses) seems to shew that these were later additions to an existing arch. We find then the true arch fairly widely used in Etruria in the third century; and it is fair to assume that the principle was discovered much earlier, both from the

[1] Dennis, I. p. 38; Canina, *Etruria Maritima*, pl. xxxv. 2.
[2] Dennis, II. p. 42.
[3] Ducati, *L'Arte Classica*, p. 534, dates it in 387 B.C.; but Zonaras, VIII. 18, clearly puts the destruction of the old Falerii and the foundation of the new after the first Punic War.
[4] On this gate cf. Dennis, II. 140 ff.; Durm, *Baukunst der Etrusker und Römer*, pp. 34–5, who regards it as entirely Etruscan if not all contemporaneous.
[5] So Noack in *Röm. Mitt.* XII (1897), pp. 174–81, noting Etruscan parallels to the decoration of these arches, and pp. 196–7; Dennis, II. p. 421, and Durm, *op. cit.* pp. 35–8, regard only the lower parts of these gates as Etruscan. Frothingham, *Roman Cities*, pp. 132–8, agrees with Noack.

perfection of the extant examples and from the fact that
in the Orvieto necropolis[1] the central stone of the vaults
is really a keystone, which by its weight prevents the projecting courses of the sides from falling in, although these
are still laid horizontally. However some little-known true
arches of an early date exist in the Roman Forum—e.g.
a drain under the Temple of Saturn, which appears from
its material (the gray *cappellaccio* already mentioned) to
date from the sixth or fifth century, and thus to be the
earliest extant arch in Italy[2]. Possibly it dates from the
Etruscan dominion in Rome; at any rate it does not impair
the general conclusion that the Etruscans freely used the
arch and vault at an earlier period than the Romans did,
and are therefore to be credited with their introduction
into Italy[3].

Closely akin to the arch and vault is the dome, a method
of construction which only appears in Roman work at the
end of the Republic, while no true dome is found in extant
Etruscan buildings. Yet the idea may have been suggested
by the false domes which were used by the Etruscans from
very early times[4], and probably introduced by them from
the East. Such "beehive-tombs" dating from the seventh
and sixth centuries are the Pietrera and Diavolino tombs at

[1] This necropolis is entirely pre-Roman, and at least previous to
the third century, and mainly of the sixth and fifth centuries. Gamurrini in *Not. scav.* 1900, p. 442: an illustration, *ibid.* tav. xv. 2.

[2] The existence of these arches and their significance were pointed
out to me by Dr Ashby. Possibly we have another Roman example in
the arch (now destroyed) referred to by Lanciani (*Not. scav.* 1886,
p. 274), see p. 55 above.

[3] So Rivoira, *Architettura Romana*, p. 37; and Cultrera in *Not. scav.*
1916, p. 23. Many arches which are called Etruscan are later Roman
work, e.g. the "drain" at Graviscae (Dennis, I. p. 430, Martha, p. 245)
really a bridge of the Via Aurelia (cf. Pasqui in *Not. scav.* 1885, p. 519);
bridges near Viterbo and at Bieda (Durm, *op. cit.* p. 56; on Bieda see
Röm. Mitt. xxx. pp. 161 ff.); the arches of the theatre at Ferento
(Dennis, I. p. 159, Durm, p. 25), etc.

[4] Rivoira, *op. cit.* p. 39.

Vetulonia[1], a tomb at Quinto Fiorentino[2], and (perhaps the best example) one from Casal Marittimo near Volterra, and now in the garden of the Florence Museum[3], in which the "dome" is formed by eleven rings of masonry each smaller than the one below, with a circular stone on top[4]. Here we have the germ from which centuries later sprang the Pantheon and other Imperial and Byzantine domed buildings, and through them again the domes of Brunelleschi and Michelangelo. In Rome the traces of a similar "beehive" structure of the Mycenaean type are to be seen in the Tullianum, or lower cell of the Mamertine Prison[5]. This was originally circular, but a chord has been cut off by a later wall on the side towards the Forum; the circular wall consists of three courses of tufa converging towards the top, but is interrupted by a very flat vault (of a different stone and clamped with iron) which serves as the floor of the upper room of the *Carcer*. This upper room rests in part on the circular wall below, but has a different plan from the lower chamber[6]. There is thus every reason to suppose that the original structure was a cone, the top and one side of which were cut off when the room above was built, and it is highly probable (from the difference in plan) that at that time the lower and older part, previously unknown, was rediscovered and adapted. Pinza[7] has shewn the im-

[1] Falchi, *Vetulonia*, pp. 206 ff., tav. II, and *Not. scav.* 1893, pp. 143–61; Milani, *Mus. Arch. Firenze*, p. 282, tav. CXXII.
[2] Milani, *Italici ed Etruschi*, p. 18; Montelius, II. p. 779, pl. 166.
[3] Milani, *Mus. Arch. Firenze*, pp. 286–7, tav. CXXIV; he regards the central pillar as symbolical and not serving any constructional purpose.
[4] Tholos-tombs have also been found at Populonia, cf. Minto in *Not. scav.* 1914, pp. 447 ff., 1921, pp. 202, 206, 211.
[5] Two cisterns on the Palatine, in front of the House of Livia, have the same convergence towards the top.
[6] Pinza, "Di un sepolcro a cupola di tipo miceneo," in *Rend. Linc.* XI (1902), pp. 226–39, and esp. pp. 231–2.
[7] *Ibid.* pp. 235–8. But the close resemblance to the fountain of Burinna at Cos (Saglio's *Dict. des Antiquités*, s.v. "Fons," figs. 3140–1) supports the theory that the Tullianum was a well-house.

probability that a considerable domed structure should be
made to cover a very insignificant spring, which further is
not in the middle but near the edge of the cell, and may
(he suggests) have been concealed under the original floor.
The original structure therefore, with its strong resemblance
to the Mycenaean and Etruscan θόλοι, may possibly have
been "a tomb of the kings of Rome[1]," transformed into
a dungeon when the *Carcer* above was built[2].

It is not improbable that the Romans owed to the
Tarquins not only their earliest wall, but also the earliest
laying-out of the Forum which was to be the centre of
their corporate life. The Etruscan doctrine of the celestial
templum involved certain rules for the ritual foundation of
cities and division of land which were adopted by the
Romans, who definitely refer to the pomerium as an
Etruscan institution; and it is very likely that the Romans
learnt from the Etruscans the rectangular planning of their
cities with intersecting *cardo* and *decumanus* and the paving
of the streets. Both these features are plainly discernible
in the Etruscan town of Marzabotto[3], in marked contrast
to the scattered huts of the Italic villages such as the
Villanova settlement at Bologna. Possibly the earliest
buildings in the Forum, exactly orientated east and west[4]
(e.g. the Fons and Aedicula Iuturnae, the Regia, the earliest

[1] Milani, *Rend. Linc.* IX (1900), p. 197.
[2] On tholos-tombs as prisons, cf. J. Harrison in *Essays presented to
W. Ridgeway*, p. 146, n. 1, and Plut. *Philop.* 19, there quoted.
[3] Brizio, *Mon. Ant.* I (1889), pp. 278, 284 ff., tav. I. v. Cf. too the
straight streets intersecting at right angles of the early necropolis at
Orvieto (Crocifisso del Tufo). But in a hill-town the rectangular plan
was not always possible: e.g. the main street at Vetulonia curved
considerably (*Not. scav.* 1895, pp. 274 ff.).
[4] Vaglieri in *Bull. Comm.* XXXI (1903), p. 11; Piganiol in *Mélanges*,
XXVIII (1908), pp. 233 ff., who however regards the primitive Forum
as the creation of the Sabines and previous to the occupation of the
Capitol by the Tarquins. But the Capitol was surely occupied before
the Forum, and not by the Tarquins first (cf. Dionys. II. 65; Liv.
I. 11. 6, etc.).

portions of the House of the Vestals and Temple of Vesta
and the earliest pavement of the Comitium) may be due
to the Tarquins who, according to tradition[1], constructed
the first drains in the Forum, previously a swamp.
This tradition is not shaken by the discovery that the
Cloaca Maxima in its present form is a later work, perhaps
of the time of Augustus. The zig-zag course of the cloaca
suggests that the original work was the canalization (by
strengthening the sides with masonry and by dredging) of
a winding stream; and it is possible that this was done
under the Tarquins as tradition asserts. The Etruscans
were believed to have made the first canals to drain the
swampy land at the mouth of the Po, and *cuniculi* for
drainage are numerous in south Etruria, both cut in the
rock in cities (e.g. Sutrium, Caere and others) and in the
open country[2]. The Roman Forum would not be a place
of common resort till there was some system of drainage,
but a portion of it was used as a cemetery till towards the
end of the sixth century—the very time to which tradition
ascribes the first cloacae[3]. These were originally open
ditches, hence Plautus speaks of the "canalis" in the
Forum[4]. The present "cloaca maxima," however, appears
to have been constructed with materials from demolished
buildings of the Republican period, and may therefore date
only from the repairs of Agrippa; but two earlier cloacae
have been discovered under the Basilica Aemilia [5], the lower
of which may be the work of the Tarquins.

[1] Dionys. IV. 44. 1; Liv. I. 38. 6, 56. 2; Plin. *N.H.* XXXVI. 106.
[2] Plin. *N.H.* III. 120; cf. Dennis, I. pp. 64, 90, 209, etc.; Martha,
pp. 242 ff. Cf. too the drains of Marzabotto (Brizio, *Mon. Ant.* I.
pp. 295–7).
[3] Hülsen, *Roman Forum*, p. 4. Sixth-century pottery found in the
Forum tombs: Boni in *Not. scav.* 1903, p. 107.
[4] Hülsen, *op. cit.* p. 5; Plaut. *Curc.* 476: "in medio propter canalem
ibi ostentatores meri"; cf. Festus, p. 45: "Canalicolae forenses homines
pauperes dicti, quod circa canales fori consisterent."
[5] Boni in *Not. scav.* 1900, p. 340: Vaglieri in *Bull. Comm.* XXXI
(1903), pp. 96, 99.

Reference has already been made to the traces of sixth and fifth century masonry on the site of the temple of Jupiter Capitolinus, which give some support to the universal Roman tradition which ascribed the building of that temple to the Tarquin kings[1]. From the measurements given by Dionysius (IV. 61. 3–4)—taken doubtless from the later temple of Catulus which was rebuilt on the old foundations—the temple corresponded fairly closely to the "Tuscan" type with three cellae described by Vitruvius (IV. 7), except that it had an extra row of columns along the front and two sides. Hence there were six columns (as shewn on coins[2]) in each of the three rows in front of the temple, which faced south as apparently did the various temples on the acropolis of Marzabotto[3]. Tradition expressly asserts the large part in the decoration of the Capitoline temple which was assigned to Etruscan artists[4], the fullest information being given by Pliny (*N.H.* xxxv. 157) on the authority of Varro: "elaboratam hanc artem [*sc.* plasticen] Italiae et maxime Etruriae, Vulcam Veiis accitum cui locaret Tarquinius Priscus Iouis effigiem in Capitolio dicandam, fictilem eum fuisse atque ideo miniari solitum, fictiles in fastigio templi eius quadrigas...." The skill of the Etruscans in modelling in clay has long been recognized from the sarcophagi[5] from Caere (in the British Museum, the Louvre, and the Villa Giulia Museum at Rome) and similar works; and the accuracy of Varro's further statements has been strikingly vindicated

[1] Dionys. III. 69, IV. 59; Liv. I. 38. 7, 56. 1; Cic. *de Repub.* II. 20. 24; Tac. *H.* III. 72.

[2] E.g. those of Petilius Capitolinus (40 B.C.) in the British Museum (*Coins of the Roman Republic,* I. nos. 4217–25).

[3] Brizio in *Mon. Ant.* I (1889), p. 252.

[4] Liv. I. 56. 1: "fabris undique ex Etruria accitis"; Plut. *Poplic.* 13: ἅρμα κατὰ κορυφὴν ἐπιστῆσαι κεραμεοῦν ἐξέδωκε [*sc.* Ταρκύνιος] Τυρρηνοῖς τισιν ἐξ Οὐηίων δημιουργοῖς. Festus, p. 274 (Müller), s.v. "Ratumena porta."

[5] Martha, p. 298; Savignoni in *Mon. Ant.* VIII (1898), pp. 521 ff.

by the discovery at Veii of the Apollo-group[1], which is assigned to the end of the sixth century. Though the subject and many features of the group are undoubtedly Greek, yet it contains elements which are either characteristically Etruscan or non-Hellenic in the sharp receding profile of the Apollo, his massive (but not heavy) form and limbs, his thick rope-like strands of hair and his animated expression[2]. Hence we should probably regard the artist as an Etruscan influenced by Greek art rather than a Greek—the same applies to the artist of the Capitoline Wolf; and in any case we have here clear evidence that terracotta statuary shewing perfect command of material and of anatomical accuracy was produced at Veii about 500 B.C. or earlier; and to suggest that Vulca is a legendary duplicate of Vulcan[3] identified with Summanus, whose statue in clay stood on the roof of the Capitoline temple[4], appears unnecessary ingenuity. We need not suppose, as Pais does (*loc. cit.* and III. p. 337), that the cult and temple of Jupiter Capitolinus date from after the Gallic invasion, nor is this proved by the existence of an earlier shrine of Jupiter, Juno and Minerva on the Quirinal, the *Capitolium uetus*[5]. After the repeated destructions of the Capitoline temples it is hardly to be expected that many traces of the original work of the Tarquins should survive; part of the *cappellaccio* basement has been found, and a drain probably contemporary, together with two terracotta fragments of an antefix and a frieze which may belong to the original

[1] This is well shewn by Giglioli in *Not. scav.* 1919, pp. 30–3.
[2] Della Seta, "Antica arte etrusca," in *Dedalo*, Ann. I. Fasc. IX. pp. 559–73, traces the two notes of "corporeity" and "expression" through all Etruscan art from the Veii group and contemporary Gorgon antefixes down to the Orator in the Florence Museum.
[3] So Pais, I². pp. 523–4.
[4] Cic. *de Diuin.* I. 10. 16: "in fastigio Iouis optimi maximi," i.e. perhaps at one end of the gable (the quadriga forming the central acroterion) or in the middle of one of its sides.
[5] Varro, *L.L.* V. 158.

temple[1]. The most recent excavations have revealed further portions of the *cappellaccio* basement to a depth of 20 feet (the κρηπὶς ὑψηλή of Dionysius), and have also remarkably confirmed the accuracy of the measurements which he gives[2].

Some reference must here be made to the temples of south Etruria and Latium, where numerous terracotta decorations[3] have been discovered in recent years, and are now mainly in the Villa Giulia Museum. The form of these temples and the different phases and types discernible in their decorations are fully and well discussed by A. Della Seta in his *Museo di Villa Giulia* (Rome, 1918), pp. 120–66[4]. He there shews that these early temples whether found in or out of Etruria by no means conform to the Vitruvian type of the "Tuscan" temple with three cellae, the one-celled form being apparently earlier[5]. It is evident too from an inspection of the terracottas that no distinction can be drawn between those from Faliscan and from Latin temples: the Sileni and Maenads of Falerii (sixth and fifth centuries) are indistinguishable from the

[1] *Bull. Comm.* 1875, pp. 165 ff., esp. pp. 178–84; *ibid.* 1876, pp. 31–4; *ibid.* 1896, pp. 116–20, tav. IX–XIII; *J.R.S.* IV. p. 183.

[2] Paribeni in *Not. scav.* 1921, pp. 38 ff. The terracotta antefix (p. 47) which was found does not appear to belong to the original temple.

[3] The sites in Etruria which have yielded these terracottas are in the main Falerii (from the remains of five temples), Caere and Veii; the Faliscan terracottas shew the strongest resemblance to those from Latian temples.

[4] See, too, an article on these decorations by Mrs Strong in *J.R.S.* IV (1914), pp. 157–81; and *Figurative Terracotta Revetments in Etruria and Latium*, by Mrs E. Van Buren. I adopt for convenience Della Seta's general designation of these temples as "Italic."

[5] The triple cella appears in the temple of Juno at Falerii (see *Not. scav.* 1887, pp. 92 ff.), but this may be due to a restoration in the fourth and third century of an earlier temple; and also (it seems) in the temple under the south side of Veii, where the Apollo-group was found. At Marzabotto (*Mon. Ant.* I. p. 262) the best-preserved temple had one cella, but one of the larger temples may have had three.

earlier ones from Satricum, and the warriors in a Faliscan acroterion (Della Seta, p. 168, tav. xxxiv) have the same armour as the warriors in a fragment from Satricum (*ibid.* p. 269)[1]. The question arises, what connexion (if any) these terracottas have with the Etruscan occupation of Latium. It must be recognized in the first place that they shew much greater affinities with Greek art than with Etruscan, even in their earlier phases; thus the Sileni and Maenads, of which numerous examples have been found in the temple of Satricum (Conca), are unknown to Etruscan art[2], as is also the so-called "Juno Sospita" with goats' horns. The armour of the warriors is also Greek, even the unusual thigh-pieces being shewn on some black-figure vases[3], but the curved sword shewn in the Faliscan acroterion of two warriors fighting seems to be rather oriental (cf. Hdt. VII. 92 on the δρέπανα of Carians and Lycians). It has further been shewn by G. Rizzo that the early architectural terracottas of Satricum are similar (and in some cases identical) with contemporary terracottas from Capua and Cumae, and with others from various parts of Asia Minor[4]; while the series of friezes from Velletri, Pitigliano, Tuscania and elsewhere, which of all early terracottas of Etruria and Latium shew clearest

[1] S. B. Luce in *Amer. Journ. Arch.* 1920, pp. 27 ff., publishes some antefixes from Caere (now in the University Museum, Philadelphia) which appear to be quite unlike those in the Villa Giulia, and more archaic, and *ibid.* 1921, pp. 266 ff., some architectural terracottas from Corneto (Tarquinii) of the Hellenistic period.

[2] See *J.R.S.* IV. pp. 168–9, pl. xxvii. For the subject cf. archaic Macedonian coins, e.g. Gardner, *Types of Greek Coins*, p. 92, pl. III. 1, 2. Similarly non-Etruscan are the Harpies and Typhons (*J.R.S. ibid.*), for the Typhon of the Grotta del Tifone at Tarquinii is entirely different in type. As a rough standard of what is or is not Etruscan I take the tomb-paintings and stone reliefs of Etruria proper.

[3] Rizzo in *Bull. Comm.* xxxix (1911), p. 33. Illustrations in *J.R.S. cit.* figs. 19–21.

[4] *Bull. Comm.* xxxviii (1910), pp. 312–9.

Etruscan traits[1], yet has some very close similarities to a frieze from Larissa, near Phocaea in Asia Minor[2]. But oriental and Ionic influences are so strong in early Etruscan art that close parallels between Assyrian, Hittite and early Ionian monuments, and the terracotta friezes of central Italy, by no means exclude the Etruscan origin of the latter[3]. Further the Italic temples, even if the details of their decoration shew Greek influence or even the work of Greek artists, have in their general construction some common features which distinguish them from contemporary Greek temples in south Italy and Sicily—notably a much greater use of timber and of terracotta, the round bases of their columns, and the apparent absence of triglyphs and metopes[4]. Such distinctive features may be due to the Etruscans, whether they represent a tradition imported from Asia Minor or merely an independent development; but such a cultural influence of Etruria in Latium is not in itself a proof of Etruscan rule[5].

---

[1] E.g. the curved *lituus*, pointed boots, the whip instead of a goad, the form of the chariots, the banquet scenes, etc. On these friezes cf. Pellegrini in *Studi e Materiali*, I. pp. 87–118, who regards them as of Etruscan make.

[2] Rizzo, *ibid.* p. 318; Van Buren, *Terracotta Revetments*, etc. pp. 57 ff.

[3] The gorgon-antefixes common in the Italic temples are paralleled in Greece, e.g. Athens (Casson, *Catal. Acrop. Museum*, p. 426) and Miletus (Koch in *Röm. Mitt.* xxx. p. 35): but cf. Della Seta in *Dedalo loc. cit.* on the Etruscan character of the Veientine gorgoneia.

[4] On the distinctive form of the pediment in the earlier Italic temples cf. Rizzo in *Bull. Comm.* 1910, pp. 286–303; 1911, pp. 48–61. Tuscan columns: Vitruv. IV. 7, Durm, *Baukunst der Etrusker und Römer* (1905), pp. 64–5. Vitruvius (*loc. cit.*) makes no mention of triglyphs and metopes in his Tuscan temple and no remains of them have been found in any of the known Italic temples, though they appear in some Etruscan monuments, e.g. the sculptured tombs at Norchia and late sarcophagi; see Durm, *op. cit.* pp. 66–8, 98.

[5] Cf. T. Frank, *Roman Imperialism*, p. 15, on "remains of an Etruscan temple at Satricum"—i.e. a temple in the "Tuscan" style—and "Etruscan remains in abundance at Palestrina and Velletri," where

It would thus be hazardous to base any historical conclusions on the art of these temples; the earliest, however,
are thought to date from the sixth century B.C. when
Etruscan influence was strongest south of the Tiber, and
we may suggest that it was the presence of Etruscan
immigrants whether as invaders or merchants which led
in Latium as at Rome to the erection of regular temples
with walls and roofs, a practice which was not native to
the Latins. And we have the testimony of Varro that till
the temple of Ceres (493 B.C.) was decorated by Damophilus
and Gorgasus, the Tuscan style of decoration had held
the field[1]. In Rome as elsewhere in Latium the terracottas which seem most clearly Etruscan in character are
the fragments of friezes, the best-preserved of which was
found in a chamber-tomb of Etruscan type on the Esquiline[2],
and is now in the Conservatori Museum; the antefixes and
other fragments are akin to those of the rest of Latium;
the "Wounded Warrior" from the Esquiline (perhaps an
Amazon) is Greek rather than Etruscan both in style and
in subject[3]. It seems that Greek artists were at work in
south Etruria during the seventh and sixth centuries and
influenced the native artists of Veii, Caere and Falerii,

presumably the reference is to the friezes which may be Etruscan,
and the Praenestine tombs which prove no more than commercial
relations with Etruria.

[1] Plin. *N.H.* xxxv. 154: "ante hanc aedem Tuscanica omnia in
aedibus fuisse auctor est Varro." The very use of the name "Tuscan"
for a type of temple-architecture suggests that such temples at least
originated with the Etruscans.

[2] Lanciani in *Bull. Comm.* 1875, p. 51, tav. VI. 1; Pinza, "Monumenti Primitivi di Roma e del Lazio Antico" (*Mon. Ant.* xv), p. 211,
fig. 90.

[3] E. Van Buren (on Roman terracottas of the 6th–4th cent.) in
J.R.S. IV (1914), pp. 183–92, esp. p. 187. Now in the Conservatori
Museum. The Tarquins possibly built a temple on the Palatine
near the Stairs of Cacus where fragments of sixth-century architectural terracottas have been found (*Not. scav.* 1907, pp. 273, 451,
539–42).

and some may have migrated into Latium with the Etruscan invaders[1]. But it is possible that there was also (as Rizzo holds) an independent current of Greek art from Campania entering Latium in the sixth and fifth centuries by way of Satricum, a town which was situated on a river which afforded a place for anchorage, the Storas (Strabo, v. pp. 232–6)[2], and which has yielded a large number of terracotta decorations of a strongly non-Etruscan character. And in the same way after over a century and long after the fall of the Etruscan power in Latium, a similar Greek current entered south Etruria and Latium, where clay statues were modelled shewing a marked Hellenistic influence[3].

§ 3

SOCIAL LIFE AND POLITICAL EXPANSION OF ROME UNDER THE ETRUSCANS

If we are right in regarding the union of the Roman villages into a walled city as the work of the Etruscan kings, the first development of native Roman industry also probably took place under their rule[4]. Here as elsewhere the beginnings of town-life would create fresh needs, to satisfy which fresh trades would develop, and the professional craftsman would emerge, where before each man made his own rough implements and pottery; and in view of the undoubted technical ability of the Etruscans, in working

[1] Cf. Varro *ap.* Plin. xxxv. 157 (quoted above) on the development of modelling in Etruria; and the tradition of the Greek artists who came with the elder Tarquin to Italy (*id. ibid.* 152); also the "Tuscum fictile" of Persius, ii. 60.

[2] Rizzo, *Bull. Comm.* 1911, p. 47.

[3] Della Seta, *op. cit.* pp. 144 ff., on the Italic temples of the Hellenistic age: *J.R.S.* iv. pp. 175–8 and pls. xxix–xxxi.

[4] Gummerus in Pauly-Wissowa, ix. 2, 1441 ff., s.v. "Industrie."

metals and clay particularly, it is not unlikely that the Romans learnt from them at the time when their influence on Rome was greatest. Thus as Pais suggests (I^2. p. 778) the guilds ascribed to Numa[1] may in reality have grown up gradually under the Tarquins, if not formally constituted till later. We may be certain that the professional potter working with a wheel had already appeared[2]; the same may be said of the smith. Pinza has noted in the numerous bronze tripods found in Roman tombs of the late iron age various peculiarities which distinguish them as a group from those of Veii or Falerii; the iron-work in these tombs is also marked by deficiencies of technique not found outside Latium[3]. He therefore concludes that to some extent both bronze and iron were worked in Rome, and by the same craftsmen, the forms used being identical in both metals. But the rare objects of gold and silver found in early Roman tombs were probably imported from Etruria, where they are much commoner[4]; possibly also from Praeneste, where there was long an important metal-working industry, as shewn by the gold fibula of Manios[5] and the silver cista now in the Conservatori Museum, which points forward to the later series of bronze cistae undoubtedly made at Praeneste[6].

[1] Plut. *Numa*, 17, cf. Plin. XXXIV. 1, XXXV. 159. The list consists of αὐληταί, χρυσόχοοι, τέκτονες, βαφεῖς, σκυτότομοι, σκυτοδεψεῖς, χαλκεῖς, κεραμεῖς.

[2] Cf. Pinza, *Mon. Ant.* XV. pp. 519 ff. and 530: "the great development of indigenous bucchero belongs to the latest phase of the iron age," i.e. about the sixth century B.C. Cf. too the famous triple vase with the inscription of Duenos in a Latin dialect (Conway, *Italic Dialects*, I. pp. 329–31). [3] *Ibid.* pp. 537–9, 551.

[4] Cf. Plin. XXXIII. 14: "Romae ne fuit quidem aurum nisi admodum exiguum longo tempore," and the XII Tables: "neue aurum addito."

[5] Curtis in *Mem. Amer. Acad.* 1919, p. 22, who shews that it probably does not belong to the Bernardini tomb; Conway, *op. cit.* pp. 311–2.

[6] Pinza, *op. cit.* p. 563, fig. 165; Matthies, *Praenestinischen Spiegel*, pp. 20, 35.

As we have seen, there was a strong tradition that artists and craftsmen were summoned to Rome from Etruria for the building of the Capitoline temple, and the "Tuscus uicus" between the Palatine and Capitoline hills, where later the statue of the Etruscan god Vertumnus stood[1], may have had its origin in this period. No doubt a large part in the buildings of the later kings was taken by native workmen; but it is probable that both in pottery and metallurgy—arts in which the Etruscans excelled, and which satisfied the chief material wants of an infant city— the Roman craftsmen learnt their trade largely from Etruscan immigrants.

Significant of the development under Etruscan influence of handicrafts and of urban life in Rome is the introduction of the cult of Minerva, a deity unknown to the earliest Roman calendar. It is generally agreed that this cult came from Falerii[2]; the shrine of Minerva Capta on the Caelian[3] no doubt dated from the capture of Falerii in 241 B.C., but the more important temple on the Aventine was probably much earlier, since Minerva was certainly known in Rome from the time of the Tarquins, as a member of the Capitoline triad. Minerva was at Rome pre-eminently the goddess of handicraft and hence the patroness of most of the trade-guilds, which had their religious centre in the Aventine temple[4]. According to a note in the Praenestine calendar the first day of the Quinquatrus (March 19th) was "artificum dies [quod Mineruae] aedis in Auentino eo die est [dedicata][5]." Thus we find the patroness of handi-

[1] Varro, *L.L.* v. 46.
[2] Wissowa, *Religion u. Kultus*, pp. 252–3; cf. the ancient dedication, *C.I.L.* xi. 3081 and Ovid, *Fasti*, iii. 843–4.   [3] Ovid, *ibid.* 835–8.
[4] Wissowa, *loc. cit.*; Waltzing, *Corporations Professionnelles*, i. p. 199, who quotes Lactantius, i. 18. 21: "Minerua est quae omnia reperit ideoque illi opifices supplicant."
[5] *C.I.L.* i. p. 312; cf. Festus, p. 237, s.v. "Quinquatrus": "Mineruae autem dicatum eum diem existimant quod eo die aedis eius in Auentino consecrata est."

craft entering Rome from south Etruria at a time when we read of craftsmen coming from the same region; and it is therefore highly probable that specialized guilds of native Roman workers now grew up, under the patronage of the goddess whom their Etruscan instructors had introduced. And so it was under her Etruscan kings that Rome entered on the first period of her life as a real city, when the primitive patriarchal community of farmers began to merge into the state with its varied interests and occupations, and the plebeians, their numbers increased by alien settlers and their importance by their new-found capacities, began to come into prominence[1].

There is therefore good ground for accepting the tradition of constitutional or perhaps rather military reforms under the later monarchy. Increased command of the material arts, and in particular of metallurgy, involved some shifting of wealth and so of power, and improved armour and weapons necessitated a reorganization of the army, which was the nation, according to the equipment which each man was able to provide for himself, and on a broader basis. Thus even if the pecuniary qualifications and the number of centuries which we find in later times date from the fourth century or later[2], a classification by property such as that ascribed by tradition to Servius Tullius may well have been instituted by the Etruscan rulers of the sixth century, not so much in conscious imitation of the Greek "timocratical" constitutions, as from the effect in Rome as in the Greek cities of economic changes following on the development of industry. Certainly it is not too much to say that the first real army of Rome was the creation of the later kings; there is little in the arms or organization of the army of the early Republic

[1] Minerva: Fowler, *Religious Experience*, etc. pp. 233 ff.; Carter, *Religion of Numa*, pp. 46-9.
[2] Cf. De Sanctis, II. ch. XVII.

which cannot be shewn with at least strong probability to have been derived from the Etruscans[1]; and the connexion of this fact with the Etruscan bronze and iron industry on the one hand and with the reforms of Servius on the other is obvious. The elder Tarquin was credited with the reconstitution on a larger scale of the cavalry[2], and the introduction of the chariot: according to Plutarch (*Rom.* 16 *fin.*) he was the first to use a chariot in a triumph, while triumphal statues of Romulus always represented him on foot. The "sella curulis," which was among the insignia of office which were believed to be of Etruscan origin[3], was, as Helbig shewed[4], a seat placed for the administration of justice in the two-horsed chariot in which the king (Etruscan or Roman) went to war. A similar chariot is that found in the Regolini-Galassi tomb at Cerveteri[5], and chariots of the same type bearing a driver and an armed warrior, and also warriors with spear and shield on horseback, appear in sixth-century terracotta friezes from Tuscania, Cerveteri, Pitigliano and elsewhere[6].

Besides the curule chair, most of the other marks of dignity which the Romans gave to their chief magistrates or triumphant generals were believed to have been introduced from Etruria, such as the purple toga, the ivory

[1] For a full discussion of this see E. McCartney, "The military indebtedness of early Rome to Etruria," in *Mem. Amer. Acad.* I. pp. 121 ff. Cf. Diod. XXIII. frag. 3, on the bronze shields, and Athen. VI. 273 ff. on the phalanx, adopted by the Romans from the Etruscans.
[2] Cic. *de Rep.* II. 20: "equitatum ad hunc modum constituit qui usque adhuc est retentus."
[3] Liv. I. 8. 3.
[4] "Le Currus du Roi Romain" in *Mélanges Perrot*, pp. 167 ff.
[5] Pinza in *Röm. Mitt.* XXII (1907), pp. 100–1, and *Rend. Linc.* XXI (1912), pp. 79 ff.
[6] On these see Pellegrini in *Stud. e Mat.* I. pp. 87–118. Other such friezes come from Velletri, Palestrina and Rome. In some Etruscan features are more marked, in others the elements derived from Greek vase-paintings. Pellegrini regards them as Etruscan, and designed originally at Caere.

rod and the golden wreath, the lictors' rods and axes, and also the music used on state occasions, including the famous Tyrrhenian war-trumpet[1]. According to Dionysius these insignia were brought by the rulers of the Etruscan cities as a sign of submission to Tarquinius Priscus; and later were given by the Romans to Porsena when he left Rome as a friend[2]. Whether the act ever really was a token of submission we do not know; Virgil evidently so regarded it when he represented these emblems as sent by Tarchon to Evander[3], a patriotic inversion of the actual submission of Rome to the Etruscans. But in later times some or all of the triumphal insignia were sometimes sent merely as a compliment to foreign kings[4].

A double axe with its shaft enclosed by a number of iron tubes resembling rods was found in the tomb named on that account Tomba del Littore at Vetulonia[5], the very city mentioned by Silius Italicus (VIII. 483–5) as the place of origin of the fasces. Dionysius (VII. 72) gives a description of an ancient Roman procession (on the authority of Fabius Pictor), which he regards as borrowed from the Greeks; but almost every element can be paralleled from Etruscan art—youths on foot or on horseback, chariots, athletes, dancers (some of them in armour like the Greek pyrrhichistae[6]), and players on the lyre and flutes. And Appian (*Punica*, VIII. 66) in his description of the triumph

[1] Diod. v. 40; Dionys. III. 61. 1; Strab. v. 220; Liv. I. 8. 3; Plin. VIII. 195.

[2] Dionys. v. 35. 1.

[3] *Aen.* VIII. 505–6:
    "ipse oratores ad me regnique coronam
       cum sceptro misit mandatque insignia Tarchon."

[4] J. S. Reid, "Roman Ideas of Deity," in *J.R.S.* VI (1916), p. 178 and nn.

[5] Falchi, *Not. scav.* 1898, p. 147 and fig. 26. Now in the Florence Museum, Room III. Cf. Rosenberg, *Der Staat der alten Italiker*, pp. 64 ff., 84 ff.

[6] These are represented in the Scimmia and Casuccini tombs of Chiusi.

of Scipio Africanus mentions a choir of harpists and pipers
ἐς μίμημα Τυρρηνικῆς πομπῆς, who were called Lydi,
because the Etruscans were Lydian colonists. The importance at Rome of music in sacrifices and solemn processions is illustrated by the story of the "tibicines" who
decamped in a body to Tibur, whither the Senate sent
envoys to demand their return[1]; this music, Strabo tells
us, was introduced from Etruria[2]. The Etruscan's passion
for music was notorious, as witnessed by the fragment of
Alcimus stating that the Etruscans πρὸς αὐλὸν καὶ μάτ-
τουσι καὶ πυκτεύουσι καὶ μαστιγοῦσι[3]: a piper appears in
the Sette Camini tomb at Orvieto among the slaves who
are preparing the dinner (one is apparently kneading), and
in the gymnastic scenes of the tombs at Chiusi and of
others at Tarquinii[4], while the banquets so common in
Tarquinian tomb-paintings are almost always accompanied
by the pipes or lyre.

It also appears that the Romans adopted from Etruria
their public games and shows[5] (originally as religious
observances)—races of horses and chariots, boxing and
wrestling, stage-plays and gladiators. To the times of the
elder Tarquin were ascribed the "ludi Romani" of horse-
races and boxing, and we read at the same time of stands
for spectators and the foundation of the circus between
the Palatine and Aventine, though no doubt no permanent
structure was built then[6]. There is good evidence for the
existence of these games in Etruria; they appear at Tar-

[1] Liv. ix. 35. 5-10; Plut. Qu. Rom. 55.
[2] Strab. v. 220.
[3] Athen. xii. 518 b, cf. id. iv. 154 a (quoting Eratosthenes). Other
literary references in Müller, ii. pp. 200 ff.
[4] "Letto Funebre," "Iscrizioni" and "Auguri" tombs.
[5] On these see Müller, ii. pp. 196 ff.
[6] Cic. de Rep. ii. 20. 36; Liv. i. 35 ("equi pugilesque ex Etruria
maxime acciti"); Dionys. iii. 68. But Tac. Ann. xiv. 21. 2: "a Tuscis
accitos histriones, a Thuriis equorum certamina."

quinii in the Letto Funebre, Iscrizioni, Barone and Bighe[1]
tombs, in the Scimmia and Casuccini tombs at Chiusi,
and on some funeral urns in the Florence Museum.

It may be mentioned here, though it has no connexion
with the Etruscan rule in Rome, that the earliest stage-
plays in Rome were produced by Etruscan players, even
after some 150 years of intermittent warfare between the
two peoples—an indication of what we may call the cultural
hegemony of Etruria surviving the loss of political power.
"Ea ipsa peregrina res fuit," says Livy (VII. 2. 4): "ludiones
ex Etruria acciti ad tibicinis modos saltantes haud indecoros
motus more Tusco dabant," and he proceeds to explain
the name "histrio" given to the actors "quia ister Tusco
uerbo ludio uocabatur." In the same way the Romans
adopted the Etruscan word "lanista" along with the
practice of gladiatorial combats, which first appear in Rome
at a funeral in 264 B.C.[2] Athenaeus (IV. 153 f.) quotes the
Peripatetic Nicolaus for the statement that the Romans
took from the Etruscans the practice of having single
combats in their festivals and theatres. Such scenes, however, are not common in Etruscan art; one of the most
interesting is in the Tomba degli Auguri at Tarquinii[3],
where a man in a chequered jacket, tall cap and red mask,
with the name "Phersu" above, is shewn holding a long
cord attached to a man with his head enveloped in a large
dark hood. A dog bites the thigh of the latter man, who
tries to hit the dog with a club. This brutal sport recalls
the "retiarius" of the Roman arena; the same motley
figure occurs again in the Tomba degli Auguri (with the

[1] Here stands are shewn filled with well-dressed and keenly in-
terested spectators, and with slaves beneath. Cf. Poulsen, *Etruscan
Tomb-Paintings*, pp. 23–5. The oldest of these tombs go back to the
early fifth or late sixth century.
[2] Liv. *Epit.* 16; "lanista" = "carnifex" in Etruscan: Isid. *Orig.*
x. 159. See further Müller, II. pp. 223–4.
[3] Not mentioned in Deecke's note on Müller, II. p. 224; for the
tomb cf. Dasti in *Not. scav.* 1878, p. 129, and Poulsen, *op. cit.* pp. 12 ff.

same inscription "Phersu," perhaps connected with the Latin "persona[1]"), and in the Tomba della Pulcinella. In the Roman amphitheatre as late as the second century A.D. the dying were despatched and the bodies removed by a man dressed as a demon with a mallet, which strongly suggests the Etruscan Charun[2]. Representations of combats of gladiators are much commoner in Oscan than in Etruscan art[3], and Weege therefore suggests that such shows came to Rome from Campania in the third century, rather than from Etruria itself. In the late Republic Capua was the chief centre for schools of gladiators[4]; but this form of amusement may have been introduced there originally by the Etruscans, though it was left to the Romans in later times to practise it on a large scale, even introducing gladiators at their banquets[5].

Thus side by side with the creation of the city of Rome by the Etruscan kings and a profound change in Roman religion, the new city-life of the people was diversified and enriched by music and public games and solemn processions, by the bright colours of the terracottas which adorned the temples, and no doubt by an increase of personal luxury as well. But how far the more costly Etruscan habits in dress and food took root in Rome, how far there was a reaction towards a more austere manner of life in the early Republic, we cannot tell. The poverty of the Roman tombs and the scarcity in them of oriental or Greek goods, compared with tombs of south Etruria or Praeneste, may be due in part to the constant disturbance of the soil by builders of all periods, and the consequent

[1] Skutsch in Pauly-Wissowa, VI. 775.
[2] Tertull. *Apol.* 15, where he calls him Pluto, brother of Jove; *adv. Nat.* I. 10.
[3] Weege, "Oskische Grabmalerei," in *Jahrb. k. deutsch. arch. Inst.* XXIV (1909), p. 134.
[4] Saglio, *Dict. des Ant.*, s.v. "Gladiator," p. 1578.
[5] Athen. *loc. cit.*

removal of objects of value. Certainly there is little evidence for any extensive foreign trade by the Romans in the regal period, or for the construction of a harbour for the purpose at Ostia[1]. There is no such evidence in the treaty with Carthage which Polybius (III. 22) assigns to the first year of the Republic; Carthage having a trade-agreement with the Etruscans (perhaps reserving Sardinia to the former and Corsica to the latter) merely wished to safeguard herself against the possible interference of Rome.

The moral and material development of Rome under her Etruscan rulers was accompanied by an enhancement of her prestige among her neighbours. Dionysius, but not Livy, ascribes to Tarquinius Priscus wars against all Etruria, including such distant cities as Arretium, Volaterrae, Vetulonia and Clusium, ending with the submission of these cities which yield him their royal insignia[2]. Both Dionysius and Livy recount a long war of Servius against the Etruscans, and the Fasti Triumphales record three triumphs of that king "de Etrusceis." But these wars are probably as legendary as those of Romulus or Tullus Hostilius: and in any case wars against Etruscan cities are not inconsistent with the Etruscan origin of the Tarquins.

There is somewhat stronger evidence for the supremacy among the Latins which Rome now began to claim[3]. The traditional accounts of the Latin wars of the Tarquins are, as we have seen, duplicates of a single story[4], and many of the details of the treacherous capture of Gabii are

---

[1] Cf. Frank, *Economic History*, p. 19: the evidence reduces itself to some "few fragments" of a *cappellaccio* wall, which certainly point to some early settlement at Ostia ("Rome's First Coinage" in *Class. Phil.* 1919, p. 316, n. 1), perhaps in connexion with the salt-pans.

[2] Dionys. III. 51–3, 55–61. Müller, I. p. 113, takes this tradition as representing an actual hegemony of the city of Tarquinii.

[3] De Sanctis, I. p. 365.

[4] Liv. I. 38. 4, 49. 8, 50 ff.: cf. Cic. *de Rep.* II. 24: "(Superbus) Latium omne bello deuicit."

borrowed from Herodotus. But the bronze pillar in the temple of Diana on the Aventine, which was ascribed to Servius Tullius, remained down to the time of Dionysius, who says that the rules of the annual festival and the names of the Latin cities which took part in it were inscribed on it in letters such as Hellas used in ancient times[1]; that is, the inscription was in extremely archaic Latin, perhaps like the archaic inscription under the "lapis niger." It might, of course, have been a later forgery, but it is more probable that it really dated from the time of the kings and perhaps included the name of Servius[2]. If this is so, the Roman king evidently meant to assert the supremacy of his city by bringing Diana Nemorensis, one of the chief Latin deities, within the power of Rome, so to speak, though being outside the pomerium she was not made a Roman state-goddess, and though her sanctuary at Nemi survived into historic times. The festival on the Aventine was on August 13th, apparently the same date as at Aricia[3]; but the Aventine temple contained as we have seen an image of the goddess like that at Massalia, which in turn was derived from the Ephesian Artemis[4]. Dionysius regards the Aventine festival as a Latin counterpart to the Amphictyonic and other religious gatherings in Greece, mentioning the temple of Artemis at Ephesus as the meeting-place of the Ionians; but even if there were Ionian elements in the Aventine cult, it was undoubtedly the Latin Diana of the Woods who was worshipped there; and that she held a prominent position among the Latins is shewn

[1] Dionys. IV. 26; Varro, *L.L.* 43: "commune Latinorum Dianae templum"; Liv. I. 45: "(Seruius) perpulit ut Romae fanum Dianae populi Latini cum populo Romano facerent: ea erat confessio caput rerum Romam esse."

[2] It is not likely that the Latins would join in founding a temple of Diana at Rome in the fifth century when Rome and the Latins were partners in the restored Latin League.

[3] Frazer, *Golden Bough*, I. p. 5, n. 2.

[4] Strab. IV. 180.

by a fragment of the *Origines* of Cato recording the dedication of a Lucus Dianius "in nemore Aricino" by a Latin
dictator, in which the peoples of Tusculum, Aricia, Lanu-
vium, Laurentum, Cora, Tibur, Pometia and Ardea
participated[1]. A similar religious action with a political
aim is attributed to Tarquinius Superbus, namely the
founding (or more probably renewal under Roman leadership) of the festival of Jupiter Latiaris on the Alban Mount[2].

Still better perhaps is the evidence for the submission
to Rome of the town of Gabii some 12 miles distant.
Dionysius (IV. 58. 4) tells us that

there is a memorial of this treaty (between Tarquin and the
Gabini) at Rome kept in the temple of Zeus Pistios, whom the
Romans call Sancus—a wooden shield covered with the hide
of the ox that was sacrificed at the making of the treaty, and with
the agreement written on it in ancient characters.

There is no reason to doubt the authenticity of this record,
which could hardly fail to contain the name of Tarquin,
king of the Romans; and as De Sanctis points out, there
would be still less motive for a later forgery in the case of
a treaty with the comparatively insignificant Gabii than
in the case of the festival of Diana.

The first treaty between Rome and Carthage, which
Polybius (III. 22) assigns with the utmost precision to the
first year of the Republic (509 B.C.), clearly shews that when
the treaty was made Rome claimed some sort of dominion
over the Latins and was determined to keep foreign invaders away from the Latin and Volscian coasts as far as
Tarracina[3]. The Carthaginians undertake to do no harm

[1] Cato, frag. 58, in Peter, *Hist. Rom. Rel.* This dictator was probably
the officer of the Latin League, formed after the expulsion of the
Tarquins, with which Rome made terms in 493.
[2] Dionys. IV. 49. 2, who does not say that Tarquin built the temple
there: cf. W. Fowler, *Religious Experience*, etc. p. 237.
[3] On this treaty cf. Frank, *Economic History*, pp. 29 ff.; De Sanctis,
however (II. 252–3), rejects the Polybian date.

to the people of Ardea, Antium, Laurentum, Circeii or
Tarracina, or other Latins subject to Rome (ὑπήκοοι); to
respect other Latin cities and surrender to Rome any such
that they may capture; to build no fortress in Latium; and
if they enter Latium under arms, not to stop a night there.
Thus, all the obligations assumed by Carthage are directed
to the maintenance of the integrity of Latium under
Roman hegemony—a plain proof of the expansion southwards of the Roman power[1]. It is not unreasonable to
suppose that such expansion actually took place under
the later kings, whose position the early leaders of the
Republic attempted to maintain.

§ 4

THE FALL OF THE ETRUSCAN DOMINION

Of the manner in which the Etruscan power in Latium
came to an end we know nothing. The tradition of a definite
constitutional revolution seems to be supported by the
deep-rooted antagonism of the later Romans to the very
names of "rex" and "regnum," and their insistence on
the principle of collegiality in public office. But we have
no means of judging how far the Roman revolution was
directed against a despotism which was becoming irksome
and how far against foreign rule—the iniquities of the
Tarquins are, probably, mainly invented to form a foil to
the heroes of the Republic and give a constitutional justification to the revolution.

There is no reason for doubting the historical existence
of Lars Porsena, an Etruscan chief who at some time in

[1] Cf. Polybius' comment (III. 23. 6): Ῥωμαῖοι περὶ τῆς Λατίνης
αὐτῆς χώρας ποιοῦνται τὰς συνθήκας, τῆς δὲ λοιπῆς Ἰταλίας οὐ μνημο-
νεύουσι διὰ τὸ μὴ πίπτειν ὑπὸ τὴν αὐτῶν ἐξουσίαν.

the last years of the sixth century marched against Rome
and reduced it to surrender by famine[1]; he also demanded
hostages from the Romans, the cession of a piece of land
on the right bank of the Tiber known as the Septem Pagi,
and the surrender of all their iron except agricultural
implements[2]. Such appear to be the facts which patriotic
imagination attempted to conceal with the legends of
Horatius, Scaevola, Cloelia, with Porsena as the chivalrous
foe who departs with admiration for the Romans. Nor
can we accept the tradition that the exiled Tarquins sought
help from all possible quarters to return to Rome—from
Veii and Tarquinii[3], the king of Clusium, the Latin League.
Tarquinii first appears in arms against Rome in 397 B.C.;
Clusium enters the political horizon of Rome about the
same time[4]. Cicero only mentions Veii and the Latins
as allies of the Tarquins[5], and there is no reason why a
king of Clusium should attack Rome by way of the Janiculum instead of the far more vulnerable region of the
Colline Gate, nor why he should demand the cession of
the Septem Pagi[6]. If, however, the invaders came from
Veii, both difficulties disappear; and there is therefore

[1] Tac. *Hist.* III. 72: "(sedes I. O. M.) quam non Porsenna dedita
urbe neque Galli capta temerare potuissent." Famine at Rome:
Dionys. v. 26; Liv. II. 11. 1–3, 12. 1; Plut. *Popl.* 17. A siege by
Etruscans and famine are recorded again in 477–6, Liv. II. 51.
[2] Plin. *N.H.* xxxiv. 139; Dionys. v. 3. 4; Liv. II. 13. 4; Plut. *Popl.* 18;
Dionys. v. 65. 3: διδόντες καὶ ἀγορὰν καὶ ὅπλα καὶ τἆλλα ὅσων ἐδέοντο
Τυρρηνοὶ παρασχεῖν ἐπὶ τῇ καταλύσει τοῦ πολέμου. Graffunder in *Klio*
XI (1911), p. 105, suggests that Porsena destroyed a portion of the walls
of Rome. [3] Liv. II. 6. 2.
[4] Liv. v. 16. 2: "eo anno Tarquinienses noui hostes exorti";
v. 35. 4: the Clusini ask help against the Gauls at Rome: "quanquam
aduersus Romanos nullum eis ius societatis amicitiaeue erat."
[5] *Tusc. Disp.* III. 12. 7: "(Tarquinius) cum restitui in regnum nec
Veientium nec Latinorum armis potuisset, Cumas contulisse se
dicitur."
[6] Pais, II. 97–8. The recent discovery of the chamber-tombs of the
Etruscan type on Monte Mario points to an Etruscan settlement there
—the nearest to Rome of which we have indications.

strong ground for the suggestion of Pais that there was
a chieftain of Veii bearing the name (or title) of Porsena,
as there was according to legend at Volsinii[1]. The temporary submission of Rome to Lars Porsena thus appears
as an incident in the long struggle between Rome and her
nearest Etruscan neighbour.

For the traditional alliance of Porsena with the exiled
Tarquins is an invention of the annalists[2]. It is clear that
though Rome was defeated the Tarquins were not restored;
our historians give a different interpretation to this fact[3],
as they give different reasons for the breach between the
Tarquins and Porsena which has to be imagined to account
for it[4]. We cannot even say whether the invasion of
Porsena followed the expulsion of the Tarquins, seizing
the opportunity of Rome's weakness, or whether it was
not Porsena himself who overthrew the Tarquins and made
himself master of Rome in their place[5]. In any case, after
the conquest of Rome he or his followers penetrated further
into Latium, and laid siege to Aricia on the western edge
of the Alban hills (and so situated on the direct road to
Campania—the later Via Appia), where they were defeated
by the Latins aided by an army from Cumae under Aristodemus, who on his return made himself tyrant[6].

The facts as stated above appear to be mainly historical
and stand in connexion with the Etruscan attack on Cumae
some years before[7]. Dionysius (VII. 3 ff.) gives a long

[1] Plin. N.H. II. 140.
[2] Meyer, II. § 500; De Sanctis, I. p. 450.
[3] Cf. Dionys. v. 31. 4: περὶ καθόδου Ταρκυνίων μηδένα ποιεῖσθαι
λόγον, and Liv. II. 13. 4: "iactatum in condicionibus nequiquam de
Tarquiniis in regnum restituendis."
[4] Dionys. v. 33–4; Plut. Popl. 18.
[5] I see no difficulty in supposing that one Etruscan chief drove out
or killed another.
[6] Dionys. v. 36, VII. 5–7; Liv. II. 14, who mentions the Cumaean
help but not Aristodemus.
[7] On this cf. De Sanctis, I. pp. 451–2.

account of this attack which he ascribes to "the Etruscans who lived round the Ionian gulf and had been driven thence by the Celts," together with Umbrians, Daunians and other barbarians; more probably it was simply an attempt by the Etruscans perhaps with Italian allies or mercenaries already settled in Campania to gain possession of the prosperous port of Cumae. According to Dionysius Aristodemus shewed especial valour in the battle and became after it a popular leader, hated and feared by the nobles; who twenty years later made him commander of the army which was sent to relieve Aricia, hoping to be rid of him. It is clear that twenty years is a long interval for the maturing of a tyranny, and if Aristodemus really took a prominent part in repelling the attack on Cumae (which Dionysius dates precisely)[1], the battle of Aricia was probably not many years later. In this battle the Romans had no part, as is clear from the silence of Dionysius and Livy[2]; the former in fact (v. 61. 4) represents the Aricians as accusing the Romans before the Latin League of giving the Etruscans free passage through their land and other assistance in their aggression against Aricia; and in all probability Rome, newly subdued by Porsena, was not in a position to do otherwise.

How long this final Etruscan domination lasted which is associated with the name of Lars Porsena, and how it came to an end, we cannot ascertain. With the campaign against Aricia the Etruscans, perhaps Veientines, who had occupied Rome under Porsena, attempted to gain for themselves the supremacy among the Latin cities which the preceding Etruscan dynasty (the Tarquins) had won: they failed, and probably their hold on Rome was broken soon

[1] "In the 64th Olympiad and the archonship of Miltiades," VII. 3. 1; the words imply a Greek source.
[2] Only Plut. de muliebri uirtute, p. 261 E, Ῥωμαίοις ἐπικουρίαν ἄγων, mentions the Romans in connexion with the battle.

afterwards. The Latins seized the opportunity offered by the expulsion of the Tarquins to form a league from which Rome was excluded; there is no reason to doubt that they went to war with Rome, and subsequently made the equal compact known as the "foedus Cassianum" of 493 B.C.[1] We must reject, however, the traditional connexion of the Latin war with the Tarquins—why should the Latins take up arms to restore the king who had fought to take away their independence?—and the victory of Lake Regillus is clearly exaggerated, being followed by a treaty on equal terms.

Thus the Tarquins lost their dominion in Rome and Latium; another Etruscan, Porsena, succeeded them for a time in Rome but came to grief in Latium, and henceforward Etruscan communications with Campania by land were blocked by the new Latin League which was soon associated with a liberated Rome. The fate of the Etruscan power in central Italy was sealed, and their colonies in Campania condemned to isolation by the great sea-fight of 474 B.C., when the Etruscans, profiting by the fall of the tyranny of Aristodemus to make another attack on the coveted position of Cumae, were utterly defeated by the fleet of Hiero of Syracuse[2].

[1] De Sanctis, II. pp. 91–102, who shews that the fragment of Cato (*ap*. Prisc. IV. p. 129 H, frag. 58) gives a more trustworthy list of the constituent cities of the League than Dionys. V. 61.
[2] Diod. XI. 13. 51; Pind. *Pyth*. I. 72; Hicks and Hill, *Greek Historical Inscriptions*, no. 22.

PART THREE

THE ROMAN CONQUEST OF ETRURIA AND UMBRIA

§ I

FROM 490 TO 340 B.C.

THE military advance of Rome into Etruria and Umbria may be divided into two main stages, the conquest of south Etruria up to the Saltus Ciminius, accomplished between the years 490 and 340 B.C., and the conquest of the rest of Etruria and of Umbria (310–264 B.C.). In the former period the chief events are the wars with Veii and Fidenae culminating in the capture of Veii: the collapse and rapid recovery of Rome in the Gallic War and the occupation of the frontier-fortresses of Sutrium and Nepet. As the most powerful foreign neighbours of Rome, the Veientines were bound to look with jealousy on the growing ascendancy of Rome in the Latin League, and on any attempts to extend Roman dominion beyond the Tiber. Ancient writers[1] have much to tell us of the strength and riches of Veii; the city itself occupied a large area, defended on the north and south by the deep ravines of the Fosso di Formello and Fosso dei Due Fossi which meet below the old acropolis (Piazza d'Armi) and form the Cremera torrent; while its territory at the time of its

---

[1] Dionys. II. 54. 3: τὴν μεγίστην ἰσχὺν ἔχουσαν τότε πόλιν...κεῖται δ' ἐφ' ὑψηλοῦ σκοπέλου καὶ περιρρῶγος μέγεθος ἔχουσα ὅσον Ἀθῆναι. *id.* frag. XII. 10: γῆν πολλὴν καὶ πολύκαρπον ἔχουσα. Liv. V. 22: "urbs opulentissima Etrusci nominis"; *id. ib.* 24: "ager Veiens uberior ampliorque Romano agro"; Plut. *Camill.* 2.

capture was larger than that of Rome. The tombs of Veii do not disclose such extensive foreign trade as those of the maritime towns of Etruria[1]; but, though the material found in them is very similar to that found in the Esquiline necropolis at Rome, the Veientine necropolis yielded much greater quantities of the precious metals, especially gold-work, than were found on the Esquiline[2]. And more recent excavations have revealed the works of Veientine artists influenced by Greek traditions, which are among the masterpieces of early modelling[3].

Apart from the natural hostility of two powerful com-munities with a common frontier, there may well have been further grounds of enmity between Veii and Rome. It is probable that the traditions[4] which refer to the salt-pans at the mouth of the Tiber in connexion with the early wars and treaties between the two cities have some historical basis; the importance of the possession of salt to a people (especially if such possession amounts to a monopoly) is well known, and according to Pliny[5] the inhabitants of central Italy came for salt to the mouth of the Tiber. There is good reason[6] to accept the tradition of an early Roman settlement at Ostia—a small body of salt-workers

[1] There were, however, tombs at Veii which belong to the same "orientalizing" group as those of Vetulonia, Caere and Praeneste, see Garrucci in *Archeologia*, XLI. 1, pp. 196–9. Thus the bronze wheeled tray called an incense-burner (pl. IV. 2) found at Veii is very similar to those found at Caere (Pinza, *Röm. Mitt.* 1907, p. 110) and Vetulonia (Milani, *Mus. Arch.* pp. 221–2, tav. LXX).

[2] Lanciani in *Not. scav.* 1889, p. 158.

[3] On the Apollo-group of Veii see Giglioli in *Not. scav.* 1919, pp. 13–37, and above, p. 65.

[4] Liv. I. 33. 6: "in ore Tiberis Ostia urbs condita: salinae circa factae" (by Ancus). Cession of the salt-pans to Rome: Dionys. II. 54. 3, III. 41. Etruscan raid up to "salinae" in 357: Liv. VII. 17. 6.

[5] *N.H.* XXXI. 89.

[6] So De Sanctis, I. p. 283, who remarks on the absence of any tradition of a later colonization of Ostia. Pais, I². p. 470, regards the early tradition as an anticipation.

however, and not till later a maritime colony. Again, from the geographical position of Veii, one of its main ways of communication with the outer world must have been down the Cremera valley and then down the Tiber to the sea; another way was the ancient "Via Veientana" which can still be traced in part winding[1] down from the acropolis of Veii and joining the later Via Clodia not far from Rome. Both these routes were commanded by Rome, and the constant contact of Romans and Veientines would breed strife and intermittent reprisals by one city on the other. A third approach to Veii was the old Etruscan road[2] thither from Caere and its port of Pyrgi; but the silence of tradition regarding any help given by Caere to Veii in war suggests that the two towns were on hostile terms; and Caere we know to have been friendly to Rome. I have referred above to the attractive suggestion that the Porsena to whom Rome surrendered towards the end of the sixth century was king of Veii.

The importance of Fidenae in the wars between Rome and Veii is easily explained by its situation. I have no doubt that the hill of Castel Giubileo, which rises conspicuously on the left bank of the Tiber almost exactly opposite the mouth of the Cremera, was the site of the citadel of Etruscan Fidenae[3], though the later Roman town seems from remains, e.g. a reservoir on top of the hill, and inscriptions (*C.I.L.* XIV. 4057-8, etc.) to have been further south on the hill of Villa Spada. Thus the control of Fidenae was of considerable importance to Veii, and without accepting in their details the traditions of numerous captures of Fidenae by the Roman kings, we may believe that the stronghold was frequently taken, lost and re-taken

[1] Dennis, I. p. 2, on the "serpentine course" of this road: Anziani in *Mélanges*, XXXIII (1913), pp. 206-7.

[2] Anziani, *op. cit.* p. 231.

[3] So Dennis, I. p. 49; Nissen, II. p. 605; cf. Liv. IV. 22: "urbs alta et munita."

by either side. Fidenae is sometimes described as a "bridge-head," but it is worth remarking that there is no indication that there ever was a bridge there in ancient, medieval, or modern times till the recent construction of a military bridge; but of course there may have been some kind of crossing by means of rafts[1].

The first war between republican Rome and Veii which appears in our historians is put between the years 484 and 474 B.C., and is chiefly remarkable for the episode of the Fabii at the Cremera[2]. Much of the tradition is no doubt untrustworthy, the invention of Fabian annalists (e.g. the heroism of Caeso Fabius, Liv. II. 43. 6 and of Q. Fabius, *ibid.* 46); but it is not improbable that the Romans occupied a strong position on Veientine territory whence they could ravage the land and command the approach to Veii up the Cremera valley, cutting off Veii from Fidenae, a more daring form of a plan of campaign often adopted by Rome, namely, the occupation of Fidenae[3]. It is credible also that the Etruscans retaliated by raiding Roman territory from the Janiculum (Liv. II. 51), but the striking Roman victories of the succeeding years, which led the Veientines to ask for a truce and pay an indemnity, are to be treated with some scepticism. An interval of peace followed: Rome, with her Latin and Hernican allies, was occupied with constantly recurring wars against the Aequians and Volscians, while the Etruscan power at sea and in Campania was shattered by the defeat at Cumae in 474 (Diod. XI. 51), which was followed about twenty years later by a series

[1] Cf. the report in "some annals" of a naval battle at Fidenae, "rem aeque difficilem atque incredibilem," which Livy suggests may be an exaggeration of a conflict of boats in preventing a crossing: Liv. IV. 34. 6–7.

[2] Dionys. VIII. 82—IX. 36; Liv. II. 42–54. The former rejects the tradition that only one of the Fabian gens survived the disaster.

[3] De Sanctis, II. p. 132, notes the record of a defeat, its definite localization, and its connexion with a particular family as features in the tale which would not be likely to be invented.

of Syracusan raids on Corsica, Elba and the Etruscan coast. Thus the foreign trade of Etruria in which the wealth of the country largely lay was damaged to the advantage of the Greek cities, with which (especially Massalia) Rome was probably already on friendly terms.

We now come to the confused narratives of the capture of Fidenae, which in Livy (IV. 17–35) are spread over the years 437–426. Two material records of this war survived into later times to support the authenticity of some details of the tradition—the statues of the murdered Roman envoys[1] and the breastplate of Lars Tolumnius dedicated to Jupiter Feretrius by A. Cornelius Cossus, the inscription of which was read by Augustus[2]. Livy himself (IV. 20 and 23) mentions discrepancies in his authorities, and records two dictatorships of Mamercus Aemilius (IV. 17 and 31), and two captures of Fidenae (IV. 22 and 34); more probably there was a single war about 426 B.C. (the record of a war in 437 being due to the consul's name, L. Sergius Fidenas)[3], and the city was finally taken by Rome at some time before the last siege of Veii: Diodorus records a war arising from the murder of Roman envoys, and a great but indecisive battle, with no mention of the capture of Fidenae[4].

The capture of Veii[5] was the first great step in the north-ward advance of Rome, and the most important military success which she had yet gained. Tradition may well be

---

[1] Liv. IV. 17. 6: Cicero says the statues survived till his own time, *Phil.* IX. 2. 4.

[2] Liv. IV. 20. On this see Dessau in *Hermes*, 41, pp. 142 ff.; Hirschfeld, *Kleine Schriften*, XXVIII; De Sanctis, II. pp. 137 ff.; Pais, II. p. 309.

[3] De Sanctis, *loc. cit.*

[4] Diod. XII. 80: πολλῶν παρ' ἀμφοτέροις πεσόντων ἰσόρροπος ὁ ἀγὼν ἐγένετο.

[5] Dated by Meyer, v. § 817 n., in 388 on the strength of Diod. XIV. 93, who says that the capture of Lipara by Rome (251 B.C.; Polyb. I. 39. 13) was 137 years after the year in which Liparaean pirates captured the gold cup made from the spoil of Veii which was being dedicated by Rome to Apollo, and sent it with an escort to Delphi. But this episode may have been a year or two after the fall of Veii.

correct in associating with the siege the introduction of
a war-tax and military pay, of the class of equites who
volunteered for service with their own horses, and of the
practice of wintering in the field. The numerous legends
which gathered round the siege shew the prominent
position which it held in the minds of the Romans. Rome
had crushed out of existence her most powerful neighbour
and made her first annexation on a large scale across the
Tiber, thereby doubling her own territory. The cause of
her success lay, no doubt, mainly in the cohesion of the
Latin alliance under Rome, in contrast with the political
disunion of Etruria. Without accepting at its face value all
that Livy tells us about the proceedings at the Fanum
Voltumnae[1], it is clear that the bulk of the Etruscan cities,
whether through preoccupation with the Gauls or not,
abandoned Veii to its fate. Only Capena and Falerii,
seeing their own danger, made common cause with Veii;
Tarquinii, if Livy speaks true (v. 16), did not get beyond
making raids on Roman territory; Caere seems to have
maintained a neutrality friendly to Rome[2].

We can see how the different fortunes of Veii and Rome
followed naturally from the contrast in their geographical
situations: Veii (and the same is equally true of Falerii)
lay off the main lines of communication, isolated among the
precipitous ravines of south Etruria, and isolation meant,
sooner or later, downfall; Rome, situated on the great
natural highway of the Tiber, and at the same time within
easy access from the sea, and at a point where, thanks to
the island of the Tiber, the river could conveniently be
crossed, was a natural meeting-place for traders and
travellers from different parts, many of whom would

---

[1] Liv. iv. 61, v. 1 and 17.
[2] The Romans "per agrum Caeretem obliquis tramitibus egressi...
Tarquinienses oppressere" (Liv. v. 16), which suggests that the *Caeres
ager* was friendly soil.

doubtless marry and settle there, contributing their abilities
and their wealth to the Republic. Thus Rome, in contrast
to the racial exclusiveness of the Etruscans, gradually
acquired that power of absorbing alien elements and im-
buing them with her own native character and traditions
which she later displayed on the larger field of a world-
wide Empire. This Roman gift of "inclusiveness" secured
the support of her allies, who saw too that her cause was
theirs; the broad and level Campagna, then densely populated, lay exposed to the power, while it looked to the
protection, of Rome. The non-Etruscan element in south
Etruria was probably large and had little in common with
its overlords, while the broken country would often make
it difficult for Veii and Falerii to control all their subjects,
many of whom deserted to Rome in time of war[1]. These
considerations of geographical position and its effect on
national character and ability to rule to a very large extent
form the key to the whole Roman conquest of Italy, and
have not always been given due recognition; I have alluded
to them here because it is in the great struggle with Veii
that they are first strikingly exemplified.

After the fall of Veii, Rome turned against Capena and
Falerii; the former was soon subdued, and the Roman
frontier was thus advanced on the right bank of the Tiber
as far as the slopes of Soracte[2]. In the same year (tradition-
ally 395 B.C.) Falerii was attacked and according to Diodorus
was sacked, but as he records a peace with the Falisci next
year it is clear that the city was neither destroyed nor
permanently taken[3]. A later version coloured by the

[1] Liv. VI. 4. 4 (389 B.C.): "in ciuitatem accepti qui Veientium
Capenatiumque ac Faliscorum per ea bella transfugerant ad Romanos
agerque his nouis ciuibus adsignatus."
[2] Liv. V. 24 (in the year after the fall of Veii). On the position of
Capena cf. Bormann in *C.I.L.* XI. 1, p. 570; Dennis, I. pp. 125–6, 131;
and Hülsen in Pauly-Wissowa, *R.E.*, s.v.
[3] Diod. XIV. 96. 5: ἐξεπόρθησαν: *ibid.* 98. 5.

Camillus-legend gives us the story of the schoolmaster and the voluntary surrender of the Falisci[1]; from which the most important fact which emerges is that the Romans failed to capture Falerii owing to its strong position[2]. The plateau on which Civitacastellana (the Etruscan Falerii) stands is still surrounded on all sides by deep and precipitous ravines, which are bridged by the three roads which lead out of the town, and there are remains of an ancient ring-wall on the cliffs above. The wealth of Falerii about this time and earlier is shewn by the contents of its cemeteries, especially the Attic vases (both black and red figure) of which there is a large number in the Villa Giulia Museum at Rome. There was also a considerable local manufacture of vases in imitation of the later Athenian styles, and this Faliscan ware is in general superior in artistic value to other Etruscan pottery. Greek influence also appears in the terracotta decorations of several temples[3] at Falerii which are ascribed to the sixth and fifth centuries B.C., though the finest terracottas of Falerii are the pediment statues of the later Sassi Caduti temple, which clearly belong to the Hellenistic age[4].

After making peace with Falerii the Romans proceeded to secure their new possessions by a further advance. The dates of the establishment of Latin colonies at Sutrium and Nepet[5], which Livy (VI. 9) describes as "loca opposita Etruriae et uelut claustra inde portaeque," are variously reported. Diodorus (XIV. 98) immediately after recording the peace with Falerii has the sentence πρὸς δ' Αἰτωλοὺς πόλεμον τὸ τέταρτον καὶ Σούτριον μὲν ὥρμησαν, which

---

[1] Dionys. XIII. 1–2; Liv. v. 27; Plut. *Cam.* 9–10, etc.

[2] Liv. v. 26 (on the Faliscan camp near the town): "asperis confragosisque circa et partim artis partim arduis uiis." Ovid, *Amor.* III. 13. 6: "difficilis cliuis huc uia praebet iter."

[3] Della Seta, *Museo di Villa Giulia*, p. 159.

[4] *ibid.* p. 148.

[5] On the form of this name cf. Bormann in *C.I.L.* XI. 1, p. 481.

Burger[1] ingeniously emends into πρὸς δ' αὐτοὺς πολίσματα Νέπετον καὶ Σούτριον κατῴκισαν: and he refers to Sutrium later (XIV. 117, after the Gallic invasion) as Σουτριανὴν οὖσαν ἀποικίαν ἢν οἱ Τυρρηνοὶ βίᾳ κατειλήφεσαν. Livy does not record the settlement at Sutrium but refers to its people as "socios populi Romani" in the year after the capture of Rome by the Gauls and he records the foundation of a colony at Nepet by triumviri in 383 B.C.[2] Velleius, however (I. 14), explicitly dates the colonization of Sutrium seven years after the Gauls took Rome, and that of Nepet a further ten years later. That Sutrium at least was strategically in the possession of Rome before the Gallic invasion is clear from Diodorus and Livy; and by founding a Latin colony there at once, Rome would be carrying out her obligation of sharing conquered land with the allies. The territory of Veii was early divided among the Roman plebs[3], bordering as it did on the *ager Romanus*; while the more distant conquered land was given to the Latins and two colonies founded upon it, Sutrium probably between the fall of Veii and the capture of Rome, and Nepet ten years later[4].

Roman influence was now dominant in south Etruria up to the well-marked natural barrier of the Tolfa and Ciminian mountains. The former are a group of mountains extending over a wide area and reaching down to the coast; they are still practically impassable save by footpaths, and south of them on the coast was the territory of Caere, friendly to Rome. On the Ciminian range the woods are

[1] *Sechzig Jahre aus der älteren Geschichte Roms*, pp. 95–6. The emendation is of course only conjectural; for others (e.g. Αἰκίκλους, ἐπολέμουν, ἐπὶ Σούτριον, or ᾤκισαν) see Drachmann, *Diodors Römische Annalen*, p. 36.   [2] Liv. VI. 3. 2; 21. 4.

[3] Liv. v. 30. 8; Diod. XIV. 102: both assign the event to the third year after the fall of Veii. The grant of land served the military purpose of securing the conquest, and afforded relief to the poor of Rome.

[4] So De Sanctis, II. p. 149, following Diod. and Livy; but Mommsen, I. p. 432, follows Velleius.

still in most places too thick to be crossed even on foot; the modern road across (the Via Ciminia of Roman times) rises steeply to a height of over 2700 feet, and its site was probably covered at this time with dense forest. An easier route between the Tolfa and the Ciminian hills was commanded at its southern outlet by the fortress of Sutrium, while between the Ciminian hills and the Tiber was the territory of Falerii, which Rome had for the time reduced to impotence. How far the political horizon of Rome at this time extended beyond the limits described above is uncertain; there is a strong tradition of Roman intervention at Clusium a few years later, and both Diodorus (XIV. 109. 7) and Livy (V. 31–2) record a war with Volsinii; there may have been some frontier raids, but the brief undetailed accounts suggest an anticipation of later events[1].

The Romans had barely time to secure their new frontier in south Etruria before the storm of the Gallic invasion burst upon them. The cause of the invasion is probably to be found in the pressure of other tribes from beyond the Alps. Diodorus indeed (XIV. 113) seems to place the first inroad into northern Italy, by which the Etruscans were driven from the region between the Alps and the Apennines, immediately before the attack on Rome; but Livy (V. 33) explicitly states that the Gauls first crossed the Alps 200 years before[2]. This period is exaggerated; even if the Gauls had already settled north of the Po, where the foundation of Mediolanum (Milan) is ascribed to them, the Etruscans of Felsina (Bologna) were still prosperous enough to be producing fine bronze-work and importing

[1] So De Sanctis, II. p. 149, but Meyer, V. § 816, accepts the Volsinian war. The Salpinates mentioned by Livy and the Γουράσιον where Diodorus records a battle are otherwise unknown. No mention of this war occurs in the Fasti Triumphales. It has been suggested that Salpinum occupied the site of Orvieto (Dennis, II. p. 40, Pais, II. p. 450).
[2] Polyb. II. 18. 2, dates the fall of Rome μετά τινα χρόνον from the Gallic settlement of the Po valley.

Attic vases up to the beginning of the fourth century B.C.[1] The record in Livy (v. 33. 6) of frequent battles between the Gauls and the trans-Apennine Etruscans is corroborated by the stelae found in the cemeteries of Felsina, many of which shew scenes of combat which (except for clearly mythological scenes) hardly occur on other Etruscan monuments. On one at least of these stelae a horseman, presumably the defunct, is represented fighting a naked long-haired opponent with a long shield, who can only be a barbarian Gaul[2]. The tradition that the Etruscan town of Melpum in the Po valley fell to the Gauls on the day that the Romans took Veii[3] represents an undoubted fact, that the decline of Etruscan power at the end of the fifth century was hastened by the simultaneous advance of the Gauls in the north and the Romans in the south, added to the loss of Campania and the disunion of the Etruscan cities.

The tradition that the Gauls, who about 387 B.C. crossed the Apennines, ravaged the territory of Clusium on their southward march is well attested (Diod., Livy) and that they were there attacked by a small Roman force is not improbable. But the crime of the Roman ambassadors in taking part in a battle seems to have been invented to account for the collapse of Rome at the Allia[4]; and the idea of the primitive barbarians (for such the Gauls appear in Polybius' description, II. 17. 9 ff.) appealing to the *ius gentium* is ludicrous. Nor is it likely that the Clusini would appeal to Rome for help, instead of to powerful and nearer neighbours of their own race such as Volsinii; the appeal

[1] The Greek vases in the Civic Museum of Bologna mainly belong to the period 510–390 B.C., and are of the later black-figure and the "severe" and "fine" red-figure styles, with a few in the "florid" style.

[2] Felsinean stelae: Ducati in *Mon. Ant.* XX (1910), pp. 360 ff.; on the scenes of combat, pp. 655–84.

[3] Corn. Nep.: cf. Plin. *N.H.* III. 125.

[4] De Sanctis, II. p. 165.

is not recorded by Diodorus, and Livy[1] remarks that they
had no claim on Rome. More probably the Romans had
heard of the invasion (not only in the supernatural manner
recorded by Livy[2]) and sent a force to Clusium to recon-
noitre, as Diodorus says[3]. From Clusium the Gauls came
down the Clanis and Tiber valleys, passing by the strongholds of Orvieto (whether this is to be identified with
Volsinii or with some other town) and Falerii; Rome was
their objective, and as they did little damage on the way
the Etruscans let them pass by without opposition[4]. Caere
proved its friendship for Rome by receiving the Roman
priests and Vestals with their "sacra" and other women
and children, when the capture of Rome was imminent;
some of the other Etruscans saw their opportunity in
Rome's adversity and made inroads on the Roman territory
north of the Tiber[5]. Meanwhile Veii, which had no doubt
been partially re-populated by the Roman settlers on its
land, became a rallying-point of survivors from the disaster
of the Allia, refugees from Rome, and Latin volunteers[6];
and a force was formed there which after repelling the
Etruscan raiders was a sufficient menace to the Gauls to
induce them to withdraw from Rome on payment of a
ransom[7]. According to Strabo the Caerites attacked and
defeated the Gauls in the country of the Sabines, and this

[1] Liv. v. 35. 4: "aduersus Romanos nullum eis ius societatis amicitiaeue erat," though the Roman envoy speaks of the Clusini as "socii
populi Romani atque amici"—clearly an anticipation of much later
Roman protectorates.

[2] Liv. v. 32. 6.

[3] Diod. xiv. 113.

[4] For different views of the site of the battle of the Allia (right or
left of the Tiber) see Hülsen and Linder, *Die Alliaschlacht*; Richter,
Die Alliaschlacht; and De Sanctis, ii. p. 169.

[5] Caere: Liv. v. 40. 10; Strab. v. p. 220, etc. Etruscan raids: Diod.
xiv. 116; Liv. v. 45. 4–8.

[6] Liv. v. 46. 4.

[7] Polyb. I. 6. 3: ποιησάμενοι Ῥωμαῖοι σπονδὰς καὶ διαλύσεις εὐδοκ-
ουμένας Γαλάταις.

is in agreement with Diodorus' record of the destruction
of a Gallic force returning from Iapygia through Roman
territory ὑπὸ Κερίων ἐν τῷ Τραυσίῳ πεδίῳ[1].

For its friendly action during the Gallic peril Caere was
given the Roman *hospitium*—an official expression of
friendship without the privileges or duties of a formal
alliance. Of the Gauls, some returned to their own
territory across the Apennines; others entered the service
of Dionysius of Syracuse[2]; others again remained in various
places in central Italy, a menace to their more peaceful
neighbours with whom they were frequently at war. Thus
we hear of them in the Alban hills in about 356 B.C. and
later[3]; and a bilingual inscription of Tuder (Todi) in
Umbria, in Gallic and Latin, points to some survival of
them there some time after the Roman conquest[4]. The
Etruscans and Volscians profiting by the disaster which
Rome had suffered invaded her territory, and the former,
acting (according to tradition) with more unanimity than
usual, crossed the Ciminian range and seized Sutrium and
perhaps also Nepet. But they had underrated Rome's
power of recovery; the frontier towns were retaken and
garrisoned, and Rome carried the war into the territory
of Tarquinii, capturing two towns[5]. The Volscian peril
was also averted and Rome could turn her attention to the
consolidation of her conquests.

The former subjects of Veii, Capena and Falerii, who
had deserted to the Roman side, were given citizenship and
a grant of land near their old homes, and were enrolled

---

[1] Strab. v. p. 22; Diod. XIV. 117 *fin.* (where Meyer reads Καιρίτων).
[2] Justin, xx. 5.
[3] Polyb. II. 18. 6; Liv. VI. 42. 6, VII. 25. 3.
[4] *C.I.L.* XI. 2. 4687.
[5] Diod. XIV. 117; Liv. VI. 3 (*ibid.* 9–10 a duplicate version) and 4;
Elogium of Camillus, *C.I.L.* I. p. 285. Pais, III. p. 91, needlessly
regards this relief of Sutrium as an anticipation of that which occurred
in 311 B.C.

in four new tribes, Stellatina, Tromentina, Sabatina, and Arniensis[1]. Of these the Stellatina seems to have been located in the territory of Capena, bordering on the Tiber, and the Tromentina in that of Veii[2]; the Sabatina would be on the south and west sides of the Lacus Sabatinus (L. di Bracciano)—on the north side was the Latin territory of Sutrium—and the Arniensis on the river Aro (Arrone, flowing into the sea near Maccarese, the ancient Fregenae), adjoining the territory of Caere. The Romans who had occupied the empty houses of Veii at the time of the Gallic invasion were recalled under severe penalties, and proposals for the migration thither of the whole state were rejected. Rome had already owed much to her position on the Tiber, and would not sacrifice its advantages for the comparative isolation of Veii, nor tolerate a schism in the body politic which might lead to civil war.

War broke out again between Rome and her Etruscan neighbours between 358 and 351 B.C., but it was probably not more than a series of raids by Tarquinii and Falerii on Roman territory and reprisals by Rome[3]; and it ended with a period of forty years' peace. With Caere, however, which had joined in these raids and received a share of the spoil, Rome (according to Livy, VII. 20) made a truce for a hundred years, in consideration of her previous good services. Nothing in Livy's account suggests that the Caerites were at this time given any form of Roman citizenship; but this must have occurred if Gellius[4] is right in saying that they were the first "municipes sine suffragii iure," since undoubtedly in 338 B.C. the Campanians,

---

[1] Liv. VI. 4. 4 and 5. 8.

[2] Bormann in *C.I.L.* XI. 1, p. 570 (Capena) and p. 557 (Veii); Kubitschek, pp. 18–19, excludes Capena, as being in the later tribus Quirina, but Festus, p. 343, s.v. "Stellatina," connects the latter tribe with Capena.

[3] Diod. XVI. 31; Liv. VII. 12–22; Fast. Tr. (356 B.C.).

[4] *N.A.* XVI. 13. 7.

Fundani and Formiani were admitted to that condition, as a reward for their friendly attitude in the Latin war[1]. Gellius therefore agrees with Livy in representing the original *ciuitas sine suffragio* as a privilege, though he describes it in terms which contradict the fundamental idea of a *municipium*—"concessumque illis ut ciuitatis Romanae honorem quidem caperent sed negotiis tamen atque oneribus uacarent pro sacris bello Gallico receptis custoditisque." Rome had already rewarded Caere with her *hospitium* and it is incredible that she ever gave the privileges of citizenship without corresponding duties. We know that in 273 B.C. the Caerites fearing an attack from Rome (evidently to punish some recent act of disloyalty) sent envoys and obtained peace by ceding half their territory[2]; which seems to shew Caere as a still independent state. The silence of Livy concerning the incorporation of Caere as the first municipium, if this occurred in 353 or soon after, is very hard to explain; the phrase "tabula Caeritum" may have become current in Roman slang because the Caerites were kept in the inferior condition of half-citizens longer than others[3], and remained in use after they became full citizens. If so, the incorporation of Caere may date from 273 B.C. as Pais[4] suggests, or at any rate the retention of Caere among the *municipia sine suffragio* was due to their disloyalty at that time. This I take to be the meaning of the scholium on Horace, which as it stands is plainly contradictory[5]; perhaps the privilege which Caere had previously received was not the citizenship, but the very

[1] Liv. VIII. 14. 10.
[2] Dio, frag. 33: in Zonaras, VIII. 7, it appears (with the name Ἀγυλλαῖοι omitted) after the Pyrrhic war, in about 273 B.C.
[3] So Tenney Frank in *Klio*, XI. p. 378 *n.*
[4] III. pp. 408 ff.
[5] Schol. Hor. *Ep.* I. 6. 62: "Caeritibus ciuitas Romana sic data ut non liceret eis suffragia ferre quia post datam ausi sunt rebellare"; whence De Sanctis, II. p. 257, says that they were given citizenship (retaining some local rights and a shadow of autonomy) in 353.

exceptional truce (100 years) which Rome granted in 353 B.C.

The exact date of the incorporation of Caere must probably remain uncertain, but there can be little doubt that by the middle of the fourth century B.C. it had declined into practical dependence on Rome. From at least the seventh century it had been rich and powerful with an extensive foreign trade through its port of Pyrgi[1]; it had cultivated friendly relations with the Greek cities as with Rome, and had dedicated a treasury at Delphi[2]. But its sea-trade and its power had declined; and in 384 B.C. Dionysius of Syracuse had plundered its port, sacking the temple there and defeating the Caerites[3]. The extension of Roman territory to the Lacus Sabatinus (see above) hemmed it in on the north-east, east, and south-east, while to the north the impassable Tolfa range separated it save for a narrow strip of coast from its nearest Etruscan neighbours. Caere was not strong enough and perhaps did not desire to form a militant Etruscan outpost, and so its absorption by Rome was only a matter of time. Falerii, which had been given a forty years' truce in 351 B.C., was in 343 bound by a treaty to Rome[4], and its potential unfriendliness was held in check by the Latin colony of Nepet, which occupied a strong natural position five miles away. Thus after the Gallic catastrophe Rome had strengthened her hold upon the extremities of her northern frontier —Caere on the coast and Falerii adjoining the Tiber—and had triumphantly maintained the line of the Ciminian hills

[1] E.g. the gold, silver and bronze treasures of the Regolini-Galassi tomb, now in the Gregorian Museum, and the fine Greek vases there and in the Villa Giulia Museum.

[2] Strab. v. p. 220, who says Caere abstained from piracy though well able to practise it. Cf. Plut. Cam. 21: the Vestals are sent εἰς τινα τῶν Ἑλληνίδων πόλεων, where the reference is to Caere.

[3] See below, p. 106.

[4] Liv. VII. 38. 1, where the request for a treaty is represented as due to the Roman victories over the Samnites.

in the centre. In forty years of peace with the Etruscans
(351–311 B.C.) she was able finally to assert her supremacy
over the Latin League, and to come through the worst of
the long struggle with the Samnites, without the fear of
any hostile intervention from the north.

For the Etruscans were exposed in this period to attacks
from several different quarters, which they were little able
to resist. In the north-west the region north of the Arno,
which at one time had belonged to the Etruscans, was over-
run by the wild Ligurian tribes: the Etruscan dominion
in the region of Pisa and Luna, asserted by Livy[1], was
probably short-lived and left few traces, but tombs which,
from the jewelry and fifth-century Attic vases which they
contained, appear to be Etruscan have been found in Pisa
itself and near Lucca[2]. Of the Pisans Strabo tells us
(v. p. 223) μαχιμώτεροι Τυρρηνῶν ὑπῆρξαν καὶ παρώξυναν
αὐτοὺς οἱ Λίγυες πονηροὶ γείτονες παρὰ πλευρὰν ὄντες:
he thus distinguishes the Pisans from the Etruscans, but
only (it seems) because he accepts the legend that Pisa
was founded by men of Pisa in the Peloponnese who lost
their way in returning from Troy. There is no adequate
ground for the suggestion of Pais that Pisa was a Phocaean
colony. Polybius speaks of the Ligurians in his time living
in the Apennines as far as Pisa, the first city of Etruria
towards the west, and inland as far as the territory of the
Arretines[3]. The two stations called "Ad Fines[4]," one on

---

[1] Liv. XLI. 13, on the foundation of the colony of Luna: "de Ligure
is captus ager erat, Etruscorum antequam Ligurum fuerat": id.
XXXV. 51, the spoil captured in the ager Pisanus by the Ligurians is
called "praeda Etrusca." Cato (ap. Serv. Aen. X. 179): "qui Pisas
tenuerint ante aduentum Etruscorum negat sibi compertum."
[2] Ghirardini in Not. scav. 1892, pp. 152–4; Rend. Linc. 1894,
pp. 81 ff. On the Etruscan occupation cf. Pais, Ancient Italy, pp. 355 ff.;
Poggi, Luni ligure-etrusca e Luna romana (Genoa, 1904); Nissen, I.L.
II. 288 ff.; Dennis, II. pp. 63, 71; Müller, I. pp. 99, 324: it is doubted
by Bormann (C.I.L. XI. 1, p. 272) and De Sanctis (I. pp. 440–1).
[3] Polyb. II. 16. 1–2.　　　[4] Tab. Peut.; Itin. Ant. p. 285.

the coast-road (Via Aurelia) between the modern Cecina and Leghorn, and the other on the Via Cassia midway between Arezzo and Florence, which no doubt were the places where the roads crossed the old frontier of Italy[1], probably also mark the border-line between the territory occupied by the Ligurians and the Etruscan cities which entered the Roman alliance in the third century B.C.

Early in the fourth century the Gauls as has been mentioned began to encroach upon the Etruscan colonies north of the Apennines, and by the middle of the century had made themselves masters of the country[2]. The Etruscan population was gradually submerged or driven into the Alps, only Mantua surviving as a relic of their former dominion north of the Po[3]. In the south, the Etruscan towns of Campania were isolated from their motherland by the independent Latins and Volscians, and fell a prey to the Samnites who defeated the Etruscans, took possession of Capua and the other Etruscan towns, and secured their hold on Campania by the capture of the Greek Cumae[4]. To the Etruscans in the first place was probably due the traditional luxury of Capua which soon distinguished the Campanians from their Samnite kinsmen, and the painted chamber-tombs of Capua, Paestum and other sites are

---

[1] On the east the Aesis was the frontier: Strab. v. p. 227: πρότερον μέν γε τὸν Αἶσιν ἐποιοῦντο ὅρον, πάλιν δὲ τὸν ʿΡουβίκωνα ποταμόν. The extension of Italian territory is generally ascribed to Sulla who in consequence extended the pomerium of Rome.

[2] Attic vases, which from their style are held to date from the early fourth century, are found in Etruscan tombs at Bologna (now in the Civic Museum). Cf. Ducati in *Atti e Mem. R. Deputazione di Storia Patria*, 1908, pp. 54–91.

[3] Plin. III. 130: "Mantua Tuscorum trans Padum sola reliqua"; *ibid.* 133: "Raetos Tuscorum prolem arbitrantur a Gallis pulsos duce Raeto." Cf. Justin, xx. 5. 9; Liv. v. 33. 11.

[4] Capua: Diod. XII. 31; Liv. IV. 371. Cumae: Diod. XII. 76; Liv. IV. 44. 12. On the chronology cf. Meyer, v. § 803 *n.*; Beloch, *Campanien*, pp. 150–1, 298–9.

clearly analogous to those of Etruria[1]. The settlements of
the Etruscans in north and south Italy had been private
ventures, the work of individual leaders or groups of
colonists, not closely attached to a strong metropolis or
to the federal league; and so they were lost one by one
when left to their own resources.

The weakness of the Etruscans was also becoming
evident at sea. Some twenty years after the battle of Cumae
the Syracusans finding their sea-trade hampered by the
rivalry of the Etruscans determined on reprisals. Phayllus
was sent out with a fleet and ravaged Elba, one of the
principal sources of Etruscan power, but was bribed by
the enemy to retire. A second expedition under Apelles
sailed along the Etruscan coast, ravaged the Etruscan towns
in Corsica and subdued Elba; the conquest was not permanent, but it shewed the weakness of Etruria and kept
alive the feud with Syracuse[2]. Hence the Athenians received promises of help from certain of the Etruscan cities
in 415 B.C., and we find Etruscan ships and land-troops
collaborating with them on several occasions in the siege
of Syracuse[3].

It was inevitable that the revived Syracusan imperialism
of Dionysius I should come into conflict with the power
which still made the Italian seas dangerous to others
though its old mastery of them was much impaired. His
activity in the Adriatic was doubtless largely directed
against the Etruscans, whose ships were still active in that
sea at a much later date even though the Po valley had
fallen into the hands of the Gauls[4]. His formal alliance

---

[1] See Weege, "Oskische Grabmalerei," in *Jahrb. k. d. Arch. Inst.*
XXIV (1909), pp. 99–162.   [2] Diod. XI. 88.
   [3] Thuc. VI. 86. 6, 103. 2; VII. 53, 2, 54, 57. 11.
   [4] Cf. Dittenberger, *Sylloge*, no. 112, an Athenian decree of 325–4
B.C. concerning a colony in the Adriatic and a φυλακὴ ἐπὶ Τυρρηνούς.
Cf. Lysias, frag. 1 (*ap*. Athen. XIII. 612 *d*) on the dangers of the Adriatic
and the titles of speeches of Hyperides and Dinarchus, περὶ τῆς φυλακῆς
τῶν Τυρρηνῶν and Τυρρηνικός.

with the Gauls (Justin, xx. 5. 4) and his colonies in Illyria, at Ancona, and above all at Adria, which if not an Etruscan town had been one of the principal ports for the trade of Felsina with the Greeks, are clear indications of his anti-Etruscan policy in the east[1]. In the Tyrrhenian Sea Dionysius in 384 B.C. sent out a fleet nominally to suppress piracy, actually to collect booty; a raid was made on Pyrgi the port of Caere, and spoil to the value of 1500 talents was taken from the rich temple of Leucothea[2]. We learn from Strabo that the expedition was also directed against Corsica, which was still apparently in Etruscan hands, and it is highly probable that Populonia and Elba were raided at the same time. A temple at Populonia of which the stone basement was excavated in 1908 was thought to shew signs of having been despoiled and destroyed in antiquity: the scattered fragments of Attic pottery found there belong to the fifth and early fourth centuries, and various of the tombs of Populonia were evidently plundered in antiquity[3]. That the Syracusans for a time regained possession of Elba is rendered probable by the story of the Sicilian who made a corner in iron ($\sigma\upsilon\nu\epsilon\pi\rho\acute{\iota}\alpha\tau o$ $\pi\acute{\alpha}\nu\tau\alpha$ $\tau\grave{o}\nu$ $\sigma\acute{\iota}\delta\eta\rho o\nu$ $\dot{\epsilon}\kappa$ $\tau\hat{\omega}\nu$ $\sigma\iota\delta\eta\rho\epsilon\acute{\iota}\omega\nu$) and without adding much to the price made a clear profit of 50 talents[4]—a considerable sum which shews that he must have disposed of a large quantity of iron, which must almost inevitably have come from Elba, the great centre of the iron mining of Italy.

[1] Dionysius and the Adriatic: cf. A. J. Evans in Freeman's *History of Sicily*, IV. pp. 220–9. Attic pottery is found at Adria of the same type as at Felsina (Bologna), cf. Grenier, *Bologne*, p. 189.

[2] Arist. *Oecon.* II. 21. 9, p. 1349; Diod. xv. 14; Strabo, v. p. 226 (speaks of the temple of Ilethyia).

[3] Milani, *Not. scav.* 1908, pp. 215, 218–31; Minto, *ibid.* 1914, pp. 447 ff. The massive walls of Populonia and the famous hydriae of Phaon and Adonis in the style of Midias (Florence Museum, Room V) which were found there shew the importance and wealth of Populonia at this period.

[4] Arist. *Pol.* I. 11, 12, p. 1259. Pais, *Ricerche storiche e geografiche,*

We have some other fleeting glimpses of events in the
Tyrrhenian Sea about this time. Thus Diodorus (XV. 27)
records a colony of 500 men sent by the Romans to
Sardinia (εἰς Σαρδονίαν) in 386 B.C., according to the
conventional Roman chronology (378 B.C. by the Greek
reckoning), and Theophrastus (*Hist. Plant.* V. 8. 2) speaks
of a Roman expedition of twenty-five ships to Corsica[1].
Neither passage has any confirmation from other authors,
but despite their difficulties they serve to some extent to
confirm one another, though we must remain ignorant of
the actual facts to which they allude. Greek pirates appear
making raids on the Latin coast from the mouth of the
Tiber southwards, perhaps in reprisals for the piracy of
Antium[2]. The Romans took measures to prevent the
Greeks from landing, but there is no allusion to a Roman
war-fleet[3]. The "duouiri nauales" are first mentioned at
Rome in 311 B.C., when it was enacted that they should be
elected by the people, but it is not certain that the office
was first constituted then[4]. A fresh commercial treaty
with Carthage was made in 348 B.C., which recognizes the
right of the Carthaginians to kidnap and rob in Latium or
by sea, provided such acts are not committed against

p. 375, n. 1. The most surprising part of the story is that Dionysius
while he banished the man from Syracuse allowed him to take his
profits with him.
[1] Unsatisfactory attempts to emend the former passage have been
made, e.g. Ταρχωνίαν (Burger, *op. cit.* p. 157, and Sigwart, *Klio*,
VI. p. 341, meaning Tarquinii), Σούτριον (Niese, *Röm. Ges.* pp. 50–4),
Σάτρικον (Pais). Meyer, V. 820 *n.*, connects it with a Sardinian revolt
against Carthage. The Romans mentioned by Theophrastus may
possibly have been really Etruscans, as the Greeks did not always
clearly distinguish the different Italian peoples.
[2] Cf. Strab. V. 232, the Antiates ἐκοινώνουν τῶν λῃστηρίων τοῖς
Τυρρηνοῖς καίπερ ἤδη Ῥωμαίοις ὑπακούοντες.
[3] Liv. VII. 25. 4, 13; 26. 13: "nec illi terra nec Romanus mari
bellator erat." Livy, though uncertain of the origin of these pirates,
inclines to connect them with the tyrants of Sicily, i.e. Dionysius II.
[4] Liv. IX. 30. 4.

persons definitely subject to Rome[1]. Rome evidently had little power at sea, though the foundation of the port of Ostia about this time shews that her thoughts were beginning to turn towards maritime trade[2]. Diodorus (XVI. 8. 2) tells us that an Etruscan sea-pirate named Postumius (the name appears Latin rather than Etruscan) came with twelve ships to Syracuse as a friend in 342 B.C. but was captured and put to death by Timoleon. The activity of the Liparaeans at sea is shewn by the episode of Timasitheus who captured the Roman gift to Apollo after the fall of Veii, and by the record of their many victories over the Etruscans[3].

§ 2

FROM 310 TO 264 B.C.

For forty years then Rome had peace on her northern frontier and could deal with her other adversaries. We may wonder why the Etruscans did not seize the opportunity offered by the Latin and still more the Samnite wars to attack Rome when she was deeply engaged with other enemies, as they had previously done at the time of the Gallic invasion. For this inaction, as for the collapse of the Etruscans when war at last broke out, several reasons may be suggested—the disunion of the Etruscan cities, internal troubles, the decline of the warlike spirit through a long period of peace, fear of a Samnite victory; it may also be suggested that the religious scrupulousness of the Etruscans restrained them from violating a sworn truce

[1] Polyb. III. 24.
[2] Ostia in the fourth century: cf. T. Frank, "Rome's First Coinage," in *Class. Phil.* 1919, pp. 314–8. The Roman colony at Antium (338) was merely defensive, cf. Liv. VIII. 14. 8.
[3] Diod. XIV. 93; Liv. V. 28; Diod. V. 10 *fin.*

even when it appeared advantageous to do so. Be that as it may, Rome was already well on the way to victory in Samnium and had founded several colonies to secure the country[1], before the Etruscan war broke out. The literary records of the war are so full of exaggerations and confusions that any attempted reconstruction of its history must be exceedingly tentative. It began with an attack by the Etruscans (probably from Volsinii and Tarquinii in particular) on the frontier colony of Sutrium, which was relieved by the Romans in 310 B.C.[2] According to Livy (IX. 32) the consul Q. Aemilius won a great victory over an army of all the Etruscans except the Arretines in 311 (though his language suggests that the victory is much exaggerated[3]), and in the next year Q. Fabius again relieved Sutrium, slaying large numbers of the enemy and driving the rest into the Ciminian Forest (IX. 35). In the brief version of Diodorus (XX. 35) the consuls Fabius and Marcius (310 B.C.) defeat the Etruscans who were besieging Sutrium and drive them back to their camp[4].

We now come to the crossing of the Ciminian range and the first appearance of Roman arms in Umbria and central Etruria. Little credit can be given to Livy's romantic story (IX. 35) of how the consul's brother and slave disguised as shepherds penetrated the dreaded and unknown

[1] E.g. Luceria in 314, Suessa and Saticula in 313, Interamna on the Liris in 312.
[2] De Sanctis, II. p. 329, n. 2, treats the events of Liv. IX. 32 as identical with those of IX. 35.
[3] Pais, IV. p. 37 *n.*: the suspicious words are "nullo unquam proelio fugae minus nec plus caedis fuisset, ni obstinatos mori Tuscos nox texisset ita ut uictores priusquam uicti pugnandi finem facerent" (IX. 32. 9).
[4] Diodorus seems to put the events of the consulship of Fabius (310 B.C.) in the same year as the censorship of Appius Claudius (XX. 36 *init.* κατὰ τοῦτον τὸν ἐνιαυτόν). The Fasti Triumphales record triumphs of Q. Aemilius in 311 and Q. Fabius in 309 over the Etruscans.

forest[1], and reaching the "Camertes Umbri" revealed
themselves to the local Senate and received promises of
help. Livy then tells us that the consul ravaged the fertile
territory north of the Ciminian, and then defeated a vast
army of Etruscans and Umbrians at Sutrium, or, according
to other versions, at Perusia. Perusia, Cortona and Arretium
asked for peace and alliance and were given a thirty years'
truce (IX. 37). We then read of a rout of the Umbrians
apparently in the same year and a defeat of the Etruscans
at Lake Vadimo (IX. 39. 4 ff.[2]), and a revolt of Perusia
which surrenders to the consul Fabius (IX. 40. 18 ff.). It
is almost incredible that all this should have taken place
in one year, and we may suspect that the family pride of
Fabian annalists is responsible for many of the successes
recorded. No way through the Ciminian Forest could
possibly lead to the Camertes[3] or any other Umbrians;
and if we imagine that the people of Clusium are meant
(following Livy, X. 25. 11: "Clusium quod Camars olim
appellabant")[4], the art and numerous inscriptions of
Clusium shew clearly that the town was completely
Etruscan at this time and earlier; and the Romans would
have had to go right across the territory of Volsinii to reach
Clusium. The disagreement of Livy's sources is shewn in
respect of the site of Fabius' victory—Sutrium or Perusia;
the stubbornly contested battle of L. Vadimo appears to
be an anticipation of the well-authenticated battle of 283
(or the earlier mention of the lake may be due to textual
corruption); while the battle of Perusia (IX. 40. 18 ff.) is

[1] Liv. IX. 36. 1: "silua erat Ciminia magis tum inuia atque horrenda
quam nuper fuere Germanici saltus, nulli ad eam diem ne mercatorum
quidem adita." On this cf. De Sanctis, II. p. 331.

[2] The text is corrupt, see Walters and Conway, ad loc.

[3] There is no evidence that "Camertes" ever meant anything but
"inhabitants of Camerinum" in eastern Umbria.

[4] So e.g. Nissen, It. Land. II, p. 323, who speaks of the Umbrian
origin of Clusium.

a duplicate of the battle recorded in chap. 37, which some
writers placed at Perusia[1].

The narrative of Diodorus affords a more intelligible
view of the events of these years (310–9)[2]. After their
defeat before Sutrium, he tells us the Etruscans mustered
against the town again but Fabius eluded them and invaded northern Etruria by way of Umbria—ἔλαθε τοὺς
πολεμίους διὰ τῆς τῶν ὁμόρων χώρας ἐμβαλὼν εἰς τὴν
ἀνωτέρω Τυρρηνίαν—and ravaged the land, defeating the
Etruscans twice, the second time near Perusia. After
making a truce with Arretium, Cortona and Perusia he
captured a city, the name of which is given as Καστόλα, and
compelled the Etruscans to raise the siege of Sutrium. The
tradition of a battle near Perusia followed by a truce with
the three powerful cities of eastern Etruria, which may
have formed a closer league within the federation of the
Twelve Cities, has thus the support both of Diodorus and
Livy.

There is good ground for believing that Fabius passed
through western Umbria and invaded Etruria from the
east, marching along the line of the later Via Amerina and
crossing the Tiber near Tuder, or along that of the Flaminia
and down the Clitumnus valley to Perusia. Such a route
would be easier, the Umbrians being largely lukewarm or
hostile towards the Etruscans[3], than a direct march through
the very heart of Etruria past the Fanum Voltumnae,
which was situated in the neighbourhood of the Lake of
Bolsena[4]. Further, the ὁμόροι of the Etruscans can only
be the Umbrians; it is not necessary, though tempting,

[1] So De Sanctis, II. p. 331, n. 3. It may be added that nothing more
is heard of the garrison left at Perusia (ch. 40. 20).
[2] Diod. XX. 35.
[3] Strab. v. p. 216.
[4] Perhaps at Montefiascone (Dennis, II. p. 33; Nissen, II. p. 341);
or Viterbo, Bolsena, or Orvieto.

to emend ὁμόρων into Ὀμβρῶν[1]. The presence of a Roman army in Umbria in 308 B.C. is attested by Diod. XX. 44, Livy, IX. 41. 8, and is therefore not incredible in 310 or 309 B.C.[2]: in fact Livy refers there to the Umbrians as "gens integra a cladibus belli nisi quod transitum exercitus ager senserat"—evidently in some previous campaign. Finally, if we suppose the Romans to have been already operating in central Umbria in 310 or 309, the alliance with the Camertes Umbri becomes intelligible; the Umbrian cities were made aware of the Roman power, and among them Camerinum hastened to secure the friendship of Rome. We may date from this time the "aequum foedus" of Camerinum[3], and perhaps also of Iguvium, the important Umbrian town which commanded the easiest pass of the central Apennines, La Scheggia[4]. According to the view set out above, the decisive event of 310-9 was the invasion of central Etruria from the east, by way of Umbria, and the battle near Perusia which caused the withdrawal of Arretium, Cortona and Perusia, and this

---

[1] Ὀμόρων is the reading of R (eleventh century), ὁμοάρχων of F (fourteenth century). Ὀμβρῶν was suggested by Haackh in Pauly's *Real-Encycl.* III. 386, s.v. "Fabia gens": Ὀμβρικῶν by Niebuhr (III. n. 488) and Dindorf. See Vogel's Diodorus (Teubner ed.) *ad loc.*, or Drachmann's *Diodors Römische Annalen* (Bonn, 1912). "Umbri" more usually appears in Greek as Ὀμβρικοί (e.g. Diod. XX. 44); but Ὀμβροί occurs in Polyb. II. 16. 3, and elsewhere, and Strab. pp. 216, 217; the latter uses Ὀμβρικοί as well, so that Diod. may have used both forms.

[2] The year 309 in which there was a dictator and no consuls (cf. *C.I.L.* I². p. 132) is passed over by Diodorus and Livy: consequently we cannot divide the events of 310-9 between the two years. Livy's sources seem to have assigned all the successes in Etruria to the credit of Fabius.

[3] So De Sanctis, II. p. 331, n. 2; who, however, thinks that Fabius marched directly across the Ciminian hills towards L. Trasimene, and not through Umbria.

[4] The "aequum foedus" of Camerinum appears in 205 B.C. (Liv. XXVIII. 45) and the treaty with Iguvium seems to have been of the same character, cf. Cic. *pro Balbo*, 20, 46-7.

again caused the siege of Sutrium to be raised, probably in 309. A raid or raids across the Ciminian range may have been made (the silence of Diodorus not being sufficient ground for denying them), but had not the importance which Livy attaches to them. We have no means of identifying the city of Castola whose capture according to Diodorus preceded the relief of Sutrium[1].

The year 308 saw the conclusion of this first period of the war in Etruria and Umbria. Diodorus records that the consuls passed through Umbria into Etruria and there captured the unknown Κάπριον: the Etruscans applied for a truce which was given for a year, except to Tarquinii which was given a forty years' peace[2]. Livy briefly records the forty years' peace with Tarquinii, the capture of some forts of the Volsinienses and a campaign very vaguely described ("circumferendo passim bello tantum terrorem sui fecit...") which led the whole federation ("omne nomen Etruscum") to ask for a treaty: on payment of an indemnity an annual truce (i.e. one which was renewed annually) was granted[3]. It is also clear that Tarquinii was obliged to cede a strip of its coast on which the colonies of Castrum and Graviscae were founded about 289 and 181 B.C.[4] The Etruscan League must have realized that the region south of the Ciminian range was irretrievably lost, and therefore willingly ended the war; while Rome had no desire for a war of aggression in Etruria, a country

[1] Pais, IV. p. 39, n. 2, mentions various possible emendations: Κλούσιον, Καρσούλας, Φαισόλαν, none of which are satisfactory both on palaeographical and geographical grounds. Carsulae lay in southern Umbria, in later times on the Via Flaminia.
[2] Diod. XX. 44.
[3] Liv. IX. 41.
[4] De Sanctis, ibid. n. 4; Liv. XL. 29: "colonia Grauiscae eo anno deducta est in agrum Etruscum de Tarquiniensibus quondam captum." Perhaps also Forum Aureli was founded on Tarquinian land: on its position on the coast-road between Graviscae and Cosa cf. Anziani, Mélanges, XXXIII (1913), p. 191.

difficult to conquer yet too weak to be a source of serious
danger any more, and could divert all her energies to
dealing with the Samnites and with the tribes of central
Italy which revolted in the following years.

After the conclusion of peace with the Etruscans Livy
gives an account in some detail (IX. 41. 8 ff.) of a rising of
the Umbrians who, drawing many of the Etruscans with
them, threatened to advance on Rome. The consul Fabius[1]
was summoned from Samnium and met the enemy near
Mevania (Bevagna, in the broad valley of central Umbria,
and later on the Via Flaminia). His arrival struck terror
into the Umbrians, but a section of them, the "plaga
Materina," compelled the rest to give battle. The Umbrians
surrendered almost without fighting, and Ocriculum, the
southernmost city of Umbria, was received into the Roman
alliance[2]. It is clear that the importance of this Umbrian
war and the Roman victory is much exaggerated; Nequinum
(Narnia), the very gate of southern Umbria, was not in
Roman hands till 299 B.C. and Diodorus and the Fasti
Triumphales record no victory over the Umbrians. We
need not, however, disbelieve the tradition of a battle in
central Umbria[3], to which the mention of a definite but
uncommon name, Mevania, lends some support; and if the
distant Camerinum already had relations with Rome, it is
not incredible that its neighbour Matelica (with which the
"plaga Materina" appears to be connected)[4] should have
taken the lead against Rome.

[1] The other consul, Decius, who was in Etruria, disappears from the
narrative and the credit for the defeat of the Umbrians is given
entirely to Fabius.

[2] Liv. IX. 41. 20: "ceteri Umbrorum populi deduntur [sc. besides
the 'primi auctores belli' who surrendered at the battle]: Ocriculani
sponsione in amicitiam recepti." Cf. Ὀκρίκολα πόλις Τυρρηνῶν, quoted
by Steph. Byz. from Dionys. XVIII.

[3] As De Sanctis does (II. p. 334), accepting only the alliances with
Camerinum and Ocriculum.

[4] Pais, IV. p. 44, n. 1: but the connexion is not certain.

For the next six years at least Rome was at peace with her northern neighbours[1], and was able to bring the long struggle with Samnium to an end and to force the tribes of central Italy to renew their alliance. To secure this territory and to maintain a line of communication across Italy, strong colonies were founded in the land of the Aequi at Alba (303) and Carseoli (298) on the line of the later Via Valeria. An Etruscan fleet appears once more in this period: in 307 B.C. twenty ships from Etruria came to the assistance of Agathocles against the Carthaginians, and enabled him to raise the blockade of Syracuse[2]. We know nothing of the circumstances which led an Etruscan city[3] to help their old enemies the Syracusans against their old friend Carthage. Livy reports at some length a fresh intervention of the Romans in Etruria in 302–1, arising out of disorders at Arretium where the powerful family of the Cilnii had been driven out. That a civil feud at Arretium may have led to Roman intervention is credible; but the version (Livy, x. 5. 13) according to which the feud was settled peaceably seems far more probable than the elaborate account of a Roman repulse followed by a great victory in the territory of Rusellae—a great distance from Arretium[4].

[1] There is a vague reference to an expedition into Umbria in Liv. x. 1. 4 ff. (302 B.C.).

[2] Diod. xx. 61.

[3] Tillyard, *Agathocles*, p. 168, suggests Tarquinii, which De Sanctis, II. p. 369, rejects on the ground that Tarquinii having just been granted a truce by Rome could hardly fight against Carthage, with which Rome was on friendly terms. We may suggest that the ships were from Vetulonia or Populonia or Volci, which are not recorded as taking any part in the war of 310–308.

[4] Liv. x. 3–5; De Sanctis, II. p. 341, n. 6, regards the victory of the dictator Valerius (which appears in the Fasti) as a pure invention of Valerius Antias. It is, however, misguided ingenuity to see in Liv. x. 4 an anticipation of Liv. x. 37. 3, where Rusellae occurs again, or to connect the events at Arretium with the *Lex Valeria de prouocatione* of 300 (as Pais does, IV. pp. 159–60, and nn.).

About this time the Romans gained control of the important position of Nequinum, later known as Narnia, and planted a Latin colony there. According to Livy the place was besieged in 300 B.C., but owing to its strength could only be taken in the following year by treachery[1]. The Fasti record a triumph of M. Fulvius in 299 "de Samnitibus Nequinatibusque": as there is no other trace of a Samnite war in this year, the victory was most probably gained over the Sabines, whose land adjoined that of Nequinum[2]. Of the circumstances of the capture of Nequinum we know nothing; it may have been in the course of a Sabine war which has disappeared from our records, or possibly it belongs in fact to the Umbrian war of 308, the colony being planted in 299. It is certainly surprising that there is no mention of a campaign against the Sabines before 290 B.C., though the Aequi, Marsi and other more distant peoples were subdued in 304[3]. The colony of Narnia, joined to Rome by a road which later became the first part of the Via Flaminia, secured to the Romans the natural route into southern Umbria; and situated on a steep and isolated rock close above the narrow gorge of the Nar it served to bar the way to any invaders advancing through Umbria upon Rome[4].

For the second period of the war in Etruria and Umbria,

[1] Liv. x. 9. 8; 10. 1 ff.

[2] B. Bruno, "La terza guerra sannitica" (Beloch's *Studi di Storia Antica*, VI), p. 16. Cf. Dionys. XVII (*ap.* Steph. Byz.): Νηκούια πόλις Ὀμβρικῶν, and *id.* XVIII: Ναρνία πόλις Σαυνιτῶν, which must mean Sabines. Narnia was in the sixth Region of Augustus (Umbria and the Ager Gallicus) but we know nothing of its ethnography before the Roman conquest.

[3] Liv. IX. 45. 18. Owing to the appearance of an unprovoked aggression by the Romans, T. Frank, *Roman Imperialism*, p. 58, rejects the capture and colonization of Narnia in 299.

[4] Cf. Liv. x. 9. 8: "locus erat arduus et in parte praeceps...nec ui nec munimento capi poterat"; Procop. *B.G.* I. 16. 17: πόλιν ἐχύραν μάλιστα...δυσπρόσοδόν τε καὶ ἄλλως ἄναντες χωρίον.

which begins in 299 B.C., the narrative of Diodorus fails us[1], but Polybius (II. 19. 20) gives a concise account of the invasions by the Gauls in this period. In 299 B.C. the Gauls of north Italy, owing to a movement among their kinsmen beyond the Alps, persuaded these to join them in an invasion across the Apennines, where, together with the Etruscans, they entered the Roman territory in south Etruria, which they raided unhindered, and retired in safety with a large amount of spoil[2]. Roman patriotism completely transformed the inglorious episode: in the version followed by Livy (x. 10. 5 ff.) the Etruscans take the initiative attempting to hire Gallic mercenaries, but the Gauls after receiving large sums of money retire without fighting owing to the refusal of the Etruscans to surrender a portion of their land. Then follows a Roman campaign in Etruria in which, after the accidental death of the consul, T. Manlius, through a fall from his horse at the very beginning of the campaign, his successor, M. Valerius, ravaged the country, burning villages, while the Etruscans in terror at his coming shut themselves up behind their fortifications[3]. There can be little doubt that this campaign of Valerius is as much an invention as the previous Etruscan campaign ascribed to him (302), the unhindered ravaging of the enemy's territory being audaciously transferred from the Gauls and Etruscans to the Romans[4]. About this time the Romans made an alliance with the Picentes, whose territory adjoined the *ager Gallicus*[5]. Thus Rome gained on the east coast a counterpoise both to the Gauls and the Sabellic peoples of central Italy.

[1] The last complete book of Diod. (xx) ends with the events of 302 B.C.

[2] Polyb. II. 19. 1–4, four years before the battle of Sentinum (§ 5).

[3] Liv. x. 11. 1–6.

[4] Cf. Bruno, *op. cit.* pp. 17–18; De Sanctis, II. p. 350, n. 4; Pais, IV. p. 57.

[5] Liv. x. 10. 12 (299 B.C.).

Evidently the Etruscans had little enthusiasm for the war, unless they were spurred on by their allies; for after the campaign of 299 in which the Gauls took the leading part, the war in Etruria seems to flicker out in the following years till rekindled by the arrival of the Samnites. Livy reports a campaign of the consul P. Cornelius Scipio: after a drawn battle near Volaterrae the Etruscans retire by night leaving their camp to be despoiled by the Romans, who then retire to Falerii (i.e. from one end of Etruria to the other) and making this their base raid the country, while the Etruscans as before keep through fear to their cities[1]. The story is suspicious enough as it stands; the Fasti only record in this year a triumph of the other consul, Cn. Fulvius Centumalus, over the Samnites and Etruscans, and above all the "elogium" of Scipio, the earliest record and one which certainly omitted no successes, does not mention Etruria at all[2]. Hence it is more credible, as Mommsen suggests, that Scipio remained in Samnium and Lucania while Fulvius, after a victory in Samnium, came north and pacified Etruria, which appears to have sued for peace in the following year[3]. But if the Etruscans were lukewarm, not so were the Samnites, who hoped to put an end to the Roman supremacy by a grand coalition of all the Italian peoples against Rome. In 296 B.C. a Samnite force under Gellius Egnatius succeeded in breaking through to the north, and in rallying to their standards the whole Etruscan League, some of the Umbrian cities, and a force of Gallic

---

[1] Liv. x. 12.

[2] *C.I.L.* I. 30, and Mommsen, *ad loc.*; Bruno, *op. cit.* p. 23, suggests that the Etruscan triumph of Fulvius is an anticipation of his successes as propraetor in Etruria in 295.

[3] Liv. x. 14. 3: the text is uncertain, see Walters and Conway, *ad loc.* To read "auctores concilii Etruriae populorum...habiti," taking "auctores" as "spokesmen," seems to suggest that not only Rome's ally Falerii but even the Latin colonies of Sutrium and Nepet were admitted to the council of the Etruscan League.

mercenaries[1]. It is not unlikely that the Sabines also joined
the alliance, as according to some of the traditions they
were defeated by Appius Claudius (consul in 296)[2] but
there is no ground for denying the presence of the Samnites
in the north altogether and assuming that the Sabines are
meant in every case[3].

The traditional account (Livy, x. 18–19) of the northern
campaign of 296 is peculiarly unsatisfactory, and Livy
himself notes disagreements in his sources[4], which are
clearly deformed by anti-Claudian spite (e.g. 18. 5–6, where
it is suggested that some of the enemy were withheld more
by fear of Rome than by any ability of the consul, whose
actions only served to encourage the enemy and sow dis-
trust between himself and his men). The long account of
the wrangle between the consuls—Appius the politician
and talker, Volumnius the blunt soldier—savours more of
political melodrama than of serious history[5]; and the
presence of Volumnius in Etruria appears to have been
invented to deprive Appius of the credit for whatever
success was gained, for it is hardly credible that in a single
season Volumnius should go to Samnium, then into Etruria
and win a battle there, return through Samnium into
Campania and gain another great victory there, and,
finally, be at Rome for the consular elections. From the
"elogium" quoted below (n. 2) and from the tradition that
the temple of Bellona was vowed by Appius in a Tuscan

---

[1] In Liv. x. 16. 2–3 this important event is absurdly represented as
the expulsion of the Samnite army, not daring to give battle, from its
own borders. The same event is reported again in chs. 18. 1–2, 21. 1–2,
and we cannot be sure whether it took place in the beginning or the
end of 296.

[2] Elogium of Appius (*C.I.L.* I². p. 192): "complura oppida de Samnitibus cepit, Sabinorum et Tuscorum exercitum fudit." *de vir.
illustr.* 34–5: "Sabinos Samnites Etruscos bello domuit."

[3] As Bruno, *op. cit.* pp. 31–2.

[4] Liv. x. 18. 7.

[5] Cf. esp. x. 19. 6–8.

war[1], it seems likely that Appius conducted a campaign against the Etruscans, who were aided by some Sabines and Samnites; but as no triumph is recorded and the battle or battles had no effect on the course of the war—in fact the coalition does not seem to have mustered its full strength till next year—the victory recorded by Livy must be grossly exaggerated, and probably only a section of the allied forces were engaged[2].

The next year (295) saw the decisive battle of the war. The forces of the allies—Samnites and Gauls, with some help from the Etruscans and Umbrians—appear to have been concentrated in eastern Umbria, while if Livy's information (X. 25. 4) is correct the Roman army, which in early spring the new consul, Fabius Rullianus, took over from Appius Claudius, was stationed at Aharna or Arna, a town near the left bank of the Tiber opposite Perusia. Fabius stationed a legion under the propraetor L. Scipio at Clusium, according to Livy, "quod Camars olim appellabant"; but Polybius in recording the destruction of this legion places the event ἐν τῇ Καμερτίων χώρᾳ[3]. There has been much disagreement on the question whether the Roman legion was lost at Clusium or Camerinum: Polybius clearly means the latter, but it has been suggested that he found the name Camars or Camers in his source and wrongly took it to mean Camerinum, while Livy saw that Clusium was meant but inserted the older name too[4]. There is no other evidence that Clusium was ever called Camars, but the alliance-coins inscribed *Pufluna-Cha-*

---

[1] Liv. x. 19. 17, cf. Ovid, *Fasti*, vi. 201 ff.: "hac sacrata die Tusco Bellona duello dicitur...."

[2] Liv. x. 19. 14 ff. speaks of 7800 of the enemy killed and 2130 captured.

[3] Liv. x. 25. 11, 26. 7; Polyb. II. 19. 5.

[4] So Nissen, *It. Land.* II. p. 323, n. 5: others who place the disaster at Clusium are Mommsen (I. p. 489), Heitland, *Roman Republic*, § 196, Hülsen in Pauly-Wissowa, *R.E.*, and Ashby in *Enc. Brit.*, s.v. "Camerinum."

Vetalu give some support to Livy's statement[1]. On geo-graphical grounds it is quite credible that the coast-towns of Populonia and Vetulonia should have had a common coinage with the inland Clusium whose territory may have adjoined theirs. But it seems natural to connect the Καμέρτιοι of 295 B.C. with the Camertes of 310 B.C., and these last, as has been shown, were more probably from Camerinum than from Clusium; and the occurrence of the great battle at Sentinum on the borders of Umbria proper and the *ager Gallicus*, a few days (as Polybius says) after the loss of the legion, suggests that the Italian allies were in that region all the time without going so far afield as Clusium. Further, one version of the disaster ascribed it to the Umbrians, not the Gauls—a version which Livy rejects for the curious reason that in that as in other years it was the Gauls who caused the Romans most alarm[2]. On the whole, therefore, it seems better to suppose that the preliminary encounter took place in the territory of Camerinum[3].

With the details of the great battle of Sentinum we are not here concerned. It is clear that the brunt of the fighting fell upon the Gauls and Samnites; the Umbrians through-out the war were never strongly opposed to the Roman supremacy and let the Roman armies pass unhindered through their territory and across the Apennines. The

---

[1] Niese, however (p. 70, n. 5), regards it as more than doubtful. On these coins cf. Sambon, *Monnaies antiques*, pp. 32, 73: the type (with head of Vulcan, and hammer and tongs) belongs to Populonia where some of the examples were found. The rare series with the single inscription Xa and an anchor is assigned by Deecke to Caere rather than Clusium (Beilage I. p. 400, in Müller, I; cf. *Etr. Forschungen*, II. p. 33).

[2] Liv. x. 26. 12–13: but Polybius only mentions Samnites and Gauls. Other divergent traditions of this year are noted by Livy, x. 26. 5, 30. 5–7.

[3] So Niebuhr, III. p. 441, n. 637; Pais, IV. p. 164, n. 3; De Sanctis, II. p. 355, n. 2; Niese, p. 70; Bruno, *op. cit.* pp. 34–5.

Etruscans were diverted by a raid on their country and appear to have been defeated separately later in the same year[1]. The slaughter at Sentinum was exaggerated by tradition[2]; but the coalition suffered a defeat from which it never recovered. The Gauls were driven back into their own territory and troubled Rome no more for ten years; the remnants of the Samnites escaped into Samnium, where they succeeded in resisting for five years more. There can be little doubt that a considerable portion of territory in central Umbria, where later there arose the "praefecture of the Fulginates[3]," the Forum Flamini, and the Latin colony of Spoletium, was now annexed by Rome as part of her territory, and most of the other Umbrian cities joined the Roman alliance. It is possible, too, that the annexation of a small portion of the Adriatic coast-land on which the colony of Sena was afterwards planted took place immediately after Sentinum[4]; Polybius first mentions Sena in connexion with the next Gallic war (284–282), but Livy appears to put its foundation about 290–288 B.C. and the words of Polybius need not necessarily imply that Sena was not founded till the whole *ager Gallicus* had been annexed[5].

The alliance against Rome had been broken at Sentinum, but the Etruscans and Samnites were still unsubdued in their own countries. The latter succeeded in inflicting a severe defeat on the Romans near Luceria[6]; but Etruria

[1] Liv. X. 30, 31, perhaps reduplications of a single event. The defeated enemies are Perusini and Clusini in ch. 30, Perusini in ch. 31.

[2] Liv. X. 30. 5; cf. Diod. XXI. frag. 6, quoting Duris for the statement that the Romans killed 100,000 of the enemy.

[3] Cic. *pro Vareno ap.* Prisc. VII. 14. 70.

[4] De Sanctis, II. p. 358, n. 2.

[5] Liv. *Epit.* XI: "coloniae deductae sunt Castrum Sena Hadria" between the triumph of M'. Curius (290) and the census of 288; Polyb. II. 19. 11–12: Ῥωμαῖοι...τῆς χώρας ἐγένοντο πάσης ἐγκρατεῖς, εἰς ἣν καὶ πρώτην τῆς Γαλατίας ἀποικίαν ἔστειλαν ("had sent"?) τὴν Σήνην προσαγορευομένην πόλιν.

[6] Liv. X. 35, 36; cf. 37. 13: "Postumium auctor est Claudius in

was pacified in the course of 294–3. The details of this pacification are uncertain, and the sources used by Livy disagreed considerably. According to Livy, Postumius defeated the Etruscans near Volsinii and again near Rusellae, capturing the latter town; but the mention of Volsinii, Perusia and Arretium, all in eastern Etruria, suing for peace which was granted for forty years on payment of an indemnity, suggests that the operations of this year were in the east rather than near the coast of Etruria[1]. The Fasti record in this year a triumph of Postumius over the Samnites and Etruscans, and of his colleague Atilius over the Volsones (which no doubt means Volsinienses) and Samnites. It seems probable that the campaign in Etruria was conducted by Atilius (as Claudius Quadrigarius related)[2] and not by Postumius at all; it is most improbable that in this year with the Samnites and Etruscans in arms at the same time either consul fought in both theatres of war "quia in Samnitibus materia belli deerat[3]." Possibly, therefore, the second campaign of Atilius was fought against the Sabines and not the Samnites[4].

Samnio captis aliquot urbibus in Apulia fusum fugatumque saucium ipsum cum paucis Luceriam compulsum." Fabius Pictor minimized the defeat ("ad Luceriam utrimque multis occisis," Liv. x. 37. 14) while other annalists whom Livy follows recorded (as usual) a Roman victory immediately afterwards, though even this was "ne Romanis quidem laeta" (36. 15).

[1] De Sanctis, II. p. 359, n. 2, remarks that Rusellae became an ally of Rome (Liv. XXVIII. 45), which was unusual for cities which had been taken by storm.

[2] Liv. x. 37. 13: "auctor est Claudius...ab Atilio in Etruria res gestas eumque triumphasse." Fabius Pictor omitted to say which consul fought in Etruria.

[3] Liv. x. 37. 1. A fragment of Dionysius (XVII. frag. 5, Teubner) relates the triumph of Postumius in opposition to the Senate (= Liv. x. 37. 6 ff.), but among its antecedents speaks only of campaigns against Cominium and Venusia, not Etruria.

[4] Bruno, *op. cit.* p. 57.

Just when the eastern Etruscans at least had submitted to Rome and probably been made permanent allies, the Faliscans, who had been loyal allies since 343 B.C., revolted, for reasons which we cannot ascertain, and we have a vague tradition of some other Etruscan cities attempting to force their neighbours to revolt. But the rebellion was soon put down: some fortresses were taken and Falerii was reduced to ask for peace and on payment of an indemnity was given a year's truce, her treaty with Rome being doubtless renewed subsequently[1]. So the war came to an end in Etruria, though it was not till 290 B.C. that the Samnites and Sabines were finally reduced to peace, the latter being at once incorporated in the Roman state as half-citizens. During the interval of peace which succeeded, the Romans planted a Latin colony at Hatria in southern Picenum, to keep watch upon the neighbouring tribes, a maritime colony of citizens at Castrum Novum in the strip of coast which had been taken from Tarquinii, and probably as we have seen also a citizen colony at Sena in the Ager Gallicus on the Adriatic[2].

But the peace of Italy was not yet secured; in the south the Lucanians were molesting a Roman ally, Thurii, while in the north we have a brief notice of hostilities with Volsinii[3]. More serious was a fresh incursion of the Gauls (apparently the Senones) into Etruria in 284 B.C.: they besieged Arretium, now a Roman ally, and a Roman army sent to relieve the town was defeated with heavy loss, the consul, L. Caecilius Metellus, being among the

---

[1] Liv. x. 45. 4 ff., 46. 10 ff.; Zonar. VIII. 1. On the unknown Troilum in Etruria, identified by some with Trossulum which was said to have been taken by Roman knights alone (Plin. *N.H.* XXXIII. 35), cf. De Sanctis, II. p. 362, n. 2. The Fasti Triumphales record no triumph over the Etruscans or Faliscans in 293.

[2] Liv. *Epit.* XI.

[3] Liv. *Epit.* XI *fin.*: "res praeterea contra Volsinienses gestas continet," mentioned after the dictatorship of Hortensius (287 B.C.).

slain¹. Manius Curius, the conqueror of the Sabines, took command (presumably as *consul suffectus*) and sent envoys to the Gauls to treat for the return of the Roman prisoners². The Gauls murdered the envoys, whereupon the Romans sent an army which defeated the Senones, killed a large number of them, and expelled the remainder in a body from the whole territory which they occupied along the Adriatic coast³. The Celtic Boii, who occupied a large area south of the Po (since Livy tells us that the colonies of Bononia, Mutina and Parma were all founded on land previously held by the Boii⁴), took alarm and (probably in the following year, 283 B.C.) marched towards Rome aided by some of the Etruscan cities. They came down the Tiber valley, as the Gauls had come who captured Rome a century before, but at the Lacus Vadimonis (Lago di Bassano, now dried up), in the narrow gap between the river and the eastern end of the Ciminian range, the Romans won a decisive victory⁵. The allies made another

¹ I follow the account in Polybius, II. 19. 7 ff., who gives the interval between the battle of Sentinum and the attack on Arretium as ten years (διαγενομένων ἐτῶν δέκα). Later writers based on Livy describe L. Caecilius as praetor (Polybius calls him ὁ στρατηγός, which is not to be taken in its technical sense as = praetor) and put his defeat in 283 B.C., e.g. Oros. III. 22. 12–14. The latter gives the number of Romans killed as over 13,000.

² ὑπὲρ τῶν αἰχμαλώτων, Polyb. II. 19. 9. Appian, *Celt.* frag. 11, who omits the defeat at Arretium, represents the embassy as protesting against the Senones fighting against Rome in Etruscan pay; but, in spite of Mommsen's acceptance of this version (II. p. 10) it is clear from Polybius that the war began with an independent invasion by the Senones. Orosius, *loc. cit.*, makes the envoys sent "ad exorandos Gallos," and the defeat of Caecilius subsequent to their murder.

³ According to Liv. v. 35, the Senones occupied the tract between the Utens (near Ravenna) and the Aesis. Appian, *loc. cit.*, ascribes the defeat and expulsion of the Senones to the consul P. Cornelius Dolabella (283).

⁴ Liv. XXXVII. 57, XXXIX. 55.

⁵ For a description see Dennis, I. p. 144. Polyb. (II. 20. 1) does not state that the invasion and defeat of the Boii were in the year following

desperate effort next year, but again being defeated were constrained to make peace, only some of the Etruscans remaining in arms. This peace, which was kept by the Gauls for 45 years, was made according to Polybius in the third year before the crossing of Pyrrhus into Italy and the fifth before the destruction of the Gauls at Delphi. The latter event is dated by Pausanias (x. 23 *fin.*) in the second year of the 125th Olympiad and the archonship of Anaxicrates, i.e. 279–8 B.C.: Pyrrhus, therefore, landed in Italy in the spring of 280 B.C., and the peace with the Boii was made in 282[1].

Our knowledge of the last years of the war in Etruria is extremely scanty; it appears, however, that Volsinii and Volci were the principal cities involved and that the war lasted till 280 B.C.[2] Some attempts were made by the Tarentines and by Pyrrhus to combine with them against Rome—in a fragment of Dio (IX. fr. 39. 1) the Tarentines are said to have instigated a revolt of the Etruscans, Umbrians and Gauls, but it is clear from the account given by Polybius that this is incorrect. The victory and peace which the Romans attained in Etruria in 280 enabled them to reinforce their army in the south after the defeat of Heraclea with a second army under the consul, Ti. Coruncanius, and Pyrrhus advancing towards Rome was dis-

the expulsion of the Senones: but the events recorded seem too much for one year, the peace with the Boii was almost certainly in 282, and later writers (App. *loc. cit.*, Diod. frag. 39. 2, Dindorf, Eutrop. II. 10) assign the victory of L. Vadimo to one or other of the consuls for 283, Domitius and Dolabella.

[1] Elsewhere Polybius more vaguely dates the arrival of Pyrrhus in the 124th Olympiad (II. 41. 11), and τῷ πρότερον ἔτει τῆς τῶν Γαλατῶν ἐφόδου (I. 6. 5).

[2] The Fasti record triumphs of [Q. Mar]cius Philippus "de Etrusceis" in 281, and [Ti.] Coruncanius "de Volsiniensibus et Volcientibus" in 280. Cf. Dionys. XVIII. frag. 6 (281 B.C.) on the opposition in the Roman senate to war with Tarentum ἕως...Τυρρηνία παρ᾽ αὐταῖς οὖσα ταῖς θύραις ἔτι ἀχείρωτος ἦν.

appointed of the help which he had expected from the
Etruscans by the separate peace which they had just con-
cluded[1]. It is clear that Volci had to surrender a considerable
portion of its territory, if, as seems probable, the Latin
colony of Cosa (273) and the Forum Aureli on the coast,
and the colonies of Saturnia (183) and Heba[2] in the valley
of the Albegna were founded on land which had originally
belonged to Volci. The existing town at Saturnia, perhaps
known at that time as Auria, seems to have been made
into a *praefectura* immediately on its annexation[3]. On
grounds of position it would be natural to suppose with
De Sanctis (II. p. 398) that the "praefectura Statonensis"
was also in Volcentine territory, but the passages which
mention this *praefectura* describe it as being in that of
Tarquinii[4].

The peace of 280 B.C. might be taken as the conclusion
of the military conquest of Etruria; but a more suitable
limit is given by the destruction of the great metropolis
of Volsinii—the last campaign which the Romans under-
took before the opening of their long struggle with Carthage. To the period immediately following the departure

[1] Zonar. VIII. 4; App. *Samn.* frag. 10. 3.
[2] The existence of this colony is proved by an inscription, *Not. scav.*
1919, pp. 199 ff. The "ager Caletranus" in which the colony of
Saturnia was founded (Liv. XXXIX. 55) points to the existence of Caletra,
a town otherwise unknown and probably a dependency of Volci.
[3] Plin. III. 32: "Saturnini qui ante Aurini uocabantur." Festus,
p. 233, includes Saturnia among the *praefecturae* of the second class
(along with Caere): "in quas ibant quos praetor urbanus quotannis in
quaeque loca miserat legibus."
[4] Vitruv. II. 7. 3: "lapicidinae complures in finibus Tarquiniensium
...quarum officinae maxime sunt circum lacum Volsiniensem, item
praefectura Statonensi," and similarly Plin. *N.H.* XXXVI. 138. Modern
writers agree in identifying the Lake of Statonia (Sen. *quaest. nat.*
3. 25. 8, Plin. II. 209) with L. di Mezzano, five miles west of the Lake
of Bolsena: Bormann in *C.I.L.* XI. p. 444; Nissen, *I.L.* II. p. 335;
Solari, *Top. Stor.* I. p. 30. I can, however, testify that there is no stone
worth quarrying round Lago di Mezzano, and the Lacus Statonensis
may be one of the numerous ancient lakes which have now dried up.

of Pyrrhus belongs the punishment of Caere, to which I
have already alluded, when that town was compelled to
cede half its territory to avert an invasion by Rome,
doubtless provoked by some recent act of disloyalty¹. The
land taken from Caere, as from Tarquinii and Volci, lay
along the coast, as is shewn by the subsequent foundation
of colonies at Alsium, Fregenae and Pyrgi. Shortly afterwards the Romans had to quell another revolt in the north-
east, that of the Picentes and the north Umbrian tribe of
the Sarsinates. The circumstances of the revolt are unknown to us²; it appears to have begun in Picenum in 269
and ended there next year, while Sarsina resisted till 266³.
A considerable amount of land was annexed by the Romans
in different parts of Picenum, on which the colonies of
Castrum Novum and Firmum (264), Potentia (184) and
Auximum (157) were founded; but the tradition of a whole-
sale deportation of the population to the gulf of Salerno⁴
is open to suspicion. It is also doubtful whether Picenum
proper (i.e. south of the R. Aesis) was allotted by the law of
Flaminius in 232 B.C. which Cicero⁵ calls "de agro Piceno
et Gallico uiritim distribuendo," as it appears that the

¹ Dio, X. frag. 33: ὅτι ᾿Αγύλλαιοι (ἀγύλλαι codd.) ἐπειδὴ ᾖσθοντο
τοὺς ῾Ρωμαίους σφίσι πολεμῆσαι βουλομένους πρέσβεις τε ἐς ῾Ρώμην
ἔστειλαν...καὶ εἰρήνης ἐπὶ τῷ ἡμίσει τῆς χώρας ἔτυχον, which Zonaras
(VIII. 6) inserts with the subject omitted after the census of 273 B.C.
² De Sanctis, II. p. 422, connects it with the establishment of a Latin
colony at Ariminum (268), which might be resented by the neighbouring
Sarsina, but hardly by the Picentes.
³ The Fasti record triumphs "de Peicentibus" in 258, and "de
Sassinatibus" in 266: cf. Liv. Epit. xv, where the submission of the
Picentes and of the "Umbri et Sallentini" appear respectively before
and after the foundation of Ariminum and Beneventum and the
introduction of silver coinage (268): Eutrop. II. 16.
⁴ Strabo, V. p. 251, accepted by De Sanctis, II. p. 423, n. 5.
⁵ Brutus, 57; Cato, 11. Beloch, It. Bund, p. 55, holds that Flaminusi
allotted Picenum in the usual sense of the name, and is followed by
De Sanctis, II. p. 423. Conway, It. Dial. p. 449; Ferrero, I. pp. 16–17
(E.T.): cf. however, T. Frank, "Roman settlement of Picenum," in
Klio, XI (1911), p. 273.

coast-land up to and including Ariminum was sometimes called Picentine[1].

The destruction of Volsinii in 264 B.C. was an event of great significance, both as a palpable proof of the reality of the Roman supremacy and from the causes which led to the intervention of Rome. The identification of the Etruscan Volsinii with the site of Orvieto, first proposed by Müller, has been widely, though not universally, accepted[2], and remains the most probable conjecture. That the natural fortress of Orvieto was the seat of an important Etruscan city is proved by the extensive necropolis, rich in Greek and particularly fine native pottery which has been found under the north side of the town. It is especially significant that nothing subsequent to the fourth century B.C. has been found in this necropolis[3] or in the isolated tombs, some of them remarkable for their paintings, at the Sette Camini a few miles outside Orvieto. The Latin inscriptions of Orvieto are scanty in comparison with those of Bolsena, where all authorities agree in locating the Volsinii of the Roman period, the place of origin of many of them is doubtful, and the only one which can be certainly dated is a dedication to the emperor Constantius in the fourth century A.D. (C.I.L. XI. 1. 2697). We need not suppose that during the whole of the Roman supremacy the site was entirely uninhabited: but the town is first mentioned by Procopius, with the name of Οὐρβίβεντος, and a little later there are letters of S. Gregory the

[1] Liv. Epit. xv: "Ariminum in Piceno." Polyb. II. 21. 7: κατεκληρούχησαν ἐν Γαλατίᾳ τὴν Πικεντίνην προσαγορευομένην χώραν ἐξ ἧς νικήσαντες ἐξέβαλον τοὺς Σήνωνας, which clearly excludes land taken from the Picentes in 268.

[2] It is accepted by De Sanctis, I. p. 151; Nissen, It. Land. II. p. 338; Bormann in C.I.L. XI. 1. p. 423; Solari, Top. stor. I. p. 268; Milani, Mus. Arch. Firenze, I. p. 344.

[3] Gamurrini in Not. scav. 1880, p. 442. As far as I know, later discoveries at Orvieto have not invalidated his conclusions.

Great to an "episcopus de Urbevetere[1]." There is thus good ground for supposing that an important Etruscan city on the site of Orvieto was destroyed by the Romans in the third century B.C., leaving little more than a village on the site for several centuries, and hence for the identification with Volsinii.

Various writers however have maintained that the Etruscan Volsinii cannot, or need not, be sought at a distance of nine miles from its Roman successor, and accordingly have located the Etruscan Volsinii in the immediate neighbourhood of Bolsena, proposing some other identification for Orvieto[2]. This view has gained some support from the discovery of Etruscan remains in various places close to Bolsena itself; thus Gamurrini, previously a supporter of Müller's opinion, was led to admit that an Etruscan city or large fort must have existed on the hill of Montebello above Bolsena, though he did not definitely identify this city with Volsinii[3]. It is also noteworthy that the tombs and cippi in the Bolsena region which inscriptions shew to be Etruscan, are widely scattered in different localities, in strong contrast to the necropolis of Orvieto, and do not shew the same indications of having belonged to an important city; and there is always the possibility that some of them are subsequent to 264 B.C. It is hazardous to argue much from the fragments of a wall found on the site of the Roman town, as it also may have been built

[1] Procop. *B.G.* II. 11, 18, 19, 20, etc.; Greg. Mag. *Epist.* I. 12, II. 5.

[2] E.g. Salpinum (Niebuhr, Pais, II. p. 450, n. 1; Kiepert, *Formae Orbis Antiqui*, xx; Dennis, II. p. 40), Herbanum (Cluver, *It. Ant.* p. 553), or the Fanum Voltumnae (Perali, *Orvieto*, pp. 12, 43—a recent view which has received little or no support).

[3] *Not. scav.* 1896, pp. 324–5. Other Etruscan remains near Bolsena: *Not. scav.* 1877, pp. 260–1, 310; 1878, p. 179; 1880, pp. 284–5; 1881, p. 55; 1882, pp. 263, 409–10; 1883, pp. 419–20; 1884, p. 101; 1885, p. 65; 1893, pp. 64–8; 1896, pp. 284–5; 1903, pp. 588–600; 1906, pp. 59–70; 1910, pp. 543–5.

by the transported inhabitants[1]. And the Etruscan inscriptions of Bolsena are very scanty in comparison with
those of Orvieto, or with the Latin inscriptions of Bolsena.

I assume therefore that the Etruscan metropolis of
Volsinii was situated on the isolated tufa rock, rising sheer
out of the valley of the Paglia, where now is Orvieto. The
city is mentioned by Livy as one of the "tres ualidissimae
urbes, Etruriae capita," which submitted to Rome in
294 B.C.; its wealth is shewn by the well-known tradition
in Pliny of the 2000 statues which were captured there[2].
The rare gold coins bearing a female head on one side,
and a running dog with "Velsu" in Etruscan characters
on the reverse, are generally held to belong to Volsinii[3].
That Volsinii was in Etruscan times a religious centre is
suggested by the rescript of Constantine which speaks of
the festival of the Etruscan and Umbrian cities as being
held "aput Volsinios[4]"; whence the Fanum Voltumnae
is generally held to have been somewhere in the territory
of Volsinii[5].

The destruction of Volsinii was due to internal strife.
According to the accounts which have come down to us,
the citizens had degenerated into idleness and luxury,
allowing their slaves to fight for them in war, to share in
the management of the city and to intermarry with the
ruling class: till finally the slaves seized the whole power
in the state, tyrannizing over their former masters with

[1] *Not. scav.* 1903, pp. 359–62. Gabrici well remarks (*ibid.* p. 374)
that as Etruscan tombs have been found on all the hills between
Bolsena and Orvieto, it is no wonder if Etruscan remains are found
on the site of Roman Volsinii.

[2] Liv. x. 37. 4; Plin. *N.H.* xxxiv. 34. In all probability Plin. ii. 139
("Volsinii oppidum Tuscorum opulentissimum totum concrematum
est fulmine") also refers to the old town, as there is no other indication
that the Roman Volsinii was remarkable for its riches.

[3] Deecke in Müller, i. pp. 386–7; *Etr. Forsch.* ii. p. 6.

[4] *C.I.L.* xi. 2. 5265.

[5] Perhaps at Montefiascone: Dennis, ii. p. 32.

the utmost insolence and licence[1]. How far this story is coloured by aristocratic bias or by the imagination of later writers, we cannot tell; perhaps the revolt was no more than a democratic upheaval due to the necessity of employing the lowest classes in war, which led to the attainment by them of *conubium* with the aristocracy and of political equality[2]. But there is every reason to believe that in Etruria the ruling aristocracy was less ready than at Rome to save itself by timely concessions; so that the traditions of the outrage of the slaves are not incredible. In any case the dispossessed nobles appealed to Rome on the ground of their alliance[3] (probably dating from 280 B.C.), and in 265 an army was sent under the consul Q. Fabius to restore them. Fabius died of wounds received in an attack on the city, which was reduced by famine in the following year. The new consul, M. Fulvius Flaccus, put to death the leaders of the revolt and destroyed the city, removing the old citizens and the loyal slaves to another site where the city began a new life with the old name[4].

The removal of the Volsinienses to a less strong and defensible site is paralleled by the similar action of the Romans after the six days' revolt of Falerii in 241[5], when according to Zonaras the ancient city built on a strong

[1] Zonar. VIII. 7, who gives the fullest account of the whole episode; Oros. IV. 5. 3–5; Val. Max. IX. 1. 2.

[2] Beloch, *It. Bund*, pp. 162–3; De Sanctis, II. pp. 424–5; Rosenberg, *Der Staat der alten Italiker*, pp. 136–7. The details given by our authorities that the slaves compelled the free-born to make wills in their favour and to give them free women in marriage might be merely an aristocratic version of the winning by the plebs of the rights of intermarriage and succession.

[3] Zonar. *loc. cit.*: ἔνσπονδοι γὰρ ἦσαν αὐτοῖς.

[4] Fast. Triumph. (264 B.C.): "M. Fulvius Flaccus cos de Vulsiniensibus." Liv. *Epit.* XVI *fin.*: "Res contra Poenos et Volsinios prospere gestas continet." The destruction of the city and removal of inhabitants occur only in Zonaras (τὴν πόλιν κατέσκαψε...ἐν ἑτέρῳ κατῴκισε τόπῳ).

[5] Polyb. I. 65; Liv. *Epit.* XIX; Zonar. VIII. 18: κατεσκάφη. We know nothing of the origins of this revolt.

hill was razed[1] and another was built, easy of access. It is now universally agreed that the Etruscan Falerii was on the site of Civitacastellana, a rock practically isolated by deep ravines, where remains of several Etruscan temples have been found dating from the sixth to the third centuries B.C., and that the Roman town lay three miles away in the neighbourhood of the church of S. Maria di Falleri, where extensive walls and other remains are visible[1]. There is also some ground for supposing that the Arretium of Roman times occupied the site of the modern town, while the Etruscan city was on higher ground[2]. It has been plausibly suggested that similarly in Umbria the inhabitants of the ancient town at Cesi, which is known to us from the extensive remains of its polygonal walls, but which seems to have lost all importance under the Empire, if it was inhabited at all, were removed to form the flourishing town of Carsulae on the Via Flaminia, and that Vicus Martis on the same road was the successor of an older settlement on the neighbouring hill-fortress of Massa Martana[3]. It is clear that the migration of inhabitants from the strong hill-towns which are so common in central Italy to new dwelling-places on lower or level ground was an event not uncommon in the period of the Roman conquest; sometimes as at Volsinii and Falerii it was done under compulsion; but often it may have been a gradual process, which took place when an impregnable situation was made needless through the security from attack which the Roman supremacy gave, and when it became advantageous to live on or near one of the great Roman highways[4]. It is also interesting to note how in the time

---

[1] On Falerii, old and new, see Dennis, I. pp. 87–114.
[2] Dennis, II. pp. 389–93; Nissen, II. p. 317.
[3] Giglioli in *Not. scav.* 1913, p. 161, on the discovery of archaic tombs close to Massa.
[4] Cf. Forum Flamini, Nuceria and Forum Semproni, on the Via Flaminia, which Strabo mentions as κατοικίαι διὰ τὴν ὁδὸν πληθυνό- μεναι μᾶλλον ἢ διὰ πολιτικὸν σύστημα (V. p. 227).

of the barbarian invasions, when the *pax Romana* broke up, the old strongholds regained their importance; so that to-day Orvieto and Civitacastellana, the old Etruscan sites, are flourishing towns, while Bolsena is insignificant and Falleri is occupied by one farm-house.

The Roman supremacy in Etruria was solemnly declared by the removal to Rome of the god Vortumnus, "deus Etruriae princeps" as Varro calls him[1], whose special seat was at Volsinii, but who must have been closely connected if not identical with the federal deity Voltumna[2]. Over a century before Rome had summoned Juno Regina from conquered Veii; now M. Fulvius Flaccus, the conqueror of Volsinii, dedicated on the Aventine a temple of Vortumnus, thereby bringing the chief divine patron of the Etruscan race under the aegis of the Roman state[3]. The goddess Nortia, who was also specially worshipped at Volsinii, appears to have migrated with the remnant of her people to their new town[4]; when Falerii, however, was destroyed not many years later, one of the city's deities was removed and given a shrine on the Caelian with the title of "Minerva Capta," while the cult of Juno Quiritis persisted in its old site, though that goddess had also a temple in Rome[5].

[1] Varr. *L.L.* v. 46.

[2] Prop. IV. 2. 3–4: "Tuscus ego Tuscis orior, nec paenitet inter proelia Volsinios deseruisse focos." Voltumna and Vortumnus were perhaps only variants of a single name, the former having a markedly Etruscan termination, while the latter is more Latin in form.

[3] A painting in the temple represented Flaccus as triumphator, wearing the purple toga (Fest. p. 209, s.v. "Picta"). A statue of Vortumnus stood in the Etruscan quarter at Rome, the Vicus Tuscus between the Forum and the Tiber; Varr. *loc. cit.*; cf. Wissowa, *Religion und Kultus der Römer*, p. 287.

[4] Cf. the dedication "deae Nort(iae)," *C.I.L.* XI. 2682, and Tert. *Apol.* 24; and a votive pit near Bolsena which perhaps belonged to a shrine of Nortia. (Gabrici in *Not. scav.* 1906, pp. 70 ff.)

[5] Ov. *Fast.* III. 843 ff. (Minerva); *Amor.* III. 13 (Juno: "difficilis cliuis huc uia praebet iter," seems to apply better to the old than the new Falerii). *C.I.L.* I². p. 331: "Junoni Curriti (or Quiriti) in campo," on Oct. 7th. Wissowa, *op. cit.* pp. 188, 253.

§3

CAUSES OF THE DECLINE OF ETRURIA

Various causes have been suggested for the decline of
the Etruscans into dependence on Rome, and their practical disappearance from subsequent history, which is in
such remarkable contrast to the supremacy in Italy which
they had once held. We have already noticed the lack of
a strong central authority in Etruria, which led to the
conquests and settlements outside Etruria proper being
made by individual cities or chieftains, and later falling an
easy prey to invasion because the nation as a whole felt
no responsibility for their fate. Till the Gallic invasion at
the beginning of the fourth century no invader ever
menaced the heart of Etruria, and the various cities were
never obliged by a common danger to sink their jealousies
or yield some part of their independence to a common
executive[1]. So Veii was left to its fate, and Etruria was
not prepared to face, when the time came, a strong and
united enemy such as Rome; and the alliances of cities
which appear to have been made towards the end of the
fourth century were too late and too narrow in their scope
to avert defeat[2].

While it is clear that Etruria as a whole was weakened
in the face of external danger by the particularism of its

---

[1] Little reliance can be placed on the Roman annalists' accounts of
proceedings at the annual meeting at the Fanum Voltumnae (Liv. IV.
23. 5, 25. 7, 61. 2; VI. 2. 2; Dionys. III. 57, etc.). The Roman treaties
were all made with separate cities and not with any body representing
the whole nation.

[2] E.g. the alliance of Populonia, Vetulonia and (?) Clusium mentioned above; perhaps also there was a league of the northern cities
Perusia, Cortona and Arretium which submitted together, Liv. IX.
37. 12.

component cities, there are also indications that the cities themselves were not free from serious internal dissensions. The most conspicuous example of these is given by the events which led up to the Roman intervention at Volsinii in 265 B.C.; another example is the feud at Arretium in 302, when the powerful family of the Cilnii was driven out because of its wealth[1], and we have an uncertain tradition regarding an unknown town Oenarea in Etruria, in which through fear of a tyranny (as the town occupied a strong position, 30 stades uphill from the plain), the government was entrusted annually to a body of freedmen[2]. All that is known of the constitution of the Etruscan cities[3] shews that the power lay in the hands of a hereditary aristocracy—the "principes" often mentioned by the Latin historians—which was also a priesthood and had sole possession of the peculiar religious lore of the Etruscans[4]. This theocratical basis, so different from Roman practice, made impossible any gradual equalization of privilege, so that the lowest classes, permanently excluded from power, had less interest in the welfare of their city than Roman citizens in theirs; or if as at Volsinii they succeeded in gaining control of the state, they used their

---

[1] Liv. x. 3.

[2] [Arist.] *de mir. ausc.* 94. Pais, IV. p. 307, identifies Οἰναρέα with Volaterrae, as being the highest Etruscan city.

[3] On this see Müller, I. pp. 337 ff., esp. p. 350. Cf. Rosenberg, *Der Staat der alten Italiker*, esp. pp. 69 ff.

[4] Censorinus, *de die nat.* IV. 13: "lucumones tum Etruriae potentes exscripserunt" (of the code of Tages); on the sacred books of the Etruscans see Müller, II. pp. 19 ff. The celebrated mummy-wrappings in the Agram Museum belong to such a book, apparently containing a sacrificial ritual; see Skutsch in Pauly-Wissowa, *R.E.* VI. pp. 777–8, and literature there quoted; also Lattes, *Saggi e appunti intorno alla Iscrizione Etrusca della Mummia* (Milan, 1894); Torp, *Etruskische Beiträge*, II. pp. 1–83; Bugge, *Das Verhältnis der Etrusker zu den Indogermanen und den vorgriechischen Bevölkerung Kleinasiens und Griechenlands*, pp. 157 ff. A. Grünwendel's *Tusca* appears to me fantastic on the subject of the Agram text.

power to avenge themselves on their former masters. In either case the strength of the city was gravely impaired.

In an earlier chapter I have attempted to shew how the power of the Etruscans in the sixth century was due to their superiority in wealth and in the use of natural resources over their neighbours. The skill and the knowledge which they brought with them from the East combined with the richness of their country and the mixture of their race with the vigorous Italic people among whom they settled, to produce an extraordinarily rapid development. But the Etruscan civilization, so rapidly matured, had less depth than that of the Latins which was won slowly and laboriously; it was more a faculty for imitating the arts and crafts of others—Phoenicians and still more Greeks—than something evolved from within, out of the soul of the people. This is best illustrated by the dependence of Etruscan upon Greek art without ever entering upon an individual line of development, which shews that the Etruscan genius for all its great ability was fundamentally lacking in initiative. At the same time the economic strength of Etruria had declined during the fifth and fourth centuries with the fall of the Etruscans' sea-power and the rise of Syracuse as a maritime and commercial rival through the energy of the Dinomenid tyrants and later of Dionysius I.

But while Etruscan culture came to a standstill, that of Rome absorbing various elements from Etruria itself gradually advanced. The Romans of the fourth century had progressed far since the beginning of their city-life under the Tarquins. The city-wall of tufa blocks built after the Gallic invasion, the high road to Capua and the first aqueduct which were constructed under the direction of the progressive leader Appius Claudius, were no mean monuments of Roman skill in the material arts. At the same time the horizon of Rome had expanded; she had entered into relations with foreign cities such as Massalia and Carthage, and sent embassies to ask counsel or to bring offerings to the shrine of Apollo at Delphi; her ships were beginning to appear on the sea, and a port was growing up at Ostia[1]. Still more important was the spirit of discipline and order, deep-rooted in the Romans and strengthened by two centuries' struggle for existence. Respect for authority, for the *imperium* of the magistrate, had been kept alive by danger from without; the strife of factions was often fierce and bitter, but it never imperilled the safety of the State, and no party ever made common cause with a foreign foe as so frequently happened in the Greek cities. The instability often amounting to chaos which was common to Greek city-states was abhorrent to the Roman respect for *mos maiorum*; on the other hand, the Roman patricians knew when to give way with a timely concession, while the Etruscan aristocracy fortified by religion kept the reins of government entirely in its own hands.

It was largely due to her geographical position that Rome and not Capua or Volsinii or some other city to north or south was to become the centre of Italy. Situated on the Tiber, the great natural highway into central Italy, and at the last convenient crossing-place above its mouth, and midway between the mountains and the sea, Rome was the natural meeting-place of travellers from all parts of the country; and in fact practically all the land-routes leading from Etruria and Umbria to the plains of Campania and from the central Apennines down to the sea converged on Rome. The coast-towns of southern Etruria had declined when the mastery of the sea passed to the Greeks after the battle of Cumae in 474, and the great

---

[1] The *duouiri nauales* first appear in 311 (Liv. IX. 30. 4); on Ostia cf. Tenney Frank, "Rome's First Coinage," in *Class. Phil.* 1919, p. 314.

inland cities such as Volsinii, Perusia, Volaterrae, for all their wealth and natural strength, were content to go their own way, having little contact with other nations. The Romans on the other hand, constantly in touch with strangers in their midst, acquired a certain sympathy and ability to deal with foreign peoples; and in the plain of Latium they were able to assert their authority in a way impossible to any city situated on some isolated mountain-top in the Apennines or among the ravines of Etruria. In this authority the Latins acquiesced, finding there a defence against the inroads of wild mountaineers or Gauls, and so the nucleus of the Roman confederacy was formed. Rome acquired the reputation for loyalty to her allies and for a consistent policy; and when finally the Italian peoples succeeded in forming a coalition to resist the Roman supremacy, they had nothing in common beyond this negative aim, while Rome had the advantage of a single executive whose directions were obeyed, and of interior lines so that armies could be sent to either front as occasion demanded.

The decline of the Etruscan people is often ascribed to the nature of their religion, and the depravation of their morals. Greek writers have much to tell us of the luxury and the vices of the Etruscans, of their elaborate feasts with flowery coverlets, silver vessels and numerous attendants, and Roman poets echo the taunt[1]. Timaeus and Theopompus, quoted by Athenaeus (XII. 517 *d*–518 *b*), give a lurid account of the depravity of the Etruscans and their women, and some have found a justification for their charges in the paintings of Etruscan tombs. The banquet accompanied by music and dancing, which is so common

[1] Diod. v. 40: παρατίθενται δὶς τῆς ἡμέρας τραπέζας πολυτελεῖς... ἐν πότοις καὶ ῥαθυμίαις βιοῦντες, and similarly Posidonius *ap.* Athen. IV. 153 *d*, cf. XII. 519 *b*; Dionys. IX. 16. 8; "pinguis Tyrrhenus," Virg. *G.* II. 193; "obesus Etruscus," Catull. XXXIX. 11, an epithet which is justified by the recumbent figures on various sarcophagi.

in early Etruscan tombs, no doubt stands for the bliss in Elysium which is ensured to the dead by its visible representation in their sepulchre; but the realistic details are taken from daily life[1], and lend no support to the assertion that the Etruscans were served by naked handmaidens[2]. Nor is it probable that the women who are represented reclining with men at the feast are to be taken as hetaerae, as is sometimes stated; it is not likely that hetaerae would be represented in tombs or on sarcophagi, and where, as in the Tomba degli Scudi or Tomba dell' Orco, the woman as well as the man has her name painted above, she is clearly his wife[3]. It is true that the symposium scenes are commonest in paintings of the sixth and fifth centuries and therefore afford little evidence as to the character of the Etruscans in the period of their decline; but there is certainly no indication to be found in any Etruscan monuments that their morals were more corrupt than those of contemporary Greeks or of the Romans at the end of the Republic. This is not to represent the Etruscans as patterns of virtue or to deny the decline in morals which probably did in fact occur[4]. But the assertions of Theopompus are not borne out by Roman writers who were in a better position to know the facts and had certainly no bias in favour of the Etruscans.

It is most likely that the scandalous tales collected by

[1] E.g. especially the kitchen and larder with slaves at work in the Golini tomb at Orvieto.

[2] Timaeus *ap.* Athen. IV. 153 *d*; XII. 517 *d*.

[3] Poulsen, *Etruscan Tomb Paintings*, pp. 32–7, who well remarks that in some realistic portraits from later urns "the appellation hetaera becomes as preposterous as that of matron is certain."

[4] De Sanctis however (I. p. 458) regards the Etruscan customs which shocked the Greeks as relics of barbarism; cf. e.g. Plaut. *Cist.* 562: "non enim hic, ubi ex Tusco modo / tute tibi indigne dotem quaeras corpore," referring to an Asiatic custom perhaps religious in origin, cf. Hdt. I. 93: τοῦ γὰρ δὴ Λυδῶν δήμου αἱ θυγατέρες πορνεύονται πᾶσαι συλλέγουσαί σφισι φέρνας.

Theopompus had their origin in the peculiarly free position of women in Etruria as compared with Greek customs. In Athens in the fourth century married women did not attend banquets with their husbands[1], but they certainly did so in Etruria, as we learn from Aristotle's work on the manners and customs of the Etruscans[2]; and a painting in the Tomba dei Vasi Dipinti clearly represents a family gathered together for the banquet in Elysium as they had done in their life on earth. Women also were allowed to be present at the athletic contests, another contrast to Greek practice: in a tomb at Chiusi in the midst of the games we see a lady seated under an umbrella, and in the frieze of the Tomba delle Bighe at Tarquinii there are women among the keenly-interested spectators in the raised stands, watching the chariot races, boxing and wrestling and other sports. It is well known too that the Etruscans used their mothers' names as well as their fathers'[3], or sometimes the former alone, which gave rise to the notion of the Greeks that in Etruria the children were brought up in common, their fathers being unknown. That in noble Etruscan families the women as well as the men were versed in the mysteries of divination we learn from the story of Tanaquil, wife of Tarquinius Priscus[4].

But even if we refrain from giving too much credit to the lurid accounts of Greek historians about the manners of the Etruscans, there is good evidence for a decline in the spirit of the people, which underlay their political weakness. We can discern this in their sepulchral art: to

[1] Isaeus, III. 14.

[2] Quoted by Athen. I. 23 *d*: οἱ δὲ Τυρρηνοὶ δειπνοῦσι μετὰ τῶν γυναικῶν ἀνακείμενοι ὑπὸ τῷ αὐτῷ ἱματίῳ.

[3] A large number of bilingual and Latin inscriptions in Etruria shew matronymics, e.g. *C.I.L.* XI. 1963, 2137-45, 2260, 3160. Cf. E. Lattes, *Le iscrizioni latine col matronymico di provenienza etrusca* (Naples, 1898). On matronymics in Lycia cf. Hdt. I. 173.

[4] Liv. I. 34. 9: "perita ut uolgo Etrusci caelestium prodigiorum mulier"; see further Dennis, I. p. 478, n. 9.

the latest age of Etruscan work belong the numerous rectangular urns of Volterra, Perugia and Chiusi, in which the reliefs repeat over and over again the conventional motives, drawn largely from Greek mythology with a preference for such scenes of slaughter as the death of Eteocles and Polynices, while the coarse recumbent figures on the lids of the urns seldom shew the vivacity or even the technical skill of the sixth-century sarcophagi of Cerveteri. Rarely do we find a work of real power such as the principal urn in the tomb of the Volumnii at Perugia, with its majestic winged spirits guarding the gate of Hades.

At the root of this artistic decline lay a change in the religious outlook of the people; from about the middle of the fourth century Etruscan religion shews those gloomy and repulsive features which are regarded as its particular characteristic. The tomb-paintings of banquets and sports, accompanied by music and dancing, so common in tombs of the sixth and fifth centuries, aimed at securing the bliss of the departed in the next world by visible representation; but in the latest tombs the old confidence in a happy immortality is replaced by fear and despair. The banquet is still represented, but the listless revellers have lost their gaiety; hideous demons and monsters begin to appear, and scenes of torment and slaughter. Chief among these demons is Charun[1], usually bearing a hammer as symbol

[1] Cf. Dennis, II. pp. 191–3; Milani in *Rend. Linc.* 1894, pp. 272–3, on this and other Etruscan demons. On Charun see O. Waser, *Charon Charun Charos*, and Lawson, *Modern Greek Folklore and Ancient Greek Religion*, pp. 98 ff., who shews that the original Charon was simply a death-god of pre-Hellenic origin (perhaps Anatolian, cf. A. B. Cook, *Zeus*, II. p. 647, n. 2), his function as ferryman being a purely literary idea which has not survived in popular belief. Traces of the older and wider use are found in Greek literature, e.g. Χαρώνειοι κλίμακες, Χ. θύρα, σπήλαια, ἄντρα, etc. The modern Charos "visits this upper world to carry off those whose allotted time has run" (Lawson, *op. cit.* p. 101) exactly as Charun does in Etruscan monuments.

of destruction, and coloured a livid blue; sometimes he appears merely as a witness at a scene of death, as at the slaughter of the Trojan prisoners in the François tomb at Volci[1], or accompanying a soul on its journey to the next world[2]. Sometimes, however, he has a vulture's beak, animal ears and snaky locks, or is shewn dragging away guilty souls or threatening them with his hammer[3]. Still more repulsive is the demon Tuchulcha, also painted with a hideous vulture's beak, who brandishes a large snake over the seated Theseus in the Orcus tomb; and the same tendency to dwell upon the tragic side of death is exemplified by the hideous old woman with wings who is represented on a cinerary urn from Chiusi clutching at the arm of a reclining youth[4]. We have further evidence of the demoralization of Etruscan religion in the fact that the secret Bacchic rites whose discovery in 186 B.C. caused such alarm in Rome were introduced thither from Etruria; and in this connexion the prevalence of Bacchic scenes on Etruscan vases, which were buried in the tombs, is doubtless significant[5].

Thus there are clear indications of a spiritual deterioration which came over the Etruscans in the fourth and third centuries B.C. and manifested itself in their religious outlook, their art, and probably their private life as well as their politics; the soul of the nation was weakened and its efforts exhausted, so that Etruria could offer but a half-hearted and ineffectual resistance to the still youthful and vigorous power of Rome.

[1] Cf. too the demons witnessing the farewell of Alcestis and Admetus on a vase from Volci (Dennis, II. frontispiece).

[2] Numerous urns from Volterra, e.g. Inghirami, *Mon. Etr.* I. tav. VIII: Tomba del Tifone at Tarquinii.

[3] Orcus and Cardinale tombs, Tarquinii, cf. Dennis, I. pp. 339 ff., 345 ff.

[4] Perugia Museum, no. 58; Dennis, II. p. 430.

[5] Liv. XXXIX. 8. 9. Cf. Albizzati in *Atti Ponti . Accad.* XIV (1919), pp. 180–1; *Röm. Mitt.* XXX (1915), pp. 129 ff.

PART FOUR

ETRURIA AFTER THE ROMAN CONQUEST

§ 1

CHARACTER OF THE ROMAN SETTLEMENT;
COLONIES AND ROADS

FROM the foregoing record of the conquest of central and northern Etruria it is clear that the terms of submission offered by Rome were not hard, and that most of the Etruscan cities readily acquiesced in them. Their national spirit was not strong enough to induce them to make great sacrifices for the ideal of independence; the aristocracies in power knew that they could count upon Roman support against a revolt of their subjects (as the episode of Volsinii clearly shewed) and against any serious encroachments by Gauls or Ligurians. Many of the Etruscan cities were important manufacturing centres, as is evident from the lavish contributions of arms, naval equipment and other supplies which they made to the fleet of Scipio in 205 B.C.[1], and industry naturally demanded peace and security. The demands of Rome in return were not heavy; thus in the Gallic invasion of 225 the contingent of the Etruscans and Sabines together numbered 4000 horse and something over 50,000 foot: while the total number of Romans and Campanians (the latter term probably including other "half-citizens") was 23,000 horse and 250,000 foot[2].

[1] Liv. XXVIII. 45. 14.
[2] Polyb. II. 24. 5, 14. The Etruscans must have found the bulk of the 54,000, most of the Sabines having received the citizenship by this time (Vell. I. 14).

Further, till the early part of the second century the allies shared equally with the citizens in the spoils of war, and also in the Latin colonies which were founded[1].

It is however certain that the Etruscan League of twelve cities, like the other national leagues in Italy, was either dissolved when the Etruscans entered the Roman alliance, or survived in an attenuated form for purely religious purposes. We have seen that our records speak of truces being granted by Rome to separate Etruscan cities on their submission, but never of any dealings between Rome and the League as a whole; and no doubt the same course was pursued in Umbria. It appears that as a rule the treaties with the allies did not give the latter the rights of acquiring property in Roman territory or contracting valid marriages with citizens—the rights known as *commercium* and *conubium*[2]; and since the policy of Rome was to unite the allies closer to herself than to one another, the allies cannot have had the power to make treaties among themselves which involved the reciprocal grant of private rights[3].

But in practice these restrictions were probably less irksome than in theory, owing to the development of the "ius gentium": thus an alien could acquire any property which was not a *res mancipi* and undertake most contracts and obligations except the *sponsio*[4]. He could not bequeath

[1] Liv. XLI. 7 (178 B.C.): "(diuiserunt) sociis tantundem quantum Romanis." But next year (XLI. 13) "sociis dimidio minus quam ciuibus datum."

[2] Ulpian, XIX. 5: "Mancipatio [which was involved in *commercium*] locum habet inter ciues Romanos et Latinos coloniarios et Latinos Iunianos eosque peregrinos quibus commercium datum est"; *id.* v. 4: "conubium habent ciues Romani cum ciuibus Romanis, cum Latinis autem et peregrinis ita si concessum est."

[3] De Sanctis, II. pp. 456–8; Mommsen, II. p. 53; Heitland, I. § 219. Beloch, *It. Bund*, pp. 220–1, holds that the allies had *commercium* and *conubium* with Rome and with one another.

[4] Gaius, II. 19: "res nec mancipi ipsa traditione pleno iure alterius fiunt," 65, 66; III. 93: "ceterae uero (obligationes) iuris gentium sunt."

to nor inherit from a Roman citizen[1]; but the *ius gentium* allowed him bonitary ownership (*in bonis habere*), and he could make a will under the laws of his own state[2]. If a marriage was contracted without *conubium*, the issue of such marriage could not succeed *ab intestato*, but the *fideicommissa* were instituted for their benefit, which seems to shew that such marriages became not uncommon[3]. The development of the *ius gentium* with its less cumbrous forms to serve as a body of international private law, and the introduction of a second praetor in 242 B.C. to administer this law, are clear proof that *peregrini*, among whom the allies were included, were already numerous at Rome at that time[4], and were therefore less isolated from intercourse with Romans and with each other than they might appear in strict law. Further, till the Romans began to grudge the grant of the citizenship in the second century, it was not difficult for Latins and other allies to obtain it on their migration to Rome[5].

The fusion of Etruscan and Roman (or at least Latin-speaking) families is attested by the numerous bilingual inscriptions which have been found mainly in the neighbourhood of Chiusi and Perugia[6]. Most of these are sepulchral inscriptions giving the name of the deceased in both languages: thus a funeral urn of Chiusi (*C.I.L.* XI. 2260 = Deecke, p. 59, no. XIV) is inscribed "vl. alfni nuvi/cainal" in Etruscan characters, and below in Latin

[1] Ulp. XXII. 2: "peregrinus...cum quo testamenti factio non est."
[2] Ulp. XX. 14.
[3] Muirhead, *Roman Law*, p. 217.
[4] Muirhead, *op. cit.* pp. 215, 218. Pomponius *ap. Dig.* I. 2. 2, § 28: "quod multa turba etiam peregrinorum in ciuitatem ueniret, creatus est et alius praetor qui peregrinus appellatus est ab eo quod plerumque inter peregrinos ius dicebat."
[5] Liv. XLI. 8 (177 B.C.): "lex sociis ac nominis Latini qui stirpem ex se domi relinquerent dabat ut ciues Romani fierent." The law was altered at the request of the allies.
[6] Cf. Deecke, *Die Etruskische Bilinguen* (Stuttgart, 1883).

"C. Alfius A.f./Cainnia natus[1]." There are also numerous inscriptions in the Latin alphabet but the Etruscan language[2]; and several groups of urns or tiles have been found together, some with Etruscan and some with Latin inscriptions[3]. A large number of the Latin funeral inscriptions of the Chiusi region record the name of the mother of the deceased, after the Etruscan fashion, as for example *C.I.L.* XI. 2405: "C. Publilius P.f. Arn./Vibinnia natus," which apparently dates from after the Social War, as the Clusines were enrolled in the tribus Arnensis on receiving the citizenship[4]. The Etruscan and bilingual inscriptions appear to continue till at least the end of the Republic; for the Latin inscriptions which are found with Etruscan ones shew the later forms *-i* and *-ae* in the genitive, very rarely *-ei* or *-ai*. In the celebrated tomb of the Volumnii near Perugia[5], there are six travertine urns with recumbent figures and Etruscan inscriptions, and one urn of Luna marble in the shape of a Corinthian temple decorated in the Roman style with garlands and paterae between ox-heads, and bearing in large Latin letters at one end the inscription "P. Volumnius A.f. Violens/Cafatia natus," and in Etruscan across the roof, "Pup: velimna: au: cahatial[6]." This urn is evidently considerably later than the other six, and we may conjecture that the Etruscan inscription was only added to bring it into line with

[1] Other true bilinguals from Chiusi: *C.I.L.* 2272, 2282-3, 2299.

[2] E.g. *C.I.L.* 2182-4, 2298, 2412, 2415, 2448, 2457.

[3] E.g. *C.I.L.* 2137-45, 2146-57, 2158-68, 2171-6, 2190-5, 2196-200, 2201-10, 2220-49 (Chiusi): 1990-2, 1993, 1995-6, 1997-9, 2000, 2001-10 (Perugia).

[4] Other Latin matronymics: *C.I.L.* 2139-41, 2144-5, 2208-10, 2385, 2484-5 and many more from Chiusi and Montepulciano: 1995, 1999, 2017, 2031, 2045, 2048 from Perugia.

[5] Dennis, II. pp. 438 ff., describes this tomb.

[6] Deecke, *op. cit.* p. 1, Mommsen in *C.I.L.* I. 1392 (=XI. 1963) both remark that the Latin inscription is the principal one, and is in lettering of the Imperial age.

them¹. Thus in the centre of the country as we have seen the
Etruscan language long survived; in the south Latin and
Etruscan inscriptions appear together in painted Etruscan
tombs, such as the Tomba del Tifone at Tarquinii and
the Tomba dei Tarquinii at Caere². An early Latin inscription (with the forms *-ei*, *-eis*) occurs in a chamber-
tomb near Falerii³; but the Faliscan language appears to
have survived till the end of the third century B.C. at
least, being found in inscriptions from the site of the new
Falerii which was founded after 241 B.C.⁴

It is generally agreed that the bulk of the Etruscan
cities were allies of Rome up to the Social War; the position of only the southernmost cities is open to question.
Beloch (*It. Bund*, pp. 58–61) holds that Caere, Tarquinii,
Volci and Falerii⁵ were incorporated without the right of
voting at the time of their last recorded submission to
Rome, but Prof. Tenney Frank has shewn⁶ that there is
no real evidence that any of these towns except Caere
had any form of citizenship previously to the Social War,
and that the date of the incorporation of Caere is unknown.
Particularly important in this connexion is the list of
Etruscan allies which contributed to the fleet of Scipio in
205 B.C.⁷ There is thus a marked contrast between the

¹ There is no evidence that the marble of Luna (Carrara) was
worked before the middle of the first century B.C.; cf. Plin. xxxvi.
135, on its use by Mamurra.
² Dennis, I. pp. 242, 335; *C.I.L.* xi. 3371, 3626–7.
³ Dennis, I. p. 132; *C.I.L.* I. 1313 =xi. 3160.
⁴ E.g. *C.I.L.* xi. 3081, mentioning a "pretod" (praetor). Cf.
Conway, *Italic Dialects*, I. pp. 371, 376 ff.
⁵ Bormann (*C.I.L.* xi. 1. p. 510) agrees with Beloch as to Caere
and Tarquinii, Nissen (*It. Land.* ii. pp. 349, 364) as to Caere and
Falerii.
⁶ *Klio*, xi (1911), pp. 376 ff.
⁷ Liv. xxviii. 45. 14: "Scipio...tenuit...ut quae ab sociis darentur
ad nouas fabricandas naues acciperet," followed by a list of contributions from Caere, Populonia, Tarquinii, Volaterrae, Arretium, Perusia,
Clusium, Rusellae.

action of Rome in Umbria and Etruria: in the former, as
has been shewn, a considerable territory was annexed in
the middle of the country—Forum Flamini, Fulginium,
and Spoletium (a Latin colony, 241 B.C.[1])—and some
cities received the Roman citizenship before the Social
War[2]. In Etruria, on the other hand, no cities were
admitted to the citizenship, and the Roman and Latin
colonies were nearly all in the south and on the coast. On
Tarquinian territory annexed in 308 was founded Castrum
Novum in 289, and on that of Volci the Latin colony of
Cosa in 273[3], which remained for nearly a century the
furthest colony on the Tyrrhene coast, while on the
Adriatic Ariminum was founded as early as 268. This was
a necessary barrier against the Gauls, to secure the land
from which they had been expelled and to close the easiest
route into Italy from the north[4]. In Etruria the Apennines formed a stronger barrier, and the Etruscan cities
could bear the brunt of an invasion; hence the absence
of colonies in north and central Etruria, and the comparatively late development there of the Roman road-
system.

Caere was deprived of half its territory in 273 B.C., and
on this territory there were founded during the first Punic
War (doubtless as a defence against the Carthaginian
fleet) the colonies of Alsium (247) and Fregenae (245)[5] and
probably also Pyrgi, which appears among the maritime
colonies which claimed exemption from military service

---

[1] Vell. I. 14. 8; Liv. *Epit.* xx.

[2] Certainly Asisium where the Umbrian office of "marones" survived after the Social War (*C.I.L.* xi. 2. 5389–90; Conway, *op. cit.*
pp. 396, 398).

[3] Liv. *Epit.* xiv.; Vell. I. 14. 5.

[4] Strab. v. 226–7 (after mentioning the two ways from Cisalpine
Gaul into Italy, by L. Trasimene and by Ariminum): βελτίων μὲν οὖν
ἡ ἐπ' Ἀριμίνου· ταπεινοῦται γὰρ ἐνταῦθα ἱκανῶς τὰ ὄρη.

[5] Vell. I. 14. 8; Liv. *Epit.* xx.

in 191 B.C.[1] Colonization in south Etruria was not resumed till after the Hannibalic War, when colonies were
settled at Graviscae on the Tarquinian coast (181 B.C.),
and at Saturnia (183)[2], which has a commanding position
in the valley of the Albegna, apparently the only inland
region of Etruria (north of the Ciminian range) which was
annexed by Rome. There had previously been a *praefectura* at Saturnia[3], or the original inhabitants remained
under a separate jurisdiction when the colony was planted,
and we also hear of a "praefectura Statonensis," apparently
somewhere between Tarquinii and the Lake of Bolsena[4].
Another colony in the territory of Volci was Heba[5], near
the modern Magliano; evidently the Albegna valley was
regarded as especially important to the Romans, perhaps
as forming the channel of communication between central
Etruria round Volsinii and the ports of Cosa and Telamon[6].
Finally in 177 B.C. a Roman colony was founded at Luna
in connexion with the long war against the Ligurians, on
land captured from the latter, though according to Livy
it had once belonged to the Etruscans[7].

The foundation of colonies was regularly followed by
the establishment of military roads, by which the colonies
and newly annexed regions were linked up to Rome. The

[1] Liv. xxxvi. 3.
[2] Liv. xl. 29; xxxix. 55.
[3] Festus, p. 233.
[4] Vitruv. ii. 7. 3; see p. 127 above.
[5] Cf. the inscription "Genio coloniae Hebae..." described by
Minto, *Not. scav.* 1919, pp. 199 ff.
[6] Port of Cosa: Liv. xxii. 11, xxx. 39; Caes. *B.C.* i. 34: of Telamon,
Plut. *Marius*, 41. Cf. the Ἡρακλέους λιμήν (Porto d' Ercole) below
Cosa, Strab. v. p. 225. Minto (*loc. cit.* p. 206) mentions traces of an
ancient road near Magliano which apparently led to Saturnia.
[7] Liv. xli. 13. On the question of a colony at Luca at this time,
as stated by Velleius, i. 15, cf. Madvig, *opusc.* i. p. 287; Mommsen on
C.I.L. i. 539; Bormann, *C.I.L.* xi. p. 295; Nissen, *It. Land.* ii. p. 287;
Kubitschek, *De Rom. tribuum origine*, etc., p. 65; Taylor in *Class.
Phil.* xvi (1921), pp. 27 ff.

Via Flaminia is the only one of the roads leading north-wards from Rome, the construction of which is recorded by ancient writers[1]; and that road was not so much con-nected with the conquest of the country through which it ran as with the regions to which it led. The Via Flaminia was not built by stages as the Roman power advanced in Umbria, but its construction was part of the policy of expansion advocated by Gaius Flaminius, who as tribune in 232 B.C. had carried against the opposition of the Senate the proposal to distribute in small lots the *ager Gallicus* on the Adriatic coast, and as consul nine years later first led a Roman army across the Po (also against the wish of the Senate) and defeated the Insubres in the Lombard plain. Flaminius was a political successor of Appius Claudius, the pioneer of Roman road-building; and prob-ably aimed at the conquest of the whole Po valley to be divided later among citizen small-holders. Both for distant colonization and for further conquest good communica-tions were important; and Flaminius therefore took ad-vantage of his censorship in 220 B.C. to build a high road to Ariminum, the colony which had been founded to defend the annexed *ager Gallicus* and which was the natural starting-point for a further advance.

No record survives of the construction of the three main roads of Etruria—the Viae Aurelia, Clodia and Cassia—and their historical significance can therefore only be deduced from their course. Valuable work in this con-nexion was done by D. Anziani, of the French School at Rome, in his study of the Roman roads of south Etruria (excluding the *ager Faliscus*)[2]. From the frequency of towns on the Via Clodia, which sometimes diverges from the direct line so as to touch a neighbouring town[3], and

---

[1] Liv. *Epit.* xx. On the Via Flaminia see *J.R.S.* xi (1921), pp. 125 ff.
[2] "Les voies romaines de l'Étrurie méridionale," in *Mélanges*, xxxiii (1913).   [3] *Op. cit.* pp. 205–6.

their rarity in the southern portions of the Via Cassia and the Via Aurelia[1], Anziani concludes that of the three roads the Clodia was built first (perhaps before 300 B.C.) to serve the region round L. Sabatinus, the Cassia considerably later at the end of the third century, and the Aurelia at the time of the Ligurian wars and the foundation of the colony of Luna (177 B.C.).

A completely opposite opinion is put forward by K. Miller (*Itineraria Romana*, p. 191), who holds that the Via Aurelia was built perhaps as far as Vada Volaterrana by C. Aurelius Cotta, censor in 241 B.C., and prolonged by Aemilius Scaurus in 109 B.C.[2]: the Via Cassia towards the end of the second century, and the Via Clodia about 43 B.C. by the C. Clodius Vestalis, who is known to us from coins of that year bearing his name[3]. Miller further states that the Via Clodia led from Rome through Siena and Lucca to Luna[4], and in justification of this theory corrects the line given by the Tabula Peutingeriana from Ad Nouas on the Via Cassia (9 miles north of Clusium), viz. Ad Nouas—VIII—Manliana—XVIII—ad Mensulas—XVI—Umbro fl.—VI—Sena Julia, making this road into a continuation of the Via Clodia from Saturnia. Miller himself admits that the portion of this road between Siena and Lucca does not appear in any of the Itineraries; and it may be added that there is no evidence that Siena in Imperial times lay on a main road to the north. It did, however, in the middle ages; but the Via Francesca, much fre-

---

[1] Anziani remarks that the Via Aurelia made no deviation to pass through Caere, Pyrgi, Tarquinii, or Graviscae, though all lay close to its course (*op. cit.* p. 191).
[2] *Itin. Rom.* p. 233.
[3] Cf. *C.I.L.* XI. 3310 a (from Forum Clodii in south Etruria): "C• Clodio C. f. Vestali pro cos Claudienses ex praefectura Claudia urbani patrono"; but this Clodius may have been a descendant of the founder of the road and Forum, cf. Solari, *Top. Stor.* I. p. 191.
[4] *Op. cit.* p. 295.

quented in that period by pilgrims to Rome, after reaching
Siena from Lucca continued thence through Radicofani
to join the Via Cassia at Bolsena[1]: and this road is not
known to have existed before the middle ages.

There can be little doubt that Etruria had a fairly well-
developed road-system some time before the Roman conquest. The presence of imported articles, whether oriental
or Greek, in the tombs of inland cities such as Falerii and
Volsinii, suggests that these had some means of traffic
with the coast-towns; and the rock-cut roads which are to
be found in various parts of southern Etruria (e.g. in the
neighbourhood of Viterbo and at Corchiano, where there
is an Etruscan inscription in one of these cuttings[2]) probably date from the period of Etruscan independence. The
narrative of the escape of the Vestals and other refugees
from Rome to Caere at the time of the Gallic invasion[3]
points to the existence of a track suitable for vehicles,
which afterwards became the first stretch of the Via
Aurelia. The antiquity of the direct road from Rome to
Tarquinii through Aquae Apollinares (Bagni di Stigliano[4])
is proved by the fact that it forms the *cardo* of the Etruscan
necropolis of Monterozzi outside Tarquinii[5], and from the
aes rude found at Stigliano it is clear that the warm springs
there were frequented at an early date. Another ancient
road may have connected Rome and Veii—the later Via
Veientana, of which traces are visible near the acropolis
of Veii—and Anziani records an undoubtedly pre-Roman
road from Veii to Caere and thence to Alsium (cutting the
Via Aurelia at an acute angle) and Pyrgi[6].

---

[1] See Repetti, *Dizionario Toscano*, v. p. 716.
[2] Dennis, I. p. 119.   [3] Liv. v. 40.
[4] So Garrucci, Miller, Hülsen (Pauly-Wissowa, s.v.), and Anziani
(*op. cit.* pp. 226–8); Dennis (I. p. 60) and Nissen (II. p. 354) identify
Aquae Apollinares with Vicarello on the Lago di Bracciano.
[5] See Pasqui and Cozza, *Not. scav.* 1885, pp. 513 ff.; Anziani,
op. cit. pp. 223 ff.   [6] *Op. cit.* p. 231.

The main question connected with the Roman road-system in Etruria is that of the Via Clodia. The Antonine Itinerary under the heading "Item a Luca Romam per Clodiam" gives the stations of the road through Florentia, Arretium, Clusium, Volsinii, Sutrium, which was certainly the Via Cassia[1]: this mistake is explicable on the hypothesis that there was a later Via Clodia from Florence to Lucca and thence through Forum Clodii[2] (marked here in the Tabula Peutingeriana) to Luna; or that the first eleven miles of the road from Rome to La Storta, where the Clodia and Cassia diverged, was called Via Clodia because this was the earlier of the two roads[3]. I believe that Anziani's method and general conclusions are sound; and the priority of the Via Clodia is confirmed by the fact that it is always named before the Via Cassia in inscriptions. Early in the fourth century, after the fall of Veii, the Roman power reached up to the Ciminian range and Sutrium was made a Latin colony: the tribus Sabatina, which must have touched the Lacus Sabatinus (L. di Bracciano), was one of the new tribes formed in south Etruria in 387 B.C.[4], and the Via Clodia may well have been made during the fourth century to unite the new tribe area to Rome, its original terminus being perhaps Forum Clodii, which is usually placed near S. Liberato, west of the Lake of Bracciano[5]. From whom the road and the Forum took their name we cannot guess. The Via

[1] Cf. Cic. *Phil.* XII. 22: "Etruriam discriminat Cassia." *C.I.L.* XI. 6668, a milestone from Montepulciano records repairs to the Via Cassia by Hadrian; and S. Maria di Forcassi near Vetralla preserves the name of Forum Cassii.
[2] Identified by Miller with Pietrasanta, near Lucca: not to be confounded with the other Forum Clodii near the Lake of Bracciano.
[3] Cf. Ovid, *Ex Pont.* I. 8. 44: "Flaminiae Clodia iuncta uiae" (of the junction at the Pons Milvius).
[4] Liv. VI. 5. 8.
[5] *Itin. Ant.* (p. 289) briefly mentions a road "a Roma Foro Clodio XXXII" which may be the original Via Clodia.

Clodia may have been extended through Blera (Bieda) to Tuscania—its course can be certainly traced so far—in the second century, with perhaps a further extension to Saturnia when this town received a colony in 183 B.C. A road from Saturnia down to the coast at Cosa, which the Tabula absurdly marks as a continuation of the Clodia in a straight line, instead of a branch at right angles, may have been made about the same time. Saturnia was evidently a road-centre of some importance, since there are traces of roads leading thence southwards (presumably the Via Clodia or its continuation), north-west in the direction of Rusellae, north-east (perhaps leading to Chiusi rather than Siena), eastwards towards Sovana—an Etruscan site—whence it may possibly have continued to Volsinii, and south-east down the valley of the Albegna[1].

It is highly probable that the first stretch of the Via Cassia as far as Sutrium (33 miles from Rome) was made in the course of the fourth century B.C., when Sutrium was an important frontier-fortress against the Etruscan or Gallic invader[2], and must therefore have had some direct communication with Rome. As long as the Saltus Ciminius formed the limit of the Roman advance, the road naturally went no further: but it must have been prolonged to Arretium in the third century, since that town was a military base during the greater part of the Hannibalic War, and it is hardly credible that Arretium was not directly connected with Rome when in 187 B.C. the younger Flaminius built a road across the Apennines from Bononia to Arretium[3]. There is no mention of the Via Cassia in literature before the last years of the Republic[4], but large

[1] See Pasqui in *Not. scav.* 1882, pp. 55 ff. I have seen the first three of these roads, and they all disappear completely within a few miles of Saturnia. Hence their destination cannot be stated with any certainty.

[2] Cf. the proverb "Sutrium ire," Plaut. *Cas.* 524, Fest. p. 310.

[3] Liv. XXXIX. 2.   [4] Cic. *Phil.* XII. 22, quoted above.

ROMAN CONQUEST 157

portions of it (e.g. from Clusium to Arretium and thence to Florentia and Faesulae) may well have been built by the Etruscans before the Roman conquest, and afterwards maintained by the allied cities through whose territory it ran until it was taken over by the Roman State. Various second-century consuls or censors of the name of Cassius have been suggested as the founder of the road[1], and there is no sufficient ground for choosing between them. As we have seen, the establishment of the Via Cassia meant mainly the joining up of existing roads and perhaps the paving of the whole as a direct way to northern Italy, shorter but more difficult than the Via Flaminia. From Florentia the road was continued through Pistoria to Lucca and Luna, perhaps by the Clodius who founded the Forum Clodii between the last-named towns.

The principal branch of the Via Cassia was that which diverged at Baccanae (21 miles from Rome) and led to the later Falerii, which was founded after 241 B.C., and thence across the Tiber to Ameria, Tuder and Perusia. It has been conjectured that the branch to Falerii was the Via Annia mentioned in some local inscriptions[2], and that beyond Falerii it was known as Via Amerina. Other branches were the Via Ciminia, which led from Sutrium over the crest of the Ciminian range and rejoined the Cassia near Viterbo[3], and the Via Ferentinensis which appears to have diverged near Viterbo and led to Ferentum and thence to Orvieto—perhaps a pre-Roman road joining the Etruscan Volsinii to its dependent towns[4].

[1] Thus Niese, *Röm. Ges.* p. 146, and Beloch, *It. Bund*, p. 59, date the road in 171 B.C.; Nissen, *It. Land.* II. p. 313, in 154 or 125.
[2] *C.I.L.* XI. 3083, 3126. See Nissen, II. p. 361; Solari, I. p. 149.
[3] *C.I.L.* X. 6006.
[4] *C.I.L.* XI. 3003; IX. 5155, 5833. The Ravenna Geographer (p. 284) and Guido (p. 487) appear to refer to this road when instead of Aquae Passeris on the Via Cassia between Forum Cassii and Volsinii (as in *Itin. Ant.*) they insert Beturbon, Balnea Regis, Urbevetus (i.e. Viterbo, Bagnorea, Orvieto).

The Via Aurelia cannot have been made earlier than about the middle of the third century B.C., since Rome had no territory at all on the Etruscan coast-line before her annexations at the expense of Tarquinii (308 B.C.), Volci (280) and Caere (273). It is not likely that the Romans carried their road at first beyond Cosa, their most distant colony in this region (273 B.C.), and this may have been done by C. Aurelius Cotta, censor in 241 B.C.[1] At a later date the road was prolonged northwards, perhaps as far as Pisa, which appears as a Roman base in the Ligurian wars of the first half of the second century B.C. The continuation of the Tuscan coast-road is ascribed to M. Aemilius Scaurus (censor in 109 B.C.)[2], but as the coast-road from the Rhone to New Carthage and the Via Postumia from Genua to Cremona date from the middle of the second century[3], it is hard to believe that the whole Riviera coast was not traversed by a continuation of the Via Aurelia at that time. It is further uncertain where the Via Aurelia ended and the Via Aemilia Scauri began: perhaps at the old frontier of Italy at Ad Fines, about 20 miles south of Pisa, or at Vada Volaterrana, 10 miles further south. The Itineraries give "Via Aurelia" as the heading for the whole road to Luna, but a milestone, giving the distance 188 miles from Rome and found about 18 miles south of Pisa, records a restoration of the Via Aemilia under Antoninus Pius.

We must now deal with the course of events in Etruria after the submission of the whole country to Rome.

[1] So Nissen, II. p. 301; De Sanctis, III[1]. p. 310; Beloch, *It. Bund*, p. 59, n. 2.
[2] *de uir. ill.* 72.
[3] Polyb. III. 39. 8; Strab. V. p. 226.

§ 2

HISTORY OF ETRURIA AFTER 264 B.C.;
ITS CONDITION UNDER THE EMPIRE

From 280 B.C. onwards the Etruscans made no attempt
to overthrow the Roman supremacy. The campaign of
225 B.C. against the Gauls was fought in Etruria, which
suffered from their ravages[1]; but, in contrast to former
Gallic invasions, none of the Etruscan cities now joined
the Gauls—the allies no longer thought of themselves as
fighting for the Roman hegemony but in defence of their
own land and cities[2]. A contingent of Etruscans and
Sabines was posted in Etruria under a praetor, but was
not strong enough to offer battle alone to the whole Celtic
force. The geography of this campaign raises difficulties—
in particular it is difficult to see why the Gauls, who had
turned northwards from Clusium to meet the Roman
force which had assembled in their rear[3], should retire
along the sea-coast on hearing of the arrival of the second
Roman army from Ariminum[4], instead of retreating by
the shortest and easiest northward road towards Arretium.
It is therefore an attractive conjecture that there was a
second city called Clusium situated on the coast, at the
modern Orbetello where the massive and well-preserved
polygonal walls bear witness to an ancient city whose name
has been lost[5]; but in the absence of other confirmation
this remains a conjecture.

[1] Polyb. II. 25. 1: πορθοῦντες ἀδέως.
[2] id. ib. 23. 13.   [3] Polyb. II. 25. 2 ff.
[4] id. ib. 26. 7. De Sanctis, III[1]. p. 309, takes παρὰ τὴν θάλατταν as
equivalent to ὡς ἐπὶ θάλατταν assuming that the Gauls came down
the Albegna valley: but from north of Chiusi the Ombrone valley
would be a more natural route, and this reaches the coast north of
Telamon, where the Gauls encountered the consul on his march from
Pisae.
[5] See Anziani in *Mélanges*, XXX (1910), pp. 382 ff.

In the year 217, when Hannibal marched through eastern Etruria, ravaging the country, none of the cities which he passed by—Faesulae, Arretium, Cortona, Perusia —opened their gates to him either before or after his victory by Lake Trasimene[1]; and we find a cohort of Perusini together with 500 men of Praeneste doing good service at the defence of Casilinum in the following year[2]. Later in the war, however, some unrest began to appear in Etruria where two legions were stationed annually from 212 onwards, perhaps as a precaution against the Gauls as well as against possible revolts. At the end of 209 B.C. we hear of a revolt which originated in Arretium and subsided on the arrival of Marcellus with authority to bring his army there if necessary[3]; and in the following year Arretium was occupied by a Roman legion and 120 hostages, children of Arretine senators, were sent to Rome, while another Roman force patrolled Etruria to check any incipient disloyalty[4]. We hear of fresh anticipations at Rome of an Etruscan revolt in 207 B.C., and of an enquiry at the end of the year to discover what Etruscan or Umbrian cities had given aid to Hasdrubal or even plotted to desert Rome[5], but it does not appear that any cities were found guilty. In 205 B.C. the fleet of Scipio was equipped without any expense to Rome by the allies, and in this eight Etruscan cities took the lead, furnishing corn and other provisions, timber and shipping tackle, and arms[6], as a practical demonstration of loyalty; Arretium in particular

---

[1] Zonar. (VIII. 24) says many of the Gauls, Ligurians and Etruscans murdered or surrendered the Romans who lived among them (218 B.C.), but this is not confirmed by Polybius or Livy; and his statement that Hannibal after Trasimene advanced towards Rome as far as Narnia τὰς πόλεις προσαγόμενος πλὴν Σπωλητίου is at variance with Polyb. III. 86. 8–9, which shews that he marched to the Adriatic.

[2] Liv. XXIII. 17. 11.   [3] Liv. XXVII. 21.   [4] Liv. XXVII. 21.
[5] Liv. XXVII. 38: "ne (Hasdrubal)...Etruriam erectam in spem rerum nouarum sollicitaret"; XXVIII. 10.
[6] Liv. XXVIII. 45.

which lay under the gravest suspicion provided (perhaps under pressure from its Roman garrison) 3000 shields and as many helmets, 50,000 other weapons, tackle for 40 warships, a large quantity of wheat and provisions for the crews. It therefore appears to be an exaggeration when all Etruria is represented as eager to join Mago next year[1], and many nobles are said to have suffered exile and confiscation for intriguing with him. The fact remains, amid these general statements of Etruscan disaffection, that there is no record of a single city of Etruria definitely giving help to the invaders[2].

Etruria had suffered little from the invasion of Hannibal compared with the regions of southern Italy where the war had raged continuously for many years. Only a small tract had been actually devastated by the invader in 217, and it had been able to furnish corn for the besieged garrison of Tarentum[3] and for the expeditionary force of Scipio. But there are some notable omissions from the roll of cities who gave help on the latter occasions: Volci and Volsinii had never recovered, the one from its loss of land in 280, the other from its revolution and removal in 264; nor do the once great names of Vetulonia and Cortona appear. We know little of the state of Etruria in the second and first centuries B.C., but its prosperity appears to have waned from causes largely connected with the Hannibalic War. The large imports of foreign corn in the years immediately following the war point to a decline of Italian agriculture[4], and served to aggravate the evil; the

[1] Liv. XXIX. 36: "consul...non tam armis quam iudiciorum terrore Etruriam continet totam ferme ad Magonem ac per eum ad spem nouandi res uersam."

[2] Cf. on this matter Prof. J. S. Reid, "Problems of the Second Punic War," in *J.R.S.* v. pp. 123–4.   [3] Liv. XXV. 15; XXVII. 3.

[4] Liv. XXX. 26, 38; XXXI. 50. Cf. Cic. *de Off.* II. 25. 89 (Cato): "a quo cum quaereretur quid maxime in re familiari expediret, respondit: 'bene pascere'; quid secundum: 'satis bene pascere': quid tertium: 'male pascere'; quid quartum: 'arare.'"

class of free farmers and small-holders was weakened by
the diversion of men to military service, and by the cost
of the war in life and in taxation. This favoured the
creation of large estates worked by slave-labour, to the
detriment of the poorer citizens; already in 196 we hear
of a revolt of the slaves in Etruria[1], and (according to the
memoirs of his brother Gaius) it was the condition of
Etruria which first turned the thoughts of Tiberius
Gracchus to land-reforms[2]. We have no direct evidence
of the activities of the Gracchi in Etruria, either in colon-
izing or road-making, beyond the records in the *Liber
coloniarum* of Gracchan settlements at Arretium, Ferentum
and Tarquinii[3].

The Etruscans and their neighbours the Umbrians do
not seem to have played a large part in the agitations
which led to the Social War, or in the war itself[4]. We are
told that they shared the anxiety of the Italians lest they
should be deprived of the public land which they were
occupying, and came to Rome to demonstrate against the
law of Drusus or (it is hinted) at the consul's instigation
to make away with him[5]. But there is no evidence that
the public land in Etruria was ever extensive; in eastern
Umbria some of the *ager Gallicus* may have been still
unallotted[6]. Towards the end of 90 B.C. some of the
Etruscan and Umbrian cities joined the rebellion and were

---

[1] Liv. XXXIII. 36; cf. Juv. VIII. 180: "nempe in Lucanos aut Tusca
ergastula mittas."

[2] Plut. *Ti. Gracch.* 8: τὴν ἐρημίαν τῆς χώρας ὁρῶντα καὶ τοὺς
γεωργοῦντας ἢ νέμοντας οἰκέτας ἐπεισάκτους καὶ βαρβάρους.

[3] *Lib. col.* pp. 215, 216, 219.

[4] The exaggeration of Florus, III. 18. 5, is obvious—"cum omne
Latium atque Picenum, Etruria omnis atque Campania, postremo
Italia contra matrem suam ac parentem Urbem consurgerent."
Neither people is mentioned in the list of original revolters in Liv.
Epit. LXXII.

[5] App. *B.C.* I. 36. 1–2.

[6] Certainly it was not all allocated by Flaminius in 232 B.C. Cf.
C.I.L. I. 583, and Mommsen, *ad loc.*

defeated almost at once and all gladly accepted the citizenship under the Lex Julia[1]. It has been shewn with strong probability by Kubitschek (*De Romanarum tribuum origine ac propagatione*, pp. 64 ff.) and Beloch (*Italische Bund*, p. 42) that the cities which fought against Rome in the Social War were afterwards allotted to eight tribes only (Arnensis, Clustumina, Fabia, Falerna, Galeria, Pomptina, Sergia, Voltinia), to which no colony or *ciuitas sine suffragio* or loyal ally is known to have been assigned[2]. It thus appears that in Umbria nearly all the cities in the west and south of the country revolted, and in Etruria Arretium, Clusium, Volsinii; perhaps also Pisae and Luca, if these towns were as yet even allied to Rome. There is some other confirmation of this division of the loyal and disloyal allies: thus Tuder, one of the many Umbrian towns assigned to the tribus Clustumina, was given the citizenship by a Roman magistrate[3] (and therefore did not receive it under the Lex Julia with the cities "quae arma aut non ceperant aut deposuerant[4]"), and also sided with the Marians in the civil war, as apparently did Clusium and Arretium[5]. It is well known that in the years succeeding the Social War the party of Marius, Sulpicius and Cinna were in favour of more generous treatment of the

---

[1] Liv. *Epit.* LXXIV: "A. Plotius legatus Umbros, L. Porcius praetor Etruscos, cum uterque populus defecisset, proelio uicerunt." Flor. III. 18. 11, mentions Faesulae and Ocriculum among the cities which suffered in the war. As Porcius Cato was consul in B.C. 89 (App. I. 50. 2–3) the defeat of the Etruscans must have been in 90. Appian (I. 49) speaks as if their revolt was forestalled by the grant of citizenship.

[2] Kubitschek, p. 70. Luna (tr. Galeria) is the only exception.

[3] Sisenna, fr. 119, in Peter, *Hist. Rom. Reliqu.*: quoted from Book IV of Sisenna which contained the events of 89 B.C. (Peter, *op. cit.* p. CCCXL).

[4] Vell. II. 15.

[5] Plut. *Crass.* 6; App. *B.C.* I. 89. 3, 92. 3, 91. 2.

revolting allies, who were afraid lest Sulla should deprive them of their new rights[1].

It may be that the Social War and the consequent bestowal of the Roman citizenship had the effect of bringing into power the popular parties which had long been suppressed in the Etruscan cities by the dominant aristocracies; certainly Etruria in general supported the Marian party and incurred the vengeance of Sulla. Here Marius landed from exile in 87, exciting pity by his mean attire and unkempt appearance, and promising freedom to the slaves succeeded in raising a force of 6000 men among them and the free workers[2]. In the war of 82 Clusium and Arretium appear as strongholds of Carbo, and we hear of a victory of Sulla near Saturnia; perhaps the towns of Telamon and Vetulonia were destroyed in the course of this campaign, as is suggested by traces of destruction by fire and by a break in the series of coins found in both places about the end of the first century B.C.[3] The ancient brick wall at Arretium recorded by Vitruvius (II. 8. 9), of which some traces have been discovered recently, also appears to have been partly destroyed at this time[4]. But the last and most stubborn resistance to Sulla was offered by the proscribed democrats at Volaterrae, which from its isolated situation on a precipitous hill-top was well suited to be the last refuge of a lost cause. Here the latest phase of Etruscan art is revealed by

[1] Cf. Liv. *Epit.* LXXVII, LXXXVI; Vell. II. 20. 2; App. *B.C.* I. 59. 6, 73. 4.

[2] App. *B.C.* I. 67; Plut. *Mar.* 41, who specifies his place of landing as Telamon; Flor. III. 21. 10–11.

[3] Gamurrini in *Not. scav.* 1888, pp. 682 ff., on Telamon, and in *Rend. Linc.* 1895, p. 237, on Vetulonia, cf. Falchi, *Not. scav.* 1895, pp. 272, 295.

[4] Pernier in *Not. scav.* 1920, pp. 172 ff., esp. 183–4. The fragments of pottery found under the bricks which came from the ruined wall were all of the "Etrusco-Campanian" type with no trace of the red Arretine ware which began to be produced in the first century B.C.

the hundreds of alabaster urns found in the tombs of
Volaterrae, and here the survivors of the Marian party
were besieged for two years, only capitulating in 80 B.C.[1]
Roman remains shew that Volaterrae was still a place of
some importance under the Empire[2], but Populonia,
which was also besieged about the same time, perhaps
never recovered, being nearly deserted (except for its
harbour) when it was visited by Strabo[3].

The vengeance which Sulla took upon his opponents
throughout Italy[4] fell with especial heaviness upon
Etruria. Land was confiscated to be given to his veterans
in various places, notably at Florence and Fiesole[5].
Whether Florence was formally constituted into a colony
by Sulla is uncertain; it held that position under the
Empire, but not being mentioned as such by Pliny cannot
have been founded by Augustus. From the absence of
any mention of the town in connexion with the rebellion
of Catiline, it has been conjectured that the Florentine
colony dated from the Lex Julia of 59[6]. At Arretium and
at Clusium there were later separate communities which
may date from the settlements of Sulla[7]: a dedication to
him, "L. Cornelio L. [f.] Sullai felici dic.," at Clusium

---

[1] Strab. v. p. 223; Liv. *Epit.* LXXXIX; cf. Cic. *pro Rosc. Am.* VII. 20.
[2] Dennis, II. pp. 149–51. [3] Strabo, *loc. cit.*
[4] Liv. *Epit.* LXXXVIII: "Urbem ac totam Italiam caedibus repleuit";
Plut. *Sulla*, 31: προεγράφοντο δὲ οὐκ ἐν Ῥώμῃ μόνον, ἀλλὰ καὶ ἐν
πάσῃ πόλει τῆς Ἰταλίας: App. *B.C.* I. 96.
[5] Cf. Flor. III. 21. 27: "municipia Italiae splendidissima sub hasta
uenierunt, Spoletium Interamnium Praeneste Florentia." Cic. *in Cat.*
III. 6. 14: "P. Furium qui est ex eis colonis quos L. Sulla Faesulas
deduxit," cf. *pro Mur.* 24. 49, Sall. *Cat.* 28.
[6] See Bormann, *C.I.L.* XI. p. 306; an inscription "genio coloniae
Florentinae" in *Not. scav.* 1890, p. 109; Nissen, *It. Land.* pp. 295 ff.;
Davidsohn, *Storia di Firenze*, pp. 10–16; Milani in *Mon. Ant.* VI
(1896), pp. 57–8; Solari, II. p. 295.
[7] Plin. III. 52: "Arretini Veteres, Arretini Fidentiores, Arretini
Iulienses," where the Fidentiores may represent Sulla's colony; and
"Clusini Veteres, Clusini Noui."

(*C.I.L.* XI. 1849) lends support to this view. The citizens of Arretium and Volaterrae not only suffered a loss of territory, but also (till the acta of Sulla were repealed) of citizenship. The latter measure was carried by the comitia on the motion (or rather, the command) of Sulla, but as it was unconstitutional to take away the citizenship by a popular vote, it was recognized as invalid even during Sulla's life-time[1]. Cicero was engaged in several cases in defence of the rights of the Volaterrans and Arretines; the case best known to us is that of Aulus Caecina, of an ancient family of Volaterrae, whose capacity to inherit was impugned owing to the Sullan legislation[2]. The exact status to which Sulla attempted to reduce the two cities is uncertain, depending on the interpretation of the vexed passage *pro Caec.* 35. 102, where it is stated that they were put in the position previously held by the men of Ariminum, "quos quis ignorat XII coloniarum fuisse et a ciuibus Romanis hereditates capere potuisse?[3]"

The land, however, which had been given to the Sullan veterans was not taken away from them, though some which had been declared confiscated but not actually allotted appears to have been restored to its former owners. In 60 B.C. Cicero thus describes his support of the Lex Agraria of Flavius, which was brought forward in the interest of the veterans of Pompey: "Sullanorum hominum possessiones confirmabam; Volaterranos et

---

[1] Cic. *pro Caec.* 33. 96, 97; *de domo*, 30. 79.

[2] Cic. *ll. cc.* and *pro Caec.* 7. 18 (69–8 B.C.).

[3] The generally accepted opinion is that of Mommsen (*Röm. Staatr.* III. 1, p. 624) that the last twelve Latin colonies had *commercium* but not *conubium* with Rome, like the Latins under the Empire (Ulp. XIX. 4; v. 4). Beloch, however (*It. Bund*, pp. 154 ff.), identifies the XII coloniae with those which refused aid to Rome in 209 and were reduced to a position resembling that of ciues sine suffragio (Liv. XXIX. 15. 37); so too De Sanctis, III². p. 462, n. 33. Cf. the remarks of Steinwenter in Pauly-Wissowa, s.v. "Ius Latii" (X. 1, pp. 1267–8).

Arretinos, quorum agrum Sulla publicarat neque diui-
serat, in sua possessione retinebam[1]"; and he had previously as consul in 63 resisted the proposals of the tribune
Rullus, by which (it seems) the confiscated land was to
be given to new owners[2]. The agrarian law of Caesar
(59 B.C.), according to Cicero, settled the question in
favour of the citizens of Volaterrae[3]; yet we find Cicero
in 45 B.C. interceding with Q. Valerius Orca, who was
superintending the assignation of lands in Italy, on behalf
of his good friends at Volaterrae, whose land was in
danger[4]. This must have been still a result of the Sullan
confiscation, since Caesar, we are told, did not seize any
land which had an owner[5]. It is not unlikely, however,
that he settled a colony at Arretium[6], perhaps on confiscated land whose owners had been killed; the "Arretini
Julienses" of Pliny seem to take their name from him.

The colonies of Sulla must have had a considerable
effect in bringing new blood into Etruria and hastening
the fusion of the Etruscans in the new Italian nation—an
effect which was continued by the triumviral and Augustan
colonies. But the more immediate result was to rouse dis-

---

[1] *ad Att.* I. 19. 4, cf. *de domo*, 30. 79: "Populus Romanus L. Sulla
dictatore ferente comitiis centuriatis municipiis ciuitatem ademit:
ademit eisdem agros. de agris ratum est, fuit enim populi potestas;
de ciuitate ne tamdiu quidem ualuit quamdiu illa Sullani temporis
arma ualuerunt."

[2] Cic. *ad Fam.* XIII. 4. 2.

[3] "C. Caesar...agrum Volaterranum et oppidum omni periculo in
perpetuum liberauit," *id. ib.*

[4] *ad Fam.* XIII. 4, 5.

[5] App. *B.C.* II. 94.

[6] Hence we hear of Octavian raising troops at Arretium in 44–3
B.C. (App. *B.C.* II. 42). There seems to have been a Julian colony
also at Castrum Novum, cf. *C.I.L.* XI. 3576–8: "col. Iulia Castro
Nouo"; and the town is not in Pliny's list of colonies founded by
Augustus. The colony of Saena (Siena) may have been founded on
Volaterran territory by the younger Caesar: it is in Pliny's list and is
called Sena Iulia in the Peutinger Table, and no Etruscan town is
known to have existed there.

content both among the dispossessed landowners and among the inexperienced soldier-settlers who soon squandered their spoils and failed to farm their lands profitably. The conspiracy of Catiline found its chief supporters in Etruria, among both the discontented classes[1], and its headquarters were at Faesulae, which had been chosen by Sulla, no doubt for its strong position, as the site for one of his settlements of veterans. With the history of the plot and the defeat and death of Catiline near Pistoria, I am not here concerned. We get another glimpse of the troubled condition of Etruria about this time in the charges brought by Cicero against Clodius—how he had harassed the country with troops of barbarian slaves from the Apennines, driving the despised Etruscans from their homes and lands[2]; while it is not unlikely that in the Perusine War of 40 B.C. the cause of Lucius Antonius was aided by dispossessed natives, making a final revolt against the military colonists of Etruria.

Etruria must have shared in the general depopulation of Italy during the period of civil war, since the triumvirs and later Augustus as princeps founded numerous colonies in the region. Pliny mentions as colonies Luca, Pisae, Falerii, Lucus Feroniae, Rusellae, Sena, Sutrium[3]. His words with regard to the first two—"primum Etruriae oppidum Luna portu nobile colonia Luca a mari recedens propiorque Pisae inter Auserem et Arnum"—are ambiguous: Luna according to the *Liber coloniarum* was re-colonized by the triumvirs, and an inscription refers to Octavian as its patron[4], but it is probable that Pliny means to describe Luca and Pisae as colonies. There is little

---

[1] Cic. *in Cat.* II. 8–10; *pro Mur.* 24. 49; Sall. *Cat.* 28; Plut. *Cic.* 14.
[2] Cic. *pro Mil.* p. 36; 27. 74; 32. 87.
[3] Plin. III. 50, 51.
[4] *Lib. col.* p. 223. 14; *C.I.L.* XI. 1330: "Imp. Caesari d. f. imp. v. cos. VI III uir r.p.c. patrono," which Bormann accepts as genuine despite the discrepancies of the titles.

doubt about the latter, as inscriptions of the Augustan age refer to it as "colonia" and to its citizens as "coloni," and shew that the young Caesars, Gaius and Lucius, were its patrons[1]; while there is some evidence that the triumvirs founded a colony at Luca[2]. The status of Falerii in the early Empire has been disputed, since in the first two centuries A.D. it appears in inscriptions as "municipium," not "colonia[3]": but the *Liber coloniarum* records a trium-viral settlement there, and the emperor Gallienus is called "redintegrator coloniae Faliscorum," which suggests that the town had been a colony before[4]. Augustus besides founding (as triumvir or as princeps) the military colonies mentioned above, which involved the influx of a new population, also restored the town of Perusia after its destruction, giving it the title of Augusta[5], and recon-stituted into a *municipium* the scattered dwellings on the site of Veii[6].

Thus the Augustan colonies completed the work of Romanization which the confiscations of Sulla and his settlements of veterans had begun. The Etruscan language and religion survived only artificially, as interesting relics of a dead past. The oriental religions appear in Etruria[7], and also the cult of the Emperor, as elsewhere in Italy[8]. But in the time of Cicero the "Etrusca disciplina" was

---

[1] *C.I.L.* XI. 1420, 1421.

[2] *C.I.L.* VI. 1420: "...praefectus leg. XXVI et VII Lucae ad agros diuidundos...." Cf. Henzen, *ad loc.*

[3] See Bormann, *C.I.L.* XI. p. 465.

[4] *Lib. col.* p. 217; *C.I.L.* XI. 3089, 3094.

[5] *C.I.L.* XI. 1923: "Augusto sacr. Perusia restituta"; 1924: "Augustae Perusiae" (166 A.D.), and the same inscription on the ancient gate known as the Arco d'Augusto (*C.I.L.* 1929).

[6] *C.I.L.* XI. 3797 (A.D. 1), etc.: "municipium Augustum Veiens." Cf. *Lib. col.* p. 220. 8, on assignations of Veientine land by Augustus.

[7] Especially at Florence and Faesulae, *C.I.L.* XI. 1543-4, 1577-86 (Isis and Osiris); cf. 2684, 3123.

[8] E.g. *C.I.L.* 1331, 2116.

still preserved in noble Etruscan families[1], and Pliny among the writers whom he consulted mentions Caecina, Tarquitius[2], Iulius Aquila, and Umbricius Melior as having written concerning it. The recondite lore of the Etruscan haruspices was congenial to the archaeological tastes of Claudius, and he was concerned that the craft should not die out[3]. It was probably due to him that an "ordo" of sixty haruspices was constituted, with a "haruspex maximus" as its chief, and containing men of equestrian rank[4]. And the knowledge of the craft was still not extinct even after the official adoption of Christianity: Julian was accompanied by Etruscan haruspices on his military expeditions[5], and the practice survived the edicts of Theodosius against all forms of divination, since at the crisis of 408 when Alaric was advancing on Rome some Tuscans claimed to have driven away the barbarians from another city by eliciting thunder and lightning by their ancestral ritual[6].

The union of Etruscan cities which appears in the Imperial age may also have been an antiquarian revival of Claudius. This union is known to us from the inscriptions of its officers, who bore the titles of "praetor xv populorum Etruriae" and (apparently subordinate) "aedilis Etruriae[7]." These offices were no doubt purely formal,

[1] Cic. ad Fam. VI. 6. 3 (to Caecina of Volaterrae): "ratio quaedam mira Tuscae disciplinae quam a patre...acceperas."
[2] Cf. C.I.L. XI. 3370: "Tarqu]itio...uenerandum discipul[inae Etruscae ritum?] carminibus edidit."
[3] Tac. Ann. XI. 15. Claudius also wrote a Greek history of the Etruscans in twenty books: Suet. Claud. 42.
[4] C.I.L. VI. 1. 2161-8 (from Rome); XI. 3382, 3390 (from Tarquinii); 4194 (Interamna); XIII. 1821 (Lugdunum); XIV. 164 (Ostia). See the art. "Haruspices" in Pauly-Wissowa, VII. pp. 2435-8.
[5] Amm. Marc. XXV. 4.   [6] Zosim. V. 41.
[7] Praetor: C.I.L. XI. 1. 1432, 1941, 2114, 2115, 2699, 3364; XI. 2. 5170 (founded at Bettona east of the Tiber, but perhaps originally from Etruria); XIV. 172. Aedile: XI. 2116, 3257. Uncertain are C.I.L. XI. 1. 1806, 1905, which appear to allude to these offices.

involving the presidency at periodical meetings of the
league for religious purposes; they appear usually to have
been held by men of equestrian rank, often by *quinquen-
nales* or other local magistrates. One of the known praetors
is L. Venuleius Apronianus, who was consul in 168 A.D.[1]:
an example had previously been set by the Emperor
Hadrian, who held a number of local offices[2].

Part of a monument of this revived Etruscan League is
still extant, namely a well-known relief, found at Caere
and now in the Lateran Museum, of figures symbolizing
three of the Etruscan cities, with the names of the cities
beneath[3]. Above "Vetulonenses" is a young man standing
by a pine-tree and carrying an oar or rudder, in allusion
to the maritime importance of the town; to the right is a
seated woman holding a bird, whom Milani identifies with
the goddess Voltumna, with the inscription "V...centani"
(i.e. Volcentani) beneath; while the Tarquinienses are
represented by a man wearing a toga and with veiled head
—probably the eponymous hero Tarchon, who in some
legends appears as founder of the Etruscan nation and its
religion. It can hardly be doubted that the fragment
belongs to a monument on which all the cities of the
Etruscan League were represented; and from the fact that
a colossal seated statue of Claudius (also in the Lateran)
was found together with it, it is generally supposed that
the reliefs ran round three sides of the base of the throne
on which the Emperor was represented seated. A relief
of a sow was also found which may have formed part of
the monument, standing for Alba Longa[4]. Canina and

[1] *C.I.L.* XI. I. 1432 and Bormann, *ad loc.*

[2] Hist. Aug. *Hadr.* 19. 1: "In Etruria praeturam imperator egit":
he was also a dictator in Latium, a demarch of Neapolis and an
archon of Athens.

[3] See on this Canina, *Etruria Maritima*, I. pp. 28–35 and pls. I, II;
Milani, *Mus. Arch.* I. pp. 17–19; Helbig, *Führer*, II. pp. 15–16.

[4] Milani suggests that the sow stood for Troy, and was balanced
by the Roman wolf.

Milani assume that twelve cities were represented, the other nine being Caere, Veii, Falerii, Volsinii, Perusia, Clusium, Cortona, Arretium and Volaterrae: but the number of cities in the revived League is always given as fifteen, so that perhaps there were five figures on each of three sides of the base[1]. Why the number of cities was raised from twelve to fifteen we do not know, nor what cities were added; it seems highly probable that among the new members was the flourishing Augustan colony of Pisae, and others may have been Luna or Luca (which were outside Etruria till the Augustan regions were drawn up), or Florentia. In the later Empire Etruria and Umbria formed a religious union with its centre at Volsinii, as we learn from the rescript of Constantine found at Hispellum (Spello), in which he gives the Hispellates leave to establish a local cult of the gens Flavia instead of having to send a priest as delegate on the laborious route across the mountains to Volsinii[2].

Though the Etruscan cities practically disappear from history on their absorption into the Roman commonwealth, their Latin inscriptions and extant remains bear witness to the prosperity which they enjoyed. Though a rhetorical historian might speak of Veii as utterly wiped out[3], yet records of the Augustan municipality survive in the Vatican statue of Tiberius, and in the Ionic temple-columns now visible at Rome in Piazza Colonna[4]. Similarly though Strabo (v. 220) says of Caere that νῦν ἴχνη σῴζει μόνον, the place continued to have its old magistrates,

---

[1] Bormann on *C.I.L.* XI. 1. 3609 says that Vetulonia was in the middle of a side, with Volaterrae and Volsinii (now lost) to the left.

[2] *C.I.L.* XI. 2. 5265; cf. *ib.* 5283 (also from Spello), which contains the title "coronatus Tusciae et Umbriae."

[3] Flor. I. 12: "hoc tunc Veii fuere; nunc quis meminit? quae reliquiae?"

[4] Inscriptions of Veii mention a temple of Mars (*C.I.L.* XI. 3801) and public games (3805, etc.).

a "dictator" and a "censor perpetuus[1]," and a theatre adorned with statues of members of the Claudian house. The great inland cities, Clusium, Perusia, Arretium, are shewn by their inscriptions to have flourished under the Empire, Arretium in particular being renowned for its red glazed pottery which was widely exported[2]; while cities which were comparatively unimportant in the period of Etruscan independence contain notable monuments of the Roman period—for example, the well-preserved theatres and remains of public baths at Faesulae and Ferentum[3].

The decay of Etruria was most marked in that region which had once been the earliest and most important centre of the Etruscan nation. This was the region along the coast from Vetulonia to Caere, and inland as far as the Lakes of Bolsena and Bracciano, the Tuscan Maremma, long a by-word for misery and desolation[4]. At what time the deadly malaria, which has made large tracts of the country uninhabitable for centuries, first became prevalent we do not know. From a dubious piece of etymology of Cato the censor, it appears that some parts of the Tuscan coast were already unhealthy in the second century B.C., and similar evidence is afforded for his own time by the younger Pliny[5]. Yet one of the audacities of Clodius according to Cicero (*pro Mil.* 27. 74) was that he seized a

---

[1] *C.I.L.* XI. 3593, 3614, 3616–7; cf. the calendar of Caere (*ib.* 3592) and the "commentarium cottidianum municipi Caeritum" (*ib.* 3614; 113 A.D.).

[2] Several Arretine factories are known to us, in particular those of M. Perennius and C. Vibienus; cf. Gamurrini, *Not. scav.* 1883, pp. 265 ff.; 1884, pp. 369 ff.

[3] On Ferentum cf. *Not. scav.* 1908, pp. 373 ff.; 1911, pp. 22 ff.; 1920, p. 117.

[4] Cf. Dennis, II. pp. 194–210, on the Maremma.

[5] Cato, frag. 46 (Peter, *Hist. Rom. Reliqu.*): "ideo Grauiscae dictae sunt quod grauem aerem sustinent," quoted by Servius on *Aen.* X. 184: "intempestaeque Grauiscae." Cf. Rutil. Nam. I. 281: "inde Grauiscarum uestigia rara uidemus / quas premit aestiuae saepe paludis odor"; Plin. *Ep.* V. 6. 2: "est sane grauis et pestilens ora Tuscorum quae per litus extenditur."

site and began under the owner's very eyes to build himself a house on an island of the Lacus Prilius, which has
only recently ceased to be a fever-stricken marsh[1]. And
the still malarious coast below Caere was in the late
Republic and early Empire covered with villas, which are
often mentioned in literature and inscriptions, and of
which considerable remains are extant[2].

It has been truly said that south Etruria, once fertile
and populous, is now a land of the dead, where only the
numerous sepulchres bear witness to its former greatness[3].
Such a land it appears to us in the last classical account
of the Etruscan coast, when the decline of cultivation had
favoured the spread of malaria, and this in turn had
driven the inhabitants from their cities. It is a gloomy
picture which Rutilius Namatianus gives of his homeward
journey from Rome in 416 A.D.[4] Along the Via Aurelia
the barbarian invaders have wrecked houses and bridges[5];
so he travels by sea and describes the deserted and lifeless
towns which he passes. The great harbour of Centum-
cellae (Civitavecchia) is almost the only exception to the
tale of desolation which he tells of Castrum Novum and
Graviscae, Cosa and Populonia; and his words might
serve as an epitaph to many another Etruscan city now
deserted or with some poverty-stricken village on its site
—to Veii and Caere and Volci, Vetulonia and Rusellae,
Blera, Suana and Norchia:

> cernimus exemplis oppida posse mori.

[1] Now called Palude di Castiglione, near Grosseto; cf. Dennis, II.
p. 223, who says it "realizes all your worst conceptions of the Maremma,
its putrescent fens, its desolate scenery."

[2] On villas at Alsium cf. Val. Max. VIII. 1. 7; Cic. *pro Mil.* 20. 54;
ad Fam. IX. 6. 1; Plin. *Ep.* VI. 10, etc.; on the palace of Antoninus
Pius at Lorium, Capitolinus, *Vita Ant. Pii*, I. 8; XII. 6, and the letters
of Marcus Aurelius and Fronto.

[3] Nissen, *It. Land.* II. pp. 326–7.

[4] The poem *De reditu suo* has been recently edited by Prof. V. Ussani
in *Rassegna italiana di lingue e letterature classiche* (Naples), May, 1920.

[5] *De red.* I. 39–42.

BIBLIOGRAPHY

A. HISTORICAL WORKS

MOMMSEN, *History of Rome* (Eng. trans. by Dickinson, London, 1894).

DE SANCTIS, *Storia dei Romani.*

PAIS, *Storia critica di Roma durante i primi cinque secoli.*

MEYER, *Geschichte des Altertums*, vols. III, IV, V.

HEITLAND, *Roman Republic.*

NIESE, *Grundriss der Römische Geschichte nebst Quellenkunde* (4th ed., Munich, 1910).

B. BRUNO, "La terza guerra sannitica" (vol. VI in Beloch's *Studi di storia romana*, Rome, 1906).

T. FRANK, *Roman Imperialism.*

—— *Economic History of Rome.*

BELOCH, *Der Italische Bund unter Roms Hegemonie.*

KUBITSCHEK, *De romanarum tribuum origine ac propagatione* (Vienna, 1882).

REID, *Municipalities of the Roman Empire.*

MODESTOV, *Introduction à l'histoire romaine.*

ROSENBERG, *Der Staat der alten Italiker.*

B. ETRURIA AND THE ETRUSCANS

DENNIS, *Cities and Cemeteries of Etruria* (revised ed., 1878).

MÜLLER, *Die Etrusker* (revised by Deecke, 1877).

NISSEN, *Italische Landeskunde*, vol. II.

SOLARI, *Topografia storica dell' Etruria* (Pisa, 1918). [A compilation from literary sources shewing little acquaintance with the actual sites, and somewhat superficial: good bibliography.]

MILANI, *Italici ed Etruschi* (Rome, 1909).

C. SPECIAL SITES OR REGIONS

FALCHI, *Vetulonia e la sua più antica necropole* (Florence, 1892).
GSELL, *Fouilles dans la nécropole de Vulci* (Paris, 1891).
MINTO, *Marsigliana d'Albegna* (Florence, 1921).
GRENIER, *Bologne villanovienne et étrusque* (Paris, 1912).

D. ART AND ARCHAEOLOGY

MARTHA, *L'Art étrusque* (Paris, 1889).
DUCATI, *L'arte classica* (Turin, 1920).
MONTELIUS, *La civilisation primitive en Italie* (Stockholm, 1895, vol. I; 1910, vol. II).
WEEGE, *Etruskische Malerei* (Halle, 1921).
POULSEN, *Der Orient und die frühgriechische Kunst* (Leipzig, 1912).
—— *Etruscan tomb-paintings*, trans. Anderson (Oxford, 1922).
KÖRTE, *I rilievi delle urne etrusche.*
GERHARD, *Etruskische Spiegel.*
DURM, *Baukunst der Etrusker und Römer* (2nd ed., 1905).
DELBRÜCK, *Hellenistische Bauten in Latium*, vol. II (Strassburg, 1912).
—— *Der Apollotempel auf dem Marsfelde* (Rome, 1903).
E. VAN BUREN, *Figurative terracotta revetments in Etruria and Latium* (London, 1921).
A. GARRONI, *Studi di antichità* (Rome, 1918).
DELLA SETA, *L'Italia antica.*
PINZA, *Monumenti primitivi di Roma e del Lazio antico* (=*Monumenti antichi*, xv).
GABRICI, *Cuma* (=*Monumenti antichi*, xxii).
MILLER, *Itineraria Romana.*
SAMBON, *Monnaies antiques de l'Italie* (Paris, 1906).

E. MUSEUMS

MILANI, *Il R. Museo Archeologico di Firenze.*
DELLA SETA, *Il Museo di Villa Giulia.*
PINZA, *La tomba Regolini-Galassi.*

F. RELIGION

Wissowa, *Religion und Kultus der Römer.*
Fowler, *Roman Festivals.*
—— *Religious experience of the Roman People.*
Carter, *Religion of Numa.*
—— *Religious Life of Ancient Rome.*

G. PRINCIPAL PERIODICALS, ETC.

Not. scav.	= Notizie degli Scavi.
Rend. Linc.	= Rendiconti della R. Accademia dei Lincei.
Mon. Ant.	= Monumenti Antichi, pubblicati per cura della R. Accademia dei Lincei.
Bull. Comm.	= Bullettino della Commissione archeologica communale di Roma.
Stud. e Mat.	= Studi e materiali di archeologia e numismatica (ed. Milani).
Bull. Pal.	= Bullettino di paletnologia italiana.
J.R.S.	= Journal of Roman Studies.
J.H.S.	= Journal of Hellenic Studies.
Amer. Journ. Arch.	= American Journal of Archaeology.
Mem. Amer. Acad.	= Memoirs of the American Academy at Rome.
Class. Phil.	= Classical Philology.
Röm. Mitt.	= Mittheilungen des kaiserlichen deutschen archäologischen Instituts, römische Abteilung.
Mélanges	= Mélanges d'archéologie et d'histoire de l'école française de Rome.

I N D E X

Ad Fines, 103
Adria, 106
Agathocles, 115
Ager Gallicus, 121 ff.
Alalia, 37
Allia, battle of, 98
Allies of Rome, legal status of, 146 f.
Alphabet, Etruscan, 19
Alsium, 150
Anthropoid urns, 8 f.
Apollo, statue of (Veii), 65
Arch, the, used by Etruscans, 58 ff.
Aricia, battle of, 84 f.
Ariminum, 150, 152
Aristodemus, tyrant of Cumae, 84 ff.
Arretium (mod. Arezzo): relations with Rome, 110 ff., 124, 133, 160 f.; feud at A., 115, 136; Roman roads to A., 156; in Social and Civil Wars, 163 ff.; pottery of A., 173
Asia Minor, 7, 11 ff.
Asisium, 150 n.
Atrium, development of the, 9 f.
Aules Pheluskes, stele of (Vetulonia), 10, 19
Aurelia, Via, 162 ff.
Axe, double, 10

Babylonia, 8, 17
Bacchanalia, 143
Banquets in Etruscan tomb-paintings, 139 ff.
Bilingual inscriptions, 147 ff.
Boii, 125
Bologna (Felsina, Bononia), 14, 16, 21, 25, 27, 96 f.
Bolsena, 129 ff.

Caecina, A., 166
Caelian hill, 42 ff.

Caere (mod. Cerveteri), an early Etruscan settlement, 18 ff.; tombs at, 15 f. (see also Tombs); tiles and sarcophagi, 36, 142; connexion with Tarquins, 46 ff.; friendship with Rome, 89, 92, 98 ff.; Roman citizenship of C., 100 ff.; cedes land to Rome, 128; under Empire, 172 f.
Caesar, Julius, 167
Camars, Camertes, 110 ff., 120 f.
Camerinum, 112, 120 f.
Camillus, 94
Campania, Etruscans in, 21 f., 104
Capena, 92 f., 99 f.
Capua, 21 f., 78, 104
Carthage, 37, 79, 81 f., 107, 115
Cassia, Via, 152 ff.
Castrum Novum, 124, 150
Catiline, 168
Charun, 78, 142
Chimaera, the (in Florence Museum), 34
Cicero, 166 f.
Cilnii, 115, 136
Ciminius saltus, 95 f., 109 f.
Claudius, Appius, 119 f., 152; — (Emperor), 170 f.
Cloaca maxima, 63
Clodia, Via, 152 ff.
Clodius, P., 168, 173
Clusium (mod. Chiusi): anthropoid urns at C., 8 f.; tombs, 76 f.; relations with Rome, 83, 97 f., 120 f.; bilingual inscriptions, 147 f.; in Civil Wars, 164 f.
Colonies, Roman, in Etruria, 150 f., 165 ff.
Conca (Satricum), 67 ff.
Corsica, 37, 105 ff.
Cortona, 3 f., 33, 57, 110 ff.
Cosa, 57, 150

ITALIA

For EU product safety concerns, contact us at Calle de José Abascal, 56–1°, 28003 Madrid, Spain or eugpsr@cambridge.org.

www.ingramcontent.com/pod-product-compliance
Ingram Content Group UK Ltd.
Pitfield, Milton Keynes, MK11 3LW, UK
UKHW020315140625

459647UK00018B/1892